D1568346

THE
MAN
WHO
DIVIDED
INDIA

THE MAN WHO DIVIDED INDIA

— An insight into Jinnah's leadership
and its aftermath —

RAFIQ ZAKARIA

POPULAR PRAKASHAN
MUMBAI

Popular Prakashan Pvt. Ltd.
35-C, Madan Mohan Malaviya Marg,
Popular Press Bldg., Tardeo,
Mumbai - 400 034

First Published 2001
First Reprinted December 2001
Second Reprinted February 2002

ISBN 81-7154-892-X

(3643)

PRINTED IN INDIA
By Alert Packaging House Pvt. Ltd.,
326, A to Z Ind. Estate, Ganpatrao Kadam Marg,
Lower Parel, Mumbai 400 013 and Published by
Ramdas Bhatkal for Popular Prakashan Pvt. Ltd.
35-C, Pandit Madan Mohan Malaviya Marg, Popular Press Bldg.,
Tardeo, Mumbai 400 034.

To
the memory of
Maulana Abul Kalam Azad
who tried his best to keep the Muslims
of undivided India
out of Jinnah's clutches in order to prevent
partition, but failed.

Do you remember I hailed you, you cut off my tongue. I picked up my pen, you severed my hand. I wanted to move forward, you cut off my legs. I tried to turn over, and you injured my back... I called upon you to wake you up at every danger signal. You did not heed my call... I warned you that the 'Two-Nation' theory was death-knell to a meaningful, dignified life; forsake it. I told you that the pillars upon which you were leaning would inevitably crumble. To all this you turned a deaf ear... Time sped along. And now you have discovered that the so-called anchors of your faith have set you adrift, to be kicked around by fate... — An extract from his address to the Friday congregation at Jama Masjid, Delhi, soon after partition.

Preface

I told my wife that my next book would be on Mohammed Ali Jinnah, the Quaid-i-Azam or "Great Leader" of the Muslims of undivided India. I said I plan to unearth the truth about his proclaimed love for Islam and his so-called concern for his co-religionists in the subcontinent.

Fatma was not impressed. She said, "Haven't you already written enough about him in your published works?"

I said what I had written so far was from a general political viewpoint; this book would concentrate on how and why he sought to divide Hindus and Muslims and brought about the division of India. The divide may not have been of his making; it had a historical and political background but it could certainly have been avoided had Jinnah not been so adamant about it. Was he in fact — as his followers have hailed him — a true Muslim, a defender of the faith, the saviour of Indian Muslims? For the past fifty years and more, he has been presented not only to Pakistanis but to Muslims everywhere as Prophet Muhammad's real follower who treaded faithfully the Islamic path and brought glory to Islam and prosperity to the Muslims of the subcontinent. I want to get at the truth of this claim.

"I think you should leave Jinnah alone for a while," Fatma mused, "you have badgered him enough. He was a vital force in undivided India in the early forties of the last century but he had a limited and specific goal. Events since then have so rapidly changed the geopolitical picture of this region that in many respects he and his Two-Nation theory have become somewhat irrelevant today, more so after the creation of Bangladesh." I disagreed: "That is where you are wrong. So long as Pakistan follows the Two-Nation theory, Jinnah and his thinking will be a disturbing factor in the subcontinent. It will continue to cause tension and even threat to peace in the whole of South Asia," I asserted. "Pakistan has so far waged three wars against India to annex Kashmir on that basis. Even after suffering defeat after defeat, it has not given up that path; on the contrary it is now resorting to terrorism and murder of innocent persons in the state of Jammu and Kashmir to achieve its objective," I argued.

I therefore remained convinced that a retrospect of Jinnah's leadership and its aftermath is essential in order to understand the ramifications of his politics not only for India but also for the once vibrant and united Muslim community. He divided the Indian Muslims into three — Pakistani Muslims, Indian Muslims and Bangladeshi Muslims who now have no connection with one another. He has destroyed all the ties which had once knit them together. And all this he did in the name of Islam. His life and activities are of immense importance in understanding the growing unrest in the subcontinent.

No one can of course blame Jinnah alone for the animosity that existed between the Hindus and the Muslims before partition but was division of the country the only solution? No other Muslim leader before him had ever suggested such a disastrous remedy. Why did he go to this extent? Was it the result of a deep-rooted conviction on his part or was it because of a certain vindictiveness which blinded him to the consequences of the terrible alternative he so doggedly pursued? In the evening of his life when transfer of power from the British to the Indians became inevitable, Jinnah turned his wrath on his Hindu compatriots in the Congress on the spurious grounds that the Hindus were the real enemies of the Muslims. He worked up a religious frenzy among his community warning them that after the British left, they would be reduced to being slaves of the Hindus. How far was he right in resorting to such a diabolical game that ultimately resulted in the disintegration of the country where every city, town and village was inhabited by members of both the communities; he ignored the fact they had lived together, by and large, in peace and harmony for a thousand years. By forcing a division, Jinnah not only split the Muslims of South Asia into three parts, but made them lose, along with their unity, their security as well. They found themselves out of place everywhere and at home nowhere.

Fatma did not pursue the matter further but I came to the conclusion that the present generation of Muslims must be made aware of how their forefathers, in the name of their cherished religion, were wrongly led to believe by Jinnah that partition alone would be the panacea of all their ills which would rid both the communities of the psychosis that has perpetuated hostilities between them. I am particularly concerned about the millions of Muslims who have been left

behind in India and who, because of the terrible burden of
estrangement and hatred that partition had heaped upon them,
are unable to lead a normal, peaceful life. No one has painted
more poignantly the plight of Muslims than Akbar Ahmed, a
distinguished Pakistani civilian and intellectual, who was
recently, for a short time, Pakistan's High Commissioner to
the United Kingdom: "The damning argument against
Pakistan," he says, "is that it took a community spread
throughout the subcontinent, chopped it into several
communities, gave it first one country and then two and left
the others dangling in mid-air. People who once possessed the
culture, customs and history of a whole subcontinent were
left with neither a nation nor an idea of themselves as a
community. Pakistan was a double disaster for the Muslims in
India: first they lost their sense of coherence and political
strength in the Indian union along with their leadership and
middle classes which migrated to Pakistan by the thousands;
secondly, they were forever damned in India for having voted
for Pakistan and broken the unity of India."

There are not many books on Jinnah, unlike on Gandhi
since interest in the Mahatma has never ceased; as against
hundreds of treatises and tomes that have come out all over
the world on Gandhi, the published works on Jinnah can be
counted on one's fingertips. But Jinnah's charisma continues
to cast a spell on large sections of the Muslims of the three
countries which have been freed from the yoke of the British.
Their activities in turn continue to disturb Hindus who see in
them a danger to India's security. That is why it is necessary to
awaken both Hindus and Muslims to the real cause of partition
giving them an insight into the making of Jinnah who in the
final outcome was alone responsible for the great tragedy.
The question to be answered is: what motivated Jinnah

and what led him to this fatal path? It is with this objective that I have collected all the relevant material about his life and his relentless pursuit of power. I have tried to focus on the repercussions of his politics on the fate of hundreds of millions of Muslims residing in the three countries that had once constituted undivided India.

I fervently hope my book will provide not only Muslims but non-Muslims as well, an insight into Jinnah's personality; it will show them how he mesmerised the Muslims and on the basis of their support, succeeded in dismembering the subcontinent.

Since 1937, when I was a student in Pune, I tried in my own modest way to fight against Jinnah's pernicious Two-Nation theory; in my book *The Price of Partition*, I have narrated the story of my trials and tribulations. Through other publications, speeches and writings, I have been pursuing the same theme, trying to disprove the contention that Hindus and Muslims cannot co-exist. My voice I am afraid has had little impact; nor have similar efforts by many other Muslims, far more influential than me, brought any worthwhile result. The barriers between Hindus and Muslims have in the meantime multiplied. The blunder that our leadership committed in agreeing to Jinnah's demand has deepened the grief and festered the wounds of millions of our people; even Nehru and Patel who succumbed to the ruse of the machiavellian Viceroy Lord Mountbatten, and accepted his infamous Balkan Plan of June 3, 1947, later admitted they had committed a grave wrong in agreeing to partition. But of what use were such confessions after the die was cast.

In building his power Jinnah forced a solution which on sober reflection, he himself would have perhaps regretted.

For Pakistan has become a state which negates his deep-rooted western outlook, it promotes a rigidly theological pattern of existence which he strongly abhorred. Moreover the bonds that once united the Muslims of the subcontinent have been permanently torn asunder and the ruling cliques in Pakistan have resorted to methods which have uprooted democracy and ushered in fascist rule in their land. The anti-Hindu frenzy that Jinnah had generated among the Muslims merely to gain Pakistan has in turn given rise to an anti-Muslim feeling among Hindus. This vicious circle of hate has threatened the peace and harmony of the whole of South Asia. One of the tallest among the religious leaders of the early forties, Maulana Husain Ahmed Madni, had therefore advised Muslims against partition, reminding them that the Prophet himself had preached and practised the virtues of united, composite nationhood when he ruled Medina. The harm that division had done to both Hindus and Muslims should be an eye-opener for all those who believe that hate can be the substitute for love, and distrust and enmity can be more potent than trust and friendship. Gandhi had to sacrifice his life in trying to spread this message among us; but such is the continued arrogance of those incited by Jinnah during his lifetime, and even after his death that they remain indoctrinated by his teachings and cannot see through the harm that Jinnah had done to them.

There is of late a growing realisation that the barriers which manipulative politics had erected need to be demolished if the two major communities have to live in amity. Jinnah's basis of the Two-Nation theory is crumbling fast not only in India and Bangladesh but also in Pakistan; proof of this came in the early seventies when Bangladesh liberated itself and founded its own state on the basis of language as against religion. Recently the supreme leader of the immigrants from

India who call themselves *Mohajirs* or refugees, Altaf Hussain
has publicly condemned the division of India as "the biggest
blunder in the history of the world". As for the situation in
India which at one time threatened to be polluted by hate and
venom against the Muslims in the aftermath of partition, it
has dramatically improved; the secular temper is once again
asserting itself and holding at bay the forces of Hindutva.
During a visit to America in September 2000, the Prime Minister
of India, Atal Behari Vajpayee who heads a coalition
government of twenty-one political parties which includes his
Bharatiya Janata Party, pointed this out by quoting a short
poem of the popular Urdu poet, Sahir Ludhianvi:

> Wo waqt gaya, wo daur gaya
> Jab do quomon ka naara tha
> Wo loge gaye is dharti saye
> Jinka maqsad batwara tha
> Ab aik hain sab Hindustani
> Ab aik hain sab Hindustani
> Yeh jaanle saara Pakistan
> Haan, haan jaanle saara Jahan

However the recent Summit at Agra between Prime
Minister Vajpayee and the President of Pakistan Parvez
Musharraf proved abortive because the General could not come
out of the stranglehold of the Two-Nation theory; the Kashmir
issue is, after all, nothing but its offshoot.

In this book I have attempted to probe into the true
nature of Jinnah's leadership and his supposed love for Islam.
I have presented facts and figures to show how he erected an
edifice of falsehood in the name of Islam and how he
irrevocably disrupted the union between Hindus and Muslims
in a vengeful manner merely to promote his own personal
gain. I have taken care to be as objective as possible in the

narration of the various phases of his leadership and the effect it had on the the present and the future of Muslims in the subcontinent. I have tried to follow the dictum of the noted British editor, C.P. Scott, who wrote: "Facts are sacred; comment is free." I have relied mainly on Pakistani sources to draw my conclusions. I have quoted from their speeches, writings, reports and documents profusely and at length only to prove how Jinnah put the Muslims in the subcontinent, comprising India, Pakistan and Bangladesh in a catch-22 situation from which they do not know how to extricate themselves. I sincerely hope my effort will help reorientate their outlook and assist them in finding a new way to re-establish their identity so that they may rebuild their unity in the multi-religious and composite world of South Asia.

In this endeavour of mine, my wife Fatma was, as usual, both my editor and censor; with her penetrating eye she detected every flaw and refashioned the text. I am also grateful to Savita Chandiramani, an executive editor of Marg Publications, for her help. Raghavan M.V., my Personal Assistant, typed and retyped the manuscript without raising an eyebrow.

Harsha Bhatkal, Managing Director of Popular Prakashan, Ashok Bhatt, General Manager and Jijesh Gangadharan, Production Manager, took personal interest in the publication, for which I express my thanks to them.

Mumbai, August 10, 2001   **Rafiq Zakaria**

Contents

ONE

Early Years

No one knows when Mohammed Ali Jinnah was born; there are no reliable records to testify to his date of birth. The Karachi Municipality did not maintain a register of births and deaths until 1876; Jinnah was supposed to have been born in the city in or about 1870. His father belonged to the Khoja community which owes its allegiance to the Aga Khan. This sect is technically Shiite but observes several Hindu ceremonies and customs. In fact even their prayer or their manner of praying does not strictly conform to Islamic precepts; there is a vast difference not only between them and the dominant Sunnis but also other Shiite sects notably the Asnasharis who regard the Aga Khani beliefs and practices as being at variance with theirs. Until recently the orthodox Muslims of various schools did not recognise Aga Khani Khojas as true Muslims. Jinnah therefore did not have a purely conventional Islamic background and hence in order to get proper religious acceptance among the generality of Muslims, he changed his sect much later and became an Asnashari.

Muslim children are taught to read the Quran in Arabic at a very young age; they also learn many verses from it by heart; they are taught to pray namaz and to fast during the month of Ramadan by the time they turn seven. Jinnah could neither read the Quran, nor did he say his prayers nor fast in Ramadan. Even in the heyday of his communal leadership he said his prayers only on the occasion of Eid, and that too, merely as a demonstrative gesture. He did not perform the Haj either which is one of the cardinal articles of the Islamic faith.

Jinnah's date of birth as given by his father in the application for admission to the primary school was October 20, 1875; in the school register he was named Mohammed Ali, son of Jinnahbhai. After a few years, his aunt Manubai Peerbhai who resided in Bombay took Jinnah under her wing; she got him admitted first to Gokuldas School and later to the well-known Anjuman-i-Islam. He was however not serious about his work at school and spent a great deal of time wandering in the affluent and elegant areas of south Bombay where the British had built some magnificent Gothic buildings. He also enjoyed going to the beach with friends rather than attending classes at school. The result was that his father grew apprehensive about his future; he brought him back to Karachi and admitted him in the Sind madrasa. But Jinnah's indifference to formal education persisted. Finally he was sent to the elitist Christian Mission High School where he became so anglicised that he soon changed his name in the school register to Mohammed Ali Jinnah discarding the "bhai" from his father's name. It however remained Jinnahbhai in other records. He arbitrarily altered his birth date to December 25 in order to coincide it with the birth of Jesus Christ. Even the missionary school could not make him overcome his aversion to studies and he dropped out without appearing for the final matriculation examination.

Jinnah's father grew increasingly worried about the future of his otherwise bright and smart son; some of his British friends told him the young man seemed to have a natural aptitude for law, being sharp, articulate and quick in repartee; he should therefore be sent to England to study law. The father readily agreed; being a prosperous merchant the expenses for education abroad posed no problem for him. His mother was however opposed to the decision of her son journeying across the oceans to faraway London, fearing he might marry a "white" girl there and be lost to the family forever. She insisted that Jinnah, who was not yet sixteen, should first go through an arranged marriage with Emibai, a Khoja girl, barely fourteen; Jinnah agreed. His eagerness to go to London was irrepressible; the thought of living there fascinated him. And so he readily went through the matrimonial ritual. Three days after the wedding he sailed for London but by the time he returned home three years later having qualified as a barrister-at-law, Emibai had passed away. And so had his mother.

At first Jinnah was miserable in London. He was no doubt awed by the majesty of the city but did not know how to adjust to the requirements of the new life. He later reminisced, "I did not know a soul and the fogs and winter in London upset me a great deal." Moreover "... the immensity of London as a city weighed heavily on my solitary life." But it did not take long for young Jinnah to adapt to the British way of life; he loved it and did everything to emulate it. He was greatly impressed by the pomp and pageantry associated with the Church and at one time, even toyed with the idea of converting to Christianity. In India he wore the traditional Khoja dress — a long coat and the Aga Khani cap but now he gave up these for western attire looking every inch a *burra sahib*. In fact he was often taken for an Englishman which greatly pleased him. He perfected both the English language and manners quickly and dressed most elegantly. As his renowned biographer, Stanley Wolpert has observed: "He also traded in his traditional Sindhi long yellow coat for smartly tailored Saville Row suits and heavily-starched detachable-collared shirts. His tall, lean frame was perfectly suited to display London's finest fashions."[1] The British found his company congenial and befriended him, taking him into their fold with open arms. He frequented the best clubs with them. In less than two months of his arrival in the British capital he was more at home in London than he had ever been in his native Karachi or Bombay.

At the time of seeking admission to Lincoln's Inn, Jinnah wrote in his application the family name "Jinnahbhai". Although he had changed it to Jinnah in the school register, his passport carried the name Jinnahbhai. He was not comfortable with it; it did not fit into the western style which he was so keen to adopt. Hence just before he was called to the bar he wrote a letter to the masters of the Bench of Lincoln's Inn, requesting them to change his name from Mohammed Ali Jinnahbhai to M.A. Jinnah. After some hesitation, relying on the entry in the school register, his request was granted. The document of qualification, therefore, bore the corrected name, as he desired. And so he became M.A. Jinnah ever since. He utilised most of his time to study legal tomes and worked hard to master the intricacies of the profession. He selected Lincoln's Inn out of the four Inns and Temples of Court because he believed that it bore the name of Abraham Lincoln whom he greatly admired. That was, however, not the case; Lincoln's

Inn was not named after the martyred American President but the King's Sergeant of Holborn, Thomas de Lincoln who lived in the fourteenth century. Gandhi and Nehru qualified for the bar from the Inner Temple. These Inns and Temples constituted different traditional centres and did not provide for preferences in the teaching of law.

Jinnah looked forward to his legal career and equipped himself in every way to succeed at the bar. In his two-year stay in London, he sat at the feet of some leading British lawyers and familiarised himself with various legal norms and procedures. He practised the art of oratory and specialised in cross-examination. He loved to argue and score points. He was also attracted to the theatre and rarely missed a good play. He was an ardent admirer of Shakespeare; he saw all his plays enacted on stage and learnt by heart many a passage from the bard's celebrated works. He was once offered an acting job by a theatre company which he was tempted to accept. He wrote to his father about it who sternly forbade him from entertaining such a thought. If not for that, instead of shining at the Bombay bar as Jinnah did on his return from London, he might well have become a star on London's famed West End stage! The experiences of those early days were of great benefit to him both at the bar and in politics. They taught him how to make use of the perplexities of human relationships and, in particular, to confront an opponent and turn an unfavourable situation to his advantage.

Many years later, when Jinnah was anointed *Quaid-i-Azam* (or the Great Leader) by his Muslim followers in the late thirties, he gave a different reason for his choice of Lincoln's Inn. He said it was because he saw a portrait there of Prophet Muhammad in the company of great law makers. The occasion

was a reception to felicitate him which was organised by the
Bar Association of Karachi; "I joined Lincoln's Inn," Jinnah
declared, "because there, right at the entrance, I saw a picture
of the Prophet included among the great law givers of the
world." In fact there is no such picture in Lincoln's Inn. What
is more shocking is that Jinnah did not know that any
representation of the figure of the Prophet is strictly prohibited
in Islam. Books showing any such depiction have been burnt
by zealous Muslims. But by then Jinnah had cast such a spell on
the Muslims that they overlooked his heretical pronouncement
without even a murmur of protest. There is a fresco in Lincoln's
Inn painted by G.F. Watt depicting great law givers; in these,
some Pakistanis have recently discovered a figure which they
claimed represented Prophet Muhammad, but it bears not the
slightest resemblance to him as he has been described in the
Books of Traditions. This was only a contrived attempt to justify
Jinnah's statement.[2]

Along with law, political developments in London also
began to interest Jinnah. He admired the British for their sense
of fair play and their adherence to the democratic system. Of
the books he read, Morley's *On Compromise* influenced him the
most. Ironically in the evening of his life Jinnah discarded all
the principles that the noble Lord had eloquently enunciated in
the classic. He became rigid in his approach to problems and
almost fanatical in dealing with them. Jinnah worked actively
during his stay in London for the election to the House of
Commons of Dadabhai Naoroji popularly known as "the Grand
Old Man of Indian Politics". He also acted as his private
secretary for a while. All through those years Jinnah showed
no interest in the Muslims of India or the difficulties they faced.
In fact their loyalist stance in politics appalled him. He was
then all for the Congress; its non-communal, nationalistic stand

enthused him. In private conversation he often bitterly criticised Sir Syed Ahmad Khan, the pre-eminent Muslim leader, for his opposition to the Congress and for his exhortation to the Muslims to keep away from it. That is why in the early twenties when the Muslims started a movement for turning the Muhammadan Anglo-Oriental College, founded by the Syed at Aligarh, into the Muslim University, Jinnah took no part in it, condemning it as a sectarian move to which he refused to subscribe.

Two

Political Initiation

After being called to the bar, Jinnah did not return to Karachi even though his father, ailing and heartbroken due to the huge financial losses he had suffered in business, badly needed his support. Jinnah ignored his father's pleas and landed in Bombay to chart a new life for himself. He managed to get entry into the chamber of the then Advocate-General of Bombay, the well-known British lawyer Molesworth MacPherson, but that did not help him financially. He remained briefless for over a year. Living in Bombay was expensive and he did not have other resources to sustain himself. He applied therefore for a job as presidency magistrate and got a temporary appointment for the post. But he did not relish the isolation a judge lived in and within months he gave it up and started practising law. His father, having lost everything in Karachi, came to Bombay with the entire family but Jinnah could not be of much help. Disappointed with his attitude the family went to Ratnagiri, a few hundred miles away from Bombay and settled there. Jinnah did not maintain contact with any member except his younger sister Fatima who came to live with him and served him as his companion for the rest of his life.

Apart from law, Jinnah was also drawn to politics. He had already come in close touch with Dadabhai Naoroji in London. He renewed his acquaintance with him when he came to India to preside over the annual session of the Congress in 1905. It was said that Jinnah helped Naoroji to draft his presidential address, but it was the lion of Bombay, Sir Pherozeshah Mehta, who truly inspired him and took to young Jinnah instantly. Jinnah too felt more comfortable with the westernised Parsis than the orthodox Muslims involved in politics especially since they were guided by Sir Syed Ahmad Khan whose politics he disliked. He was particularly disturbed with their subservient attitude to the British rulers. He found the Congress, which the Syed opposed bitterly, more to his liking. He attended the twentieth annual session of the Congress, held in Bombay in December 1904 and took an active interest in its deliberations. He assisted Mehta who had become chairman of the Reception Committee; their association proved immensely fruitful to Jinnah. Sir Pherozeshah sent him to London as member of the Congress delegation led by Gopal Krishna Gokhale where they pleaded for a larger share in administration for Indians. It was during their travel and stay in London that Gokhale and Jinnah came close to each other. Jinnah liked Gokhale's liberal outlook and broad humanism and Gokhale saw in Jinnah a young, progressive Muslim, free of any communal prejudice; he often spoke highly of Jinnah's nationalistic fervour.

The partition of Bengal by the Viceroy, Lord Curzon, had led to violent agitation in the province; it had also spread to other parts of India. Muslims favoured the divide since they were in a majority in the Eastern part but Jinnah took a stand against it. He stood solidly by the agitating Hindu Bengalis and denounced Lord Curzon for his unpatriotic action which had generated discord between the Hindus and the Muslims. Strangely, in 1947, he was the person mainly responsible for partitioning Bengal on the ground that Hindus and Muslims could not be lumped together. They needed separate homelands, free from the domination of each other. In 1906 Jinnah even refused to join the All-India Muslim League, founded in Dacca as a counter force to the Congress. But much later, he made the same League the instrument for dividing India and lorded over it as its supreme leader for almost a decade from 1937 to 1947. Earlier Jinnah used to be, in fact, horrified at the sycophancy exhibited by the Muslim aristocrats to the British and publicly opposed the need to form the League. He criticised its leaders for the hostility they displayed against the Hindus and the divisive stand they took in politics.

These shenanigans endeared Jinnah to the Hindus and he soon became the darling of the leaders of the Congress. They extolled his robust patriotism. Gokhale called him "the best ambassador of Hindu-Muslim unity". The poetess Sarojini Naidu, who had met Jinnah for the first time at the Calcutta Congress in 1906, paid him glowing tributes, praising his qualities of head and heart in her characteristically romantic language: "a naïve and eager humanity, an intuition quick and tender as a woman's, a humour gay and winning as a child's — pre-eminently rational and practical, discreet and dispassionate in his estimate and acceptance of life. The obvious sanity and serenity of his worldly wisdom effectually disguise a shy and splendid idealism which is of the very essence of the man."[1]

There were at this time two sets of leaders in the Congress— one, moderate and the other extremist. Among the moderates were Jinnah's friends such as Mehta and Gokhale. The extremists were led by Bal Gangadhar Tilak who was equally fond of Jinnah and whose aggressive nationalism Jinnah greatly admired. The two factions clashed violently at the next annual session of the Congress at Surat in 1906 which resulted in the first open split in the organisation. Though Jinnah's sympathies were with the moderates, he refused to condemn the revolt that Tilak had mounted against them. The bold and frank editorials of the fiery Brahmin in his newspaper *Kesari*, published from Poona, were highly appreciated by Jinnah. A year later when Tilak was arrested and charged with sedition, he defended him in the trial court but failed to get him acquitted. Ever since then Tilak developed high regard for Jinnah who appeared for him in yet another case in 1916 on a similar charge. But this time he succeeded in obtaining Tilak's release. For the Hindus, whether moderates or extremists, liberals or conservatives, secular or communal, Jinnah was then the hope for a united India and the finest embodiment of Hindu-Muslim unity.

The Muslim leadership of that time was, however, not in tune with Jinnah's unqualified nationalism. They did not like the idea of uniting with the Hindus without obtaining the maximum safeguards for the Muslims. They carved out a separate political path for the community. On October 1, 1906, over fifty Muslim leaders from all over India met the Viceroy Lord Minto in a deputation and presented him a memorandum incorporating their special demands. In his reply the Viceroy assured them that "... I am as firmly convinced as I believe you to be that any electoral representation in India would be

doomed to mischievous failure which aimed at granting a
personal enfranchisement regardless of the beliefs and
traditions of the communities composing the population of
this continent."² Minto assured them of separate electorate
which goaded them to form the All-India Muslim League in
Dacca on December 31, 1906. Jinnah reacted strongly against
it. He organised, along with a few friends, a countermove in
Calcutta at the same time to warn the Muslims not to succumb
to the British policy of "divide and rule" which was being
endorsed by the newly formed League. He said it would
eventually harm the Muslims and deprive them of participation
in national life.

The Aga Khan, who was elected as the first President
of the League, pointed out subsequently that Jinnah was "our
doughtiest opponent in 1906". He had publicly denounced
the League's communal move. In the words of the Aga Khan,
"Jinnah came out in bitter hostility towards all that I and my
friends had done and were trying to do".³ He opposed the
League's stand of favouring separate electorate for the Muslims
and described it "as a poisonous dose to divide the nation
against itself". He collaborated with the Congress and actively
worked against the Muslim communalists, calling them enemies
of the nation. He had been much influenced by the speeches
of Naoroji, Mehta and Gokhale whom he adored. Naoroji as
Congress President had emphasised the need for "a thorough
union of all the people" and pleaded with Hindus and Muslims
to "sink or swim together. Without this union, all efforts will
be in vain,"⁴ he added. Jinnah was in full agreement with this
view. He deprecated the contrary separatist policy advocated
by the League.

However despite the protest by the Congress, the
provision for separate electorate for the Muslims was made by

the British in the Indian Councils' Act of 1909. In the twenty-fifth session of the Congress at Allahabad in 1910, Jinnah moved a resolution condemning the provision of reserving separate seats for the Muslims, especially in its application to municipalities, district boards and other local bodies. He said it would sow the seed of division between the Hindus and the Muslims and keep them politically apart.

Despite his resolute opposition to the introduction of separate electorate for the Muslims, Jinnah did not hesitate to take personal advantage of it and contested the election to the Viceroy's Executive Council from the reserved Muslim constituency of Bombay and got himself elected. The voters disregarded his opposition to reservation and were carried away by his brilliant advocacy at the bar and his arresting personality. He was the first non-official Muslim to sit on the Viceroy's Executive Council in 1910. His three-year tenure on that body and the lure of Muslim representation gradually drew him away from the purely nationalist mind-set to which he had so far adhered and made him turn more to the problems of the community rather than of the country as a whole. It was a turning point in his political career but he pursued it cautiously. He cleverly managed the contradictions in the two streams of communalism and nationalism. He took care not to antagonise the Hindus while working for the Muslims. For instance he vigorously defended Gandhi when the latter was censured in the Viceroy's Executive Council for his so-called seditious activities in support of Indian settlers. Jinnah had condemned such criticism as "cruel". Lord Minto reprimanded Jinnah for using the word "cruel" against "a friendly part of the Empire". It was, he declared, "too harsh". Jinnah countered it as politely as he could: "My Lord," he said, "I should feel much inclined to use much stronger language. But I am fully aware of the constitution of this Council, and I do not wish to trespass for one single moment. But I do say that the treatment meted out to Indians (in South Africa) is the harshest and the feeling (about it) in this country is unanimous."[5] Jinnah had substituted "cruel" for "too harsh" and called the treatment "harshest". In retort and rebuttal he had no equal either at the bar or on the political forum.

Another trait in his character which was noticed especially at the bar was the manner in which he asserted himself. He was oversensitive and had his own notion of self-respect, regardless of the price he might have to pay; this often awed his opponents. He would not tolerate the slightest insult or humiliation and was quick to retaliate. Sir Chimanlal Setalvad narrates two incidents in his memoirs *Reflections and Recollections* on how Jinnah reacted in such situations: "He [Jinnah] never allowed himself to be overborne either by the judge or the opposing counsel. Once Strangman and Jinnah were briefed together in a case and Jinnah attended a consultation in Strangman's chamber. It was said that during the consultation, Strangman spoke to Jinnah in a manner which the latter regarded as insulting. Ever since, Jinnah always refused to go into Strangman's room for consultation and they never talked to each other... I remember an episode in the court of the late Justice Mirza. Jinnah and myself were appearing on opposite sides and there were other counsel appearing for some of the various parties in the suit. During the course of argument, Jinnah addressed the judge in a manner which the judge resented. Justice Mirza told Jinnah that he was committing contempt of court. Strangely enough, the judge turned to me and said: 'Don't you think Mr. Jinnah is guilty of contempt of court?' It was indeed stupid of the judge to have put such a question to me. I answered 'It is not for me to give an opinion whether Mr. Jinnah had committed contempt or not. It is your privilege to determine that but I can say that knowing Mr. Jinnah as I do, he could never have intended to insult the court'. Jinnah, thereafter, ceased to appear before this judge for some time."[6]

As Jinnah became more active in public affairs, he realised he could not make a mark there unless he reconciled his undiluted nationalism with the rising tide of Muslim communalism. He thus walked the tightrope with consummate tact and ability. Though he was a Muslim only in name, having neither practised the tenets of Islam nor studied the Quran or the traditions of the Prophet, he was fully aware of the significance of the religious label in those days of avant-garde politics. He used it not only in dealing with the British but also with the Hindus. He needed the support of his coreligionists as much as the goodwill of the Hindus to forge his leadership. In the atmosphere then prevailing, the link proved useful but he also used it to remove the barriers between Hindus and Muslims. His efforts to retain the admiration of the Muslims did not come in the way of his eagerness to keep, at the same time, the trust of the Hindus.

THREE

Efforts at Unity

By now, Jinnah had risen high in the Congress hierarchy. His work in London for greater participation of Indians in the administration was much appreciated. Gokhale praised him and gave him prominence at the annual session of the Congress held at Karachi in December 1913. Jinnah showed his keenness in bringing the Congress and the League together on one platform; his intention was applauded by most of the Congress leaders. Hence he proceeded to Agra where the League was holding its annual session and told the delegates to defer their move on separate electorate for a year. But despite his powerful presentation he did not succeed. Somewhat disappointed he once again sailed for London along with the President-elect of the Congress, Bhupendra Nath Basu and Lala Lajpat Rai. It was during this visit that Jinnah first met Gandhi who had come to London from South Africa to protest against the treatment of Indians in what was then a British colony. A reception was held in his honour to extol his brave but non-violent fight on behalf of the indentured Indian labour.

Jinnah spoke in glowing terms of Gandhi's services to the nation. Later, when Gandhi returned from South Africa for good in 1915, the Gujarat Sabha gave him a rousing welcome. Jinnah was asked to preside over it which pleased Gandhi for he saw in it a good augury for the future of Hindu-Muslim unity.

Jinnah suffered a setback in the passing away of his closest associates in the Congress — Gokhale and Mehta who died one after the other. He then came close to Tilak who was hailed as a national hero after his release from jail. Tilak had observed Jinnah's cosmopolitan stand on various issues and commended the courage that he showed in expressing them. From an aggressively pro-Hindu Tilak, this was indeed great appreciation; Jinnah also learnt from Tilak that in order to have a mass base, a leader had to cultivate his community. This was not easy for him to accomplish. He was thoroughly westernised both in his thinking and his lifestyle. He lacked the popular touch since he was not a natural mass leader. Nevertheless he started taking greater interest in the affairs of the Muslims and establishing closer contacts with their leaders. He acquainted himself with the problems that bothered them. As a member of the Viceroy's Executive Council he therefore came forward to pilot the Wakf Validating Act which won him much gratitude from a number of Muslim families. Subsequently during his election campaigns he cultivated the Muslim voters belonging to different sections. All of them were much appreciative of his sincere efforts for the welfare of the community. Jinnah was courteous and considerate to them but not easily accessible to anyone on a personal basis. He always kept the public at arm's length; he was happy to plead for them but did not want to mingle with them. Once one of his colleagues requested him to shake hands with people at receptions. Jinnah was irritated: "If I shake hands with one I shall have to shake hands with all. And there is no time for that."[1]

Jinnah's main concern during this period was to bring Hindus and Muslims together politically. He felt this would ensure him a more secure place in India's public life. He worked hard to see that the coming annual sessions of both the Congress and the League took place in Bombay. To create the right atmosphere for unity he persuaded the President-elect of the League Mazhar-ul-Haque to take the lead and extend a hand of friendship to the Hindus. For this move Jinnah received wholehearted support of the Congress but some sections of the League were strongly opposed to it for they feared that it would destroy the independence and importance of their organisation. Despite Haque's assurance that there was no question of the League merging with the Congress, Hasrat Mohani and others mounted a virulent attack on Jinnah. They denounced him as an agent of the Hindus. They said he neither looked nor behaved like a Muslim nor did he speak their language; they accused him of lacking in knowledge of the Quran and the traditions of the Prophet. How could such a Muslim speak on their behalf, they asked. Haque was aghast at the intensity of their attack; it was followed by violent demonstrations against Jinnah. In the commotion Haque adjourned the meeting; this was then held the following day behind closed doors at the Taj Mahal Hotel, Bombay. Jinnah mobilised his supporters and managed to get a resolution passed authorising the President of the League to appoint a committee to formulate a scheme of political and administrative reforms in collaboration with the Congress. It was to be then jointly presented to the British. In the game of power politics he was able to show that he could easily out-manoeuvre his opponents.

As a result of Jinnah's persistent endeavour in improving relations between the Congress and the League, the two organisations, after intense discussion among their leaders, decided to hold their respective annual sessions in the last week of December 1916 in Lucknow. This culminated in the Congress agreeing to enter into a pact with the League —the famous Congress-League Pact — under which it was provided that "no bill, nor any clause thereof, nor a resolution introduced by a non-official member, affecting one or the other community, which question is to be determined by the members of that community in the Legislative Council concerned, shall be proceeded with, if three-fourths of the members of that community in the particular Council, Imperial or Provincial, oppose the bill or any clause thereof or the resolution".[2]

For having played a vital role in forming a united front with the Congress, Jinnah was elected to preside over the annual session of the League. In his presidential address he declared triumphantly that India had been brought out of its depths. As for the Muslims, he assured them that "their gaze, like that of their Hindu fellow- countrymen, is fixed on the future". He welcomed the new spirit of patriotism which "has taken its rise from a newborn movement in the direction of national unity". It had "brought Hindus and Muslims together involving brotherly service for the common cause."[3] Jinnah had hoped that, once both the Congress and the League adhered to the provisions of the bill which had been incorporated in the pact, it would be presented to the British Parliament as the united demand of the two major communities of India. He told the Muslims that "towards the Hindus our attitude should be of goodwill and brotherly feelings. Cooperation to the cause of our motherland should be our guiding principle. India's real progress can only be achieved by a true understanding and harmonious relations between the two great sister communities."[4]

Though Jinnah aligned himself with the Muslims he was, as Gokhale had said, free "of all sectarian prejudices"; in fact he always felt more at home with the non-Muslims. In particular he enjoyed the sophisticated company of the Parsis, which brought him in close touch with Sir Dinshaw Petit. His beautiful daughter Ruttie was greatly enamoured by Jinnah and fell in love with him. Jinnah also grew fond of her. They decided to marry, despite parental opposition; Ruttie embraced Islam and became Jinnah's wife. She was warm, lively and high spirited, gregarious, tempestuous and fiercely independent. Jinnah, on the other hand, was exceedingly controlled, self-possessed, grim, cold, distant and almost a recluse in personal life. They could not cope with life together. A few years later they separated but were never divorced. Their failed relationship also gives an insight into Jinnah's complex personality. Ruttie was the only human being he ever came close to; no one else ever succeeded in penetrating through his loneliness. He himself admitted, "I seem to be losing her — she was slipping away and I resented this and felt miserable. Many of our little tiffs... were due to this background of conflicts.... In politics I was an unhappy, lonely figure and now even my home life was ending for me. Loneliness everywhere...."[5]

Jinnah worked for Hindu-Muslim unity and made every attempt to see that the Congress and the League presented a united front. He swore by the Pact and assured the British that they need not be unduly perturbed as its terms if implemented would help them as well. He welcomed the historic declaration made by the British Government in the House of Commons on August 20, 1917, which assured Indians that "the policy of

His Majesty's Government, with which the Government of India are in complete accord, is that of the increasing association of self-governing institutions with a view to the progressive realisation of responsible government in India as an integral part of the British Empire."[6] To give effect to it, the new Secretary of State for India Edward Montague visited India in the winter of that year. He along with Viceroy Lord Chelmsford conferred with the leaders of different schools of political thought to try and find a consensus on the future constitutional advance. Of all the politicians whom Montague met, he was most impressed by Jinnah. He recorded this in his diary: "Young, perfectly mannered, impressive looking, armed to the teeth with dialectics, and insistent upon the whole of his scheme.... Chelmsford tried to argue with him and was tied up into knots. Jinnah is a very clever man, and it is, of course, an outrage that such a man should have no chance of running the affairs of his own country."[7]

Jinnah's scheme to bring the Hindus and the Muslims on a common constitutional platform received good response all around; but some of his colleagues in the League were not too happy about it. They expressed the fear that the Hindus who would form the majority in the proposed arrangement might jeopardise Muslim interests. Jinnah reminded them that the voice of seventy million Muslims could not be throttled by anyone, even through the ballot box. In any legislature, he said, a minority could not be easily suppressed, much less a large minority like the Indian Muslims. They had to have confidence in their own strength. He advised them not to be "scared away ... from cooperation with the Hindus, which is essential for the establishment of self-government".[8]

The political situation however became complicated with a new development in the international arena where the

Caliph, who was also the Sultan of Turkey, joined Germany against Britain and other Allies in the First World War (1914-18). Being the custodian of the Kaaba, the holiest place of Islam, the Caliph's defeat stirred the Muslims to such religious fury that they united in protesting against the victorious British who seemed bent upon dismembering the Caliphate which was then regarded as the rallying centre of Islam. The Ali Brothers organised a massive movement to restore the Ottoman guardianship over the Kaaba; the agitation soon acquired a mass base and was deemed seditious by the British. The Ali Brothers were interned along with Maulana Abul Kalam Azad and other prominent Muslim leaders.

The constitutionalist Jinnah was outraged by this illegal action; he disassociated himself with it. In the process he became totally alienated from the Muslims who accused him of being a traitor to their cause. They attacked him publicly for letting down the community on such a crucial issue. For them the guardianship of the Kaaba was an article of faith; it could not be allowed to go into the hands of a foreign power or its agent; the Khilafat guaranteed that their sacred shrine would remain in the hands of the Muslims; to take it away from the Caliph was to strike a death nail at the very root of their religion. Jinnah who was neither steeped in the tenets of Islam nor sensitive to the emotional and spiritual significance of the Kaaba in the life of a Muslim, took a legalistic view and refused to join the massive protest against the British.

Gandhi was cast in a different mould. He did not recognise laws which flouted the aspirations of the people. He believed not only in defying them but also in overthrowing the system that nurtured them. Being a man of faith, he fully respected the religious susceptibilities of others. According to him the Hindus and the Muslims were children of the same soil; they were blood brothers who owed their loyalty to mother India. And so if one brother was in trouble and his religious faith was sought to be destroyed, it was the duty of the other brother to go to his rescue. He offered the Ali Brothers his unqualified support for the protection of the Kaaba and the restoration of the Khilafat. He placed two conditions before the Muslims: one, that non-cooperation with the Government which he planned as a protest against the British, would have to be total; and two, that it had to be non-violent. The agitated Muslims were enthused by Gandhi's spontaneous support to their stand, especially in view of the hold that he had acquired among the Hindus and the universal reverence that he commanded because of his piety, integrity and selfless service. They not only accepted his conditions but also requested him to lead them.

On behalf of the Muslims, the Ali Brothers promised unreserved loyalty and complete obedience to Gandhi. This was how the leadership of the Khilafat and Non-Cooperation movement — the first India-wide mass struggle against the British — came to Gandhi. It catapulted him to centrestage and earned him the love and devotion of millions of Hindus and Muslims. And thus from a mere rebel, Gandhi was transformed into the Mahatma. No one was more dismayed than Jinnah at this sudden development which metamorphosed the whole character of Indian politics. The Nagpur session of the Congress in 1919 put the seal of approval on Gandhi's defiance of the British raj; the British characterised it as seditious to the core. Jinnah opposed it bitterly. He said he could not be party to such an open rebellion which threatened to disrupt public life. The delegates heckled and jeered him; they refused to listen to him. He walked out in sheer disgust and never returned to the Congress. He told a representative of the press: "I will have nothing to do with this pseudo-religious approach to politics. I part company with the Congress and Gandhi. I part company with mob hysteria. Politics is a gentleman's game."[9]

The Muslims were naturally upset that while Jinnah had exhibited no qualms in opposing the Rowlatt Bill and castigating the British, he backed out when it came to standing by the Muslims. Although he was their elected representative, he showed no sympathy for them. He was not prepared to upset the British on this score. Such callousness on his part on what was to the Muslims a matter of life and death, annoyed "Big Brother" Maulana Shaukat Ali. During the Congress session at Nagpur, when Jinnah was expressing his opposition to the Khilafat movement, the Maulana lost his cool and excitedly rushed towards him to lynch him. Jinnah remained calm and refused to be provoked. Apart from the defiance of law that the Mahatma advocated, what troubled Jinnah was the prospect of going to jail; it would have entailed giving up his luxurious life. He witnessed the massive enthusiastic support that Gandhi, along with the Ali Brothers, had generated, but it did not make him change his mind. He remained aloof politically and carried on with his legal practice. He did not hesitate to criticise the introduction of religion into politics and to express his dislike of the mullahs and the pundits with their archaic views. He was totally averse to clashing with the police on the streets and organising protest marches. He found the entire movement loathsome and deliberately distanced himself from it. More than earning the displeasure of the British, what really kept Jinnah away from this movement was its religious character which was at the time anathema to him.

FOUR

The Lean Period

With the rise of Gandhi in the political arena, Jinnah's leadership suffered heavily. He became a square peg in the round hole of mass agitation. His open opposition to the Khilafat movement had already dealt a severe blow to his relationship with the Muslims. He became like a Dutch general with no soldiers. He struggled hard to regain his old position but every move that he made proved to be abortive. He therefore made a half-hearted attempt to modify his opposition to Gandhi and his movement. But such was the resentment against him that both the Congress and the Muslims paid little heed to his turnabout. He had to reconcile himself to the reverence the Mahatma commanded among both Hindus and Muslims. He thus refrained from ridiculing him any more. In his presidential address to the special session of the League at Calcutta in February 1921, Jinnah referred no more to him as Mr. Gandhi. He said, "Mahatma Gandhi has placed his programme of non-cooperation supported by the authority of the Khilafat Conference before the country. It is now for you to consider whether or not you approve of its principle and, approving of its principle, whether or not you approve of its details. The operation of this scheme will strike at the individual in each of you and therefore it rests with you alone to measure your strength and to weigh the pros and cons of the question before you arrive at a decision. But once you have decided to march, let there be no retreat under any circumstances (Shouts of no, no, never)... I do not wish to detain you any more but before I sit down I will only say this; remember... that united we stand, divided we fall (Hear, hear and applause)..."[1] Jinnah made a guarded appeal, devoid of sincerity, only because he did not want to be isolated. This is, in fact, the first solitary instance when he publicly ate humble pie and tried to appease the mob, much against his wish.

This was in sharp contrast to the stubborn stand he had taken earlier and the contemptuous manner in which he had turned down Gandhi's request, when the Mahatma had invited him to participate in the "new life" that had opened up before the country: he had told Gandhi frankly: "If by 'new life' you mean your methods and your programme, I am afraid I cannot accept them; for I am fully convinced that it must lead to disaster... Your methods have already caused split and division in almost every institution that you have approached hitherto, and in the public life of the country not only amongst Hindus and Muslims but between Hindus and Hindus and Muslims and Muslims and even between fathers and sons; people are generally desperate all over the country and your extreme programme has for the moment struck the imagination mostly of the inexperienced youth and the ignorant and the illiterate."[2] This however made little impact on Gandhi who was unable to appreciate Jinnah's legal quibbling about what was legitimate agitation and what was not, according to his perception. As for Jinnah calling him Mr.Gandhi at the Nagpur session of the Congress in 1920, it had only amused the Mahatma; but his followers were annoyed at Jinnah's deliberate discourtesy. Gandhi had, in fact, chided people for calling him Mahatma. He told them, "The word 'Mahatma' stinks in my nostrils; and, in addition to that, when somebody insists that everyone must call me 'Mahatma' I get nausea, I do not wish to live. Had I not known that the more I insist on the word 'Mahatma' not being used, the more does it come into vogue, I would most certainly have insisted. In the Ashram where I live, every child, brother and sister has orders not to use the word 'Mahatma'."[3] The people irrespective of their caste or creed, position or status, persisted in addressing him as "Mahatma" and anyone who did not do so was frowned upon, Jinnah being one of them.

After the Congress session at Nagpur, Jinnah was dumbfounded to see the tremendous response that Gandhi continued to attract. Jinnah was unable to comprehend the reason for it. He felt increasingly like a fish out of water. What shocked him was that eminent lawyers such as C.R. Das and Motilal Nehru, who like him were confirmed constitutionalists, had quietly given up their opposition to Gandhi and declared their unflinching loyalty to him. He therefore felt forlorn. But being a diehard champion of the legal system, Jinnah could not bring himself to defy it. Thus despite the popular pressure that was mounted on him, he kept aloof from the movement. He had, on several occasions, opposed the British but within the limits prescribed by the law. He thrived on encounters and enjoyed battering his opponents. However revolt against authority went against his grain; rulers could be admonished, even rebuked, but not disobeyed. He was at his best in fighting them in court and in the legislature. He had done it on many occasions with devastating effect. For instance he brilliantly defended Tilak's writings when he was arrested and put on trial. He proved to the court that what Tilak had written could not be regarded as seditious; even so Tilak was imprisoned for six years and exiled in the Andamans. The verdict did not rouse the same resentment in Jinnah as it did among millions of Indians. He believed that he had done his job as a lawyer to the best of his ability but the verdict had to rest with the judge. That was how the legal system worked.

Jinnah's disagreement with Gandhi was on the same grounds. At the Nagpur Congress session he took pains to explain that the constitutional way was the only way to attain freedom; Maulana Mohamed Ali interrupted him and narrated a story about a preacher in the Salvation Army. He was haranguing the crowd at Hyde Park in London telling them that his was the only way to reach God; someone in the audience interjected and asked him: "How long have you been saying this?" "Oh, for the past twenty years," he replied. The heckler then said: "After all these years if it has taken you where you are, I am not interested in your way." The Maulana asked Jinnah: "Where has your constitutional way taken us — only to the hell of slavery. There are no signs of the heaven of freedom."[4]

By 1922, the Khilafat and Non-Cooperation movement, because of the various oppressive measures taken against it by the British authorities, had begun to lose its élan. Gandhi himself called off the agitation after the Chauri Chaura incident when the protesters had burnt a police chowki with twelve policemen inside. Then there was the terror unleashed by the Moplahs, a Muslim sect of Kerala, who not only revolted against the authorities but also the Hindu landlords and subjected them to loot and arson; some of them were even forcibly converted to Islam. This naturally upset the Hindus terribly. To worsen the situation, the British hirelings instigated communal riots in several cities and towns in different parts of India. Jinnah had earlier warned the Congress of such occurrences but what distressed him now was the deterioration in Hindu-Muslim relations. The fault, however, did not lie with the participants who had worked for unity but with those who had engineered these riots, as one of Gandhi's lieutenants Rajendra Prasad, pointed out. The British authorities in order to suppress the massive revolt had resorted to such tactics. This was the most heinous part of their policy of "divide and rule". Jinnah was fully aware of this fact; still he blamed Gandhi for the adverse turn that politics had taken.

Subsequently in 1923 when a section of the Congress decided to abandon agitational politics and contest elections to the provincial and central legislatures under the leadership of C.R. Das and Motilal Nehru, Jinnah heaved a sigh of relief. The cooperators called themselves Swarajists and won a number of seats. Jinnah also got himself elected to the Central Legislative Assembly from his old reserved Muslim constituency in Bombay. His close associate of those days, M.C. Chagla, who later became Chief Justice of Bombay, has narrated in his memoirs *Roses in December* an interesting episode which took place in the midst of Jinnah's election campaign. Jinnah and Chagla took some time off and went to lunch at Cornaglia, then a much-patronised restaurant. Jinnah ordered "two cups of coffee, a plate of pastry and a plate of pork sausages." Just then an old bearded Muslim accompanied by his ten year old son came up to talk to them. Jinnah invited the father and son to join them. Chagla recounts: "I then saw the boy's hand reaching out slowly but irresistibly towards the plate of pork sausages. After some hesitation, he picked up one, put it in his mouth, munched it and seemed to enjoy it tremendously. I watched this uneasily... After some time they left and Jinnah turned to me, and said angrily: 'Chagla, you should be ashamed of yourself.' I said: 'What did I do?' Jinnah asked: 'How dare you allow the young boy to eat pork sausages?' I said: 'Look, Jinnah, I had to use all my mental faculties at top speed to come to a quick decision. The question was: should I let Jinnah lose his election or should I let the boy go to eternal damnation? And I decided in your favour.'⁵

After the election, Jinnah along with twenty-two other members with no affiliation to any political party formed the Independent Party under his leadership. The Swarajists who had forty-two members elected Motilal Nehru as their leader. In the Central Legislative Assembly the two groups worked in unison on most occasions; they criticised, attacked and opposed the British-controlled treasury benches. Jinnah was keen to regain his lost position as the ambassador of Hindu-Muslim unity; by joining hands with the Congress he hoped to regain it. He emphasised the need for unity by declaring, as the newly elected President of the League on the eve of its annual session in December 1923, that his aim had always been "to bring about, in due course, through and by means of the All-India Muslim League organisation once more a complete settlement between the Hindus and the Muslims as was done in 1916." He paid a rather unexpected tribute to Gandhi by stating that "the result of the struggle of the last three years has this to our credit that there is an open movement for the achievement of Swaraj for India."⁶ The changed political environment, in which the Mahatma towered above all, could not be ignored by Jinnah. He confessed, by implication, that he was wrong in his assessment of the Non-Cooperation movement; but even so he showed little inclination to follow the Mahatma. He was content to sow his lonely furrow.

Nevertheless, he made every effort to reduce the hostility between himself and the Congress. Maulana Mohamed Ali who was elected as its President at the Kokanada session in December 1923, continued to bear the old grudge against him. He was bitter about Jinnah's role in the Khilafat movement. Jinnah did not react. He went on being friendly to the Congress. He wanted the Hindus to show the same affection to him as before and not to misunderstand his motives. He assured them that "I still stand as a tried nationalist". He had no interest in communal politics; he said, "it is not with a view to prejudicing national interest, on the contrary, to bring them [the Muslims] in line with the rest of India."[7] He participated in the All-Parties Conference convened by Maulana Mohammed Ali to resolve the Hindu-Muslim tangle. In the committee that was appointed by the conference to prepare a scheme for Swaraj, he played a leading role. In the All-Parties Conference in Delhi which was held soon thereafter and over which Gandhi presided, Jinnah made valuable and constructive suggestions.

He presented a draft statement on the future political set-up, stressing that there should be a "reunion of all nationalists on a common platform". He also attended the Unity Conference called by Dr. M.A. Ansari who had by then become Congress President of the Madras session in 1927. Thus he went out of his way to go along with the party; he did not miss any occasion now to show his alignment with the Congress which had begun to somewhat drift from its agitational agenda. Earlier he had even made a public clarification to the effect that he was not anti-Congress. In a letter to *The Times of India* dated October 3, 1925 Jinnah wrote: "I wish again to correct the statement which is attributed to me and to which you have given currency more than once and now again repeated by your correspondent 'Banker' in the

second column of your issue of the 1ˢᵗ October, that I
denounced the Congress as a 'Hindu institution'. I publicly
corrected this misleading report of my speech in your columns
soon after it appeared; but it did not find a place in the columns
of your paper and so may I now request you to publish this
and oblige."[8] So eager was he then to refute that he ever regarded
the Congress as a Hindu body. The subsequent volte face on
his part, which changed the history of India, is a sad commentary
on the shape that his politics finally took.

FIVE

Decline of Clout

Despite Jinnah's frantic efforts to woo the Congress, especially after the way the Swarajists asserted themselves against the diehard Gandhians, misgivings about him persisted. As M.R. Jaykar said, the old prejudices against him were so ingrained within the entire Congress hierarchy that the change in his stance could not restore the faith they once had in him. This came out sharply on the floor of the Central Legislative Assembly when Jinnah tried to criticise the Swarajists for their obstructive activities. He had wrongly believed that their deviation from the Gandhian path of non-cooperation would help them to be constructive. He soon realised that they had hardly been cured of their old agitational habit.The Swarajist members made it clear in their speeches that they stood for wrecking the legislature and making it impossible to function as a tool of the government. Speaking on the Indian Finance Bill on March 15, 1925, Jinnah condemned this declaration saying, "I can say to my friends here and I can say to this House that standing here in the month of March 1925, I am not prepared to resort to any policy or any programme of obstruction to be put into operation here." He added: "I say if the country wants that this Legislature should be wrecked and if you want to make that clear to the country, it may be that you may not have a majority for some time; it may be that some of us may die and some of us may have to resign for their own purpose and there may be bye-elections and you will come forward before the electorates and try and get that majority — that is what I mean..."[1]

The record of the proceedings clearly establishes the alienation between Motilal Nehru and Jinnah:

Motilal Nehru interjected: Allow me to make it perfectly clear for my Honourable friend's information that we have a distinct and direct mandate from the country to destroy this Legislature if it will not mend.

M.A. Jinnah: I deny it; I challenge it.

Motilal Nehru: We came on that ticket; that was our election manifesto.

M.A. Jinnah: I challenge it; the Honourable Pandit is not yet in the majority here and I challenge that and I want the country to declare it. (An Honourable Member: "Are you in a majority?")

Shamlal Nehru: May I inform the Honourable Member that we are in a majority here. If the 30 nominated Members of the Government are not counted we are in a majority in this House. M.A. Jinnah: Sir, it is no use evading it. I put it to my Swarajist friends; I am perfectly willing to stand by what I say. If my friend Motilal Nehru's policy is that policy and if that is his programme,

that he wants in this Assembly to obstruct from
beginning to end, persistent, continuous, together with
refusal of supplies, if that is his policy, and if, as my
friend Mr. Chaman Lall very rightly said, we want to
make this Government impossible and as Mr. Abhyankar
very rightly endorsed it now, then I am opposed to it.
Sir, that is the issue before us. I feel and I am convinced,
and let me tell you here and I hope that you will believe
me, that I am honestly convinced that it is not possible
for you to make this Government impossible at present
and it will recoil on you if you make a mistake.

Pandit Motilal Nehru: Have courage.

M.A.Jinnah:My Honourable friend says, "Have courage."
My answer is that I cannot share in your recklessness at
your mature age. I say it is recklessness and that keeps
me back. But I tell you that you are not going to get me
to agree to pursue a policy of obstruction, to pursue a
policy of wrecking and recklessness by merely resorting
to these tactics.

Motilal Nehru: We do not depend upon you. [2]

The encounter clearly showed that Jinnah had not
changed; he remained as loyal to the constitutional way as
ever before. He opposed Gandhi on this score; he left the
Congress because he would not be a party to defiance. In effect
he was not prepared to overthrow the British; he would not
push them out but expect them as rulers to be generous and
accommodative. And to leave gracefully when the time came.
He attacked them verbally; but never revolted against them.
He always refrained from crossing the *laxman rekha*. He claimed
to be a nationalist but on every critical issue he compromised

with the British. He was careful not to unsettle them. Hence his bonafides were always suspect in the eyes of the Congress. From the time of the Non-Cooperation movement, he had remained for them, a renegade. Though he believed in cooperation with the government, he would not spare it for the wrongs he thought it committed; but that was always peripheral; he did not really wish for the end of their rule; he certainly wanted more Indian participation in the government but did not want to oust the British. For instance on January 25, 1925 Jinnah told the Finance Member Sir Basil Blackett during a debate in the Central Legislative Assembly on the Indian Finance Bill that he dare not deny that he had formulated a policy more helpful to Britain than to India. Sir Basil interjected to say that was not true. Jinnah told him to put his hand on his heart and say so. Sir Basil got up quietly, put his hand solemnly on his heart and repeated that what Jinnah had alleged against him was indeed not true. Jinnah retorted: "In that case I submit, Sir, that the Hon'ble Finance Member has no heart."[3] No one could really unnerve Jinnah in discussion or debate; that remained his forte till the end.

There was yet another charge levelled against Jinnah by the Hindu Mahasabha that he was more interested in being the advocate of the interests of the Muslims than a champion of freedom for all Indians. He was in reality, they said, a communalist in the garb of a nationalist. This hurt Jinnah deeply. In order to appease the Hindus and to win over his detractors, he went to the extent of abandoning the claim of the Muslims for separate electorate and suggested a scheme for general electorate. He did so while presiding over a convention called by the League in Delhi on March 20, 1927 where he presented what came to be known as the Delhi Proposals under which Muslims would give up separate electorate and accept general electorate with certain conditions. He got the Proposals adopted by the meeting calling them the most generous gesture by the Muslims to the Hindus. It was no doubt a bold and radical measure which upset many traditional Muslim leaders resulting subsequently in the break-up of the League into two groups: one led by Sir Mohamed Shafi and the other by Jinnah. The All-India Congress Committee was naturally happy at the volte face on Jinnah's part and wholeheartedly endorsed the Delhi Proposals at its meeting in May 1927.

Explaining the change in his attitude, Jinnah said in a statement to the Associated Press on March 29, that the Hindus did not fully appreciate the offer of joint electorate that he had so boldly enunciated. The two conditions that he had attached to it were most reasonable: one that Sind should be made a separate province and two, that reforms should be introduced in the North-West Frontier and Baluchistan. No prudent Hindu, having the larger interest of the country at heart, could object to it; but what thwarted Jinnah's desperate effort to win over the Hindus was the strong opposition that these Proposals evoked from a number of Muslim leaders who were not prepared to give up separate electorate under any circumstance. This considerably weakened Jinnah's bargaining position. In the Delhi session of the League, there was such rowdyism with the supporters of Jinnah and his opponents led by Sir Mohamed Shafi hurling allegations against each other that the meeting had to be adjourned. A further effort made after a few months to bring about rapprochement between the two sections also ended in a fiasco; however pressure mounted on both sides to come to an amicable settlement and restore unity in the ranks of the League. The Aga Khan was requested to intervene and preside over the next session of the League which was to be attended by both the Jinnah and the Shafi groups. At first the Aga Khan agreed but later he changed his mind. A dispute also arose on the selection of the venue for the session; Jinnah insisted on Calcutta but Shafi wanted Lahore. Shafi's supporters feared that Jinnah and his followers would push through the Delhi Proposals at Calcutta where the situation was congenial to them; the Shafi group saw through Jinnah's game and backed out of its commitment.

The Jinnah group went ahead and held the annual session of the League at Calcutta from December 30, 1927 to January 1, 1928. In his presidential address Jinnah admonished Shafi and his colleagues and co-workers for their unpatriotic stand. He was emboldened by the warm welcome the Delhi Proposals received from one of the tallest among the Hindu leaders — Pandit Madan Mohan Malaviya. This, Jinnah said, would definitely help to bring about a settlement of the long-standing Hindu-Muslim differences on the issue. He added, "I welcome the hand of fellowship extended to us by Hindu leaders from the platform of the Congress and the Hindu Mahasabha. For, to me, this offer is more valuable than any concession which the British Government can make. Let us then grasp the hand of fellowship."[4]

Apart from his opposition to joint electorate Shafi and his group worked actively to undermine the attempt by Jinnah and his League to boycott the all-white Simon Commission which was sent to India by the British Government to review the constitutional requirements. The Viceroy Lord Irwin clarified in a statement on November 8, 1928 that it would draft a new constitution for India. Jinnah had strongly censured the appointment of the Commission as it did not include any Indian as member. Hence his League joined hands with the Congress to boycott it. To the British, the stand the Congress took was understandable in view of its past history but what surprised them was the attitude of Jinnah who called upon his followers to collaborate with the Congress and non-cooperate with the Commission. He had earlier written to the Viceroy that at least one Hindu and one Muslim should be appointed on the Commission. But Lord Irwin turned down his request; in his reply to Jinnah's letter the Viceroy wrote: "I am not sure that I feel as confident as you that our path would be smoothed, even if it were possible to act upon your suggestion."[5]

Despite Jinnah's uncompromising stand, the Muslims were divided on the question of boycott of the Commission; Sir Mohamed Shafi, Sir Mohamed Zafrullah Khan and several other leaders asked them to fully cooperate with the Commission. The Hindus were however jubilant that Jinnah had taken a different position. Gandhi congratulated him on the courage that he had shown in mobilising Muslim public opinion. But Jinnah was disappointed at the lukewarm support he received from his co-religionists. Shafi had managed to enlist the help of even the eminent poet-philosopher Allama Iqbal who advised Muslims to cooperate with the Commission and use the opportunity to press their demands before it. Jinnah had also lost the support of the Anglo-Indian press which until then had demonstrated great adoration for him; *The Times*, London criticised him bitterly. Jinnah wondered why these newspapers had become so hostile to him. "Why," he asked, "this audacious attempt under the guise of friendship by these newspapers" and replied himself: "because there are people in England and India who believe that among Mussalmans there is a fertile soil for their manoeuvres and machinations."[6] He was severely attacked even by the liberals but he stood firm. His self-respect would not allow him to compromise on this issue which for him was the real test of British intention. He had supported them because he believed they wanted Indians to be partners with them. The all-white composition of the Simon Commission came as a rude shock to him.

The division in the ranks of the Muslims had no doubt dealt a blow to Jinnah's claim that he spoke for the Muslims. His opposition to the Commission was unequivocal but he realised that his hold on the Muslims had considerably weakened. He was already suspect in the eyes of the Hindus but his co-religionists had also begun to disown him. They were not prepared to accept him as a broker although he had so far played the role fairly successfully for them. Disgusted with the state of affairs in India, Jinnah concluded that for the time being there was no place for him in Indian politics. Gandhi had already sullied the atmosphere; Jinnah felt suffocated under it; but now Irwin had fallen prey to the imperial game; this made the situation worse. He therefore sailed for London on May 5, 1928 on *S.S. Rajputana* with Srinivasa Iyengar and Dewan Chamanlal as fellow passengers. On board, Jinnah forgot the humiliation he had suffered and was happy to escape the stress and strain of controversial politics as also the hurt the British had caused by not heeding him. His tragedy was that he was so full of himself that nothing else mattered to him; what he thought had to be right. As Chamanlal observed, "He has never belonged to a party unless he himself was the party."[7] He had taken little interest in the League until he became the dominant force in it. No sooner was his authority challenged than he cold-shouldered his colleagues, ignoring them and going his own way. Jinnah could never play second fiddle to anyone. He had to be the leader calling the shots. Nehru, despite his fundamental differences with Gandhi, surrendered to his mentor; he did not mind subordinating his views in order to retain the Mahatma's trust. Jinnah on the other hand was self-opinionated and self-absorbed. He regarded no one as his master. He rarely bent and never bowed. He was too strong-willed a person to be subjugated. He had his way, irrespective of the price he or anyone else would have to pay for it.

Six

Temporary Retirement

In London Jinnah renewed his acquaintance with some of the top British leaders whom he had known personally and explained to them the complexities of the situation in India. They enjoyed his company and freely exchanged views with him. They found in him a kindred soul. However before Jinnah could settle down, he was disturbed to hear about the deteriorating health of his young wife who was under treatment in Paris. He rushed to be with her. Ruttie's condition continued to worsen. She was taken back to Bombay; soon thereafter she passed away at the premature age of twenty-nine. Though they had been separated for some time, her death came as a great shock to him. It is said that the only time he was ever seen to break down and cry was at Ruttie's funeral as her body was being lowered into the grave.

During Jinnah's stay in London, political developments in India had moved fast. The deliberations of the All-Parties Conference called in July 1928 by the then Congress President Motilal Nehru, to draft a constitution for India, had come to a close. The most contentious issue before it was the Muslim demand for separate electorate. The Hindu members by and large opposed it; they insisted on general electorate for all. Though this was accepted by pro-Congress Muslim leaders like Dr. M.A. Ansari and Maulana Azad, it was vehemently opposed by other Muslim leaders such as Maulana Mohamed Ali. At one time Jinnah had agreed to general electorate for Muslims on certain conditions but since then he had begun to suspect the bona fides of the Congress and had reversed his stand. His conditions were that Muslims should agree to joint electorate provided Nehru accepted the formation of Sind as a separate province, the introduction of reforms in the North-West Frontier and Baluchistan and a certain fixed percentage of representation for the Muslims at the Centre and in the provinces of Punjab and Bengal. The Congress took an ambivalent stand. Nehru could not carry Hindu leaders like B.S. Moonje and M.R. Jaykar with him and did not therefore incorporate these provisions in his report. Though Jinnah was then away in London, Nehru was confident that he would be able to persuade him to accept the final draft in the larger interest of the nation. He therefore sent an advance copy of the report as approved by the Conference to Jinnah at the port of Aden where his ship halted en route to Bombay.

Jinnah had given serious thought to this question while in London and had come to the conclusion that unless Nehru acceded to his conditions he would not be a signatory to the report. He was no longer interested in playing a nationalist role; it had paid him no dividend. He was distrusted by the Hindus and suspected by the Muslims. He laboured hard for unity but neither community seemed keen on it. His so-called ambassadorship had come into disrepute. Thus he gave up trying to bring about reconciliation and opted for separatism which had gripped the imagination of the Muslims. He had been beaten once on the Khilafat issue, he was now cautious in unreservedly accepting the Nehru Report which he learnt had upset the Muslims.

When he landed in Bombay his colleague M.C. Chagla told him that he had committed the League to the acceptance of the Nehru Report. Jinnah lost his temper. He rebuked Chagla and told him that he had no right to do so; he immediately announced to the press that he would have to consult the League Council first. This was his way to buy time before giving his reaction. In fact, he had made up his mind to go with the majority Muslim opinion. Motilal Nehru felt let down; his friends in the Congress chided him for having trusted Jinnah who, they said, was "a communal wolf in the shape of a nationalist sheep".

Jinnah called a meeting of the League Council and conferred with members on the implications of the report; since the Congress claimed that the report would form the basis of the future Constitution of India, he stressed that the interests of Muslims had to be protected. They concurred with his views and unanimously decided that they could not abandon separate electorate unless the conditions, as chalked out by Jinnah, were accepted by Nehru. The Council resolved that a delegation headed by Jinnah should attend the All-Parties National Convention called in Calcutta by Nehru on December 22, 1928 to press for the acceptance of these conditions. At the Convention, Jinnah used his forensic skills to give expression to Muslim apprehensions and pointed out : "I am exceedingly sorry that the report of the Committee is neither helpful nor fruitful in any way whatsoever... no country has succeeded in either wresting a democratic constitution from the domination of another nation or establishing representative institutions from within, without giving guarantees for the securities of the minorities wherever such a problem has arisen. Majorities are apt to be oppressive and tyrannical and minorities always dread and fear that their interests and rights, unless clearly and definitely safeguarded by statutory provisions, would suffer and be prejudiced, but this apprehension is enhanced all the more when we have to deal with communal majority...."

Though some delegates felt uneasy at his peroration, Jinnah continued uninterrupted: "The first point that I want to place before you is a point with regard to our proposal that there should be no less than one-third of Muslim representation in the Central Legislature. We propose that one-third of the elected members of the Central Legislature should be Mussalmans, and that the seats should be reserved for them to that extent under the joint electorate of the country.... What we feel is this. If it is conceded that Mussalmans should be enabled to secure one-third of the representation in the Central Legislature, the method which is adopted (in the Nehru Report) is neither quite fair to the provinces where the Mussalmans are in a minority, nor does it guarantee that we shall obtain one-third representation in the Central Legislature. You remember, originally the proposal emanated from certain Muslim leaders in March 1927 known as the Delhi Muslim Proposals. That was debated by the All-India Congress Committee in Bombay and in the open session of the Madras Congress and endorsed by it. The Muslim League in its Calcutta session in December 1927 also confirmed the proposal.... That has been given a go-by in the Nehru Report. Our next proposal is that the form of the constitution should be federal with residuary power vesting in the Provinces. This has also not been accepted. With regard to the questions of separation of Sind and the N.W.F. Province, we cannot agree that they should await until the Nehru Constitution is established with adult suffrage."[1]

Sir Tej Bahadur Sapru spoke immediately after Jinnah and conceded Jinnah's demands, in particular those pertaining to reservation of seats for the Muslims. He said: "If you examine the figures you will find that, including nominated members, Muslim representation in the Central Legislature is 27 percent and Mr. Jinnah wants 33... Speaking for myself, I would like you to placate Mr. Jinnah, whom I have known intimately for fifteen years. If he is a spoilt child, a naughty child, I am prepared to say, give him what he wants and be finished with it."[2] M.R. Jaykar, with his strong leanings towards the Hindu Mahasabha, stood up immediately and declared that he strongly disagreed with Sapru. He said: "I have also known Mr. Jinnah for the last sixteen years in close association as a colleague in nationalist life and I can assure you that he comes before us today neither as a naughty boy nor as a spoiled child... one important fact to remember... is that well-known Muslims like the esteemed patriots Maulana Abul Kalam Azad, Dr. Ansari, Sir Ali Imam, Raja Sahib of Mahmudabad and Dr. Kitchlew have given their full assent to the compromise embodied in the Nehru Committee Report. Mr. Jinnah, therefore, represents, if I may say so without offence, a small minority of Muslims."[3]

Jinnah was quick to react: "Minorities cannot give anything to the majority. It is, therefore, no use asking me not to press for what you call 'these small points.' I am not asking for these modifications because I am a 'naughty child'. If they are small points, why not concede? It is up to the majority, and majority alone can give. I am asking you for this adjustment because I think it is the best and fair to the Mussalmans...."[4]

It was a hopeless encounter between him and Jaykar which did not help to resolve the dispute. Neither the Hindu leaders nor Nehru were in a conciliatory mood. The Convention therefore put its stamp of approval on the Nehru Report without incorporating any of the amendments proposed by Jinnah. Attired in his best Saville Row suit, Jinnah put on his hat and walked out of the Convention — a lonely, forlorn figure. He was invited to attend the Muslim All-Parties Conference to be held on December 31, 1928 at Delhi but he kept away as he felt that no useful purpose would be served by his participation. His League, meeting in its annual session, had in fact denounced the move to hold such a conference claiming that "the League was the sole representative of the Muslims" and to hold the so-called All-Parties Muslim Conference would be "an insult to the League which has looked after Muslim interests for more than two decades."[5] Jinnah was firmly of the opinion that it would be disastrous for Muslims if rival and ad hoc organisations were set up whenever the community faced a crisis. The League, Jinnah said, should be consolidated and not disrupted.

However the other Muslim leaders who had assembled in Delhi for the Conference had lost faith in Jinnah and the League; they were convinced that the League could no longer deliver the goods.The Aga Khan presided over the Conference; this was arranged by Sir Fazl-i-Husain with a purpose; he wanted to break once and for all Jinnah's hold on the Muslims. He called him a rank opportunist who ran with the Congress hare and hunted with the British hound. Jinnah on his part continued to insist that the Conference lacked representative character and claimed that the League alone was "the sole representative of the Muslims". The Conference turned down the claim asserting that they, and not the League, were the real voice of the Muslims. The presence of most Muslim leaders, representing different shades of political and religious thought turned it into a grand spectacle of unity. Later even the League had to concede supremacy to the Conference and endorsed its decisions. Jinnah was completely sidelined; he was also ignored by Nehru and outmanoeuvred by the Conference. Only the Aga Khan, to whose religious sect Jinnah once belonged, showed some regard for him. He said: "The unanimity of this conference was especially significant for it marked the return — long delayed and, for the moment private and with no public avowal of his change of mind, of Mr. M.A. Jinnah to agreement with his fellow Muslims. Mr. Jinnah had attended the Congress Party's meeting in Calcutta shortly before, and had come to the conclusion that for him there was no future in the Congress or any camp — allegedly on an all-India basis — which was in fact Hindu-dominated. We have at last won him over to our view."[6] This was far from correct. Jinnah did not participate in that gathering nor did he come near any of its leaders. But it was true that he had finally broken with the Congress.

Despite the setback, Jinnah was determined to retrieve his position by maintaining his own separate status; it was no doubt a difficult task because Shafi and Fazl-i-Husain were intensely hostile to him. They had become diehard separatists who wanted nothing to do with the Hindu nationalists. Jinnah took a contrary stand. He explained that his communalism was never incompatible with nationalism. The two were complementary to each other. He came out openly in support of preserving the unity of India, stressing that it was as much in the interest of the Muslims as of the Hindus. In an interview to the special correspondent of London's *Daily Telegraph*, Ellis Bartlett, he reiterated his undying commitment to united India. Bartlett reported, "Mr. Jinnah refuses absolutely to admit that India is not a single geographical unit forming one homogeneous nation. He declares he considers himself to be a citizen of India, and not one of a particular province; he regards the entire country as his native land; and he declines to allow that the existence of so many different races, creeds, and languages constitute an insuperable obstacle to unity and self-government."[7] Jinnah gave a personal example by citing his experience in the High Court of Bombay to prove that Hindus and Muslims could function together. He narrated how Hindus and Muslims at the bar worked side by side. He told Bartlett: "During the whole of my thirty years' experience at the Bar I have never known of a single case where a Mohammedan complained that he could not obtain justice from a Hindu judge or vice-versa."[8]

Jinnah maintained that the Hindus in their own interest should agree to his demands and exhibit that spirit of communal accommodation and political realism which alone would cement the bond between the two communities. He entertained some hope that he might still be trusted by both Hindus and Muslims in view of his past record and, therefore, came out with a series of proposals which were characterised by the press as the "Fourteen Points"; therein he pleaded for their acceptance by the Hindus as he asserted that they would pave the way to break the political deadlock and usher in a new era of unity and harmony. There was really little new in these proposals; Jinnah had proposed these from time to time. Now he cleverly catalogued them under one cover. This was his last desperate effort to bring the two communities together. The proposals were as follows and in a way contained the gist of all his labours of the last two decades. They are reproduced here in his own words:

1. The form of future constitution should be fedral with residuary powers vested in the province, Central Government to have the control only of such matters of common interest as may be guaranteed by the Constitution.

2. Uniform measures of autonomy shall be granted to all provinces.

3. All legislatures in the country and other elected bodies should be reconstituted in the definite principle of adequate and effective representation of minorities in every province without reducing the majority of any province to a minority or even equality.

4. In the Central Legislature Muslim representation should not be less than one-third.

5. The representation of communal groups should continue to be by means of separate electorates as at present, provided that it should be open to any community at any time to abandon its separate electorate in favour of a joint electorate.

6. Any territorial redistribution that might at any time be necessary should not in any way affect the Muslim majority in the Punjab, Bengal, and North-West Frontier Province.

7. Full religious liberty, that is, liberty of belief, worship, observances, propaganda, association and education should be guaranteed to all communities.

8. No bill or resolution, or any part thereof, should be passed in any legislature or any other elected

body, if three-fourths of the members of any community in that particular body opposes such a bill or resolution or part thereof, on the ground that it would be injurious to the interest of that community or, in the alternative, such other methods be devised as may be found feasible and practicable to deal with such cases.

9. Sind should be separated from the Bombay Presidency.

10. Reform should be introduced in the North-West Frontier Province and Baluchistan on the same footing as in other provinces.

11. Provision should be made in the Constitution giving the Muslims an adequate share along with other Indians in all the Services of the State and in self-governing bodies, having due regard to the requirements of efficiency.

12. The Constitution should embody adequate safeguards for the protection of Muslim religion, culture and personal law, and the promotion of Muslim education, language, religion, personal laws, Muslim charitable institutions, and for their due share in grants-in-aid given by the State and by self-governing bodies.

13. No cabinet, either Central or Provincial, should be formed without there being a proportion of Muslim ministers of at least one-third.

14. No change to be made in the Constitution by the Central Legislature except with the concurrence of the states constituting the Indian federation.[9]

To Jinnah's consternation, the publication of these proposals did not produce any impact; in fact the author was ridiculed. Motilal Nehru advised the Congress "to ignore them"; the Aga Khan refused to take notice of them; Sir Fazl-i-Husain described them as the same old wine, which had soured, only the bottle was new. Speaking on behalf of nationalist Muslims, Dr. Ansari characterised them as lacking in vision. Maulana Mohamed Ali was charitable; he called Jinnah "the arch-compromiser". Never before had Jinnah been subjected to such contemptuous treatment by his contemporaries. Stanley Wolpert observes, "He took the Aga Khan's 'four principles', patched them together with his Delhi Muslim Proposals of 1927, hammered a few more planks onto either end, and hoped it would float, an ark in which all of them might survive the coming flood."[10] Jinnah's ego was badly hurt, he decided to retire from what he called "the messy politics" and settle in London. He said goodbye to India and to "the confusion worse confounded" caused by his opponents, who were too self-opinionated, according to him, to see reason and the good of the country. For more than three decades he had tried to play the role of a unifier but it was neither. appreciated by the Hindus nor favoured by the Muslims; each community was interested in obtaining the maximum benefits for their own people; neither was keen in a give-and-take solution; each wanted all or nothing.

Hence Jinnah, the compromiser and the reconciler, became increasingly irrelevant. On noticing the unfavourable Muslim reaction to the Nehru report, the Mahatma also realised that the Congress should concentrate instead on confronting the British and making it clear to them that if they were not inclined to grant even dominion status, India would have no alternative but to struggle for achieving complete independence. Gandhi anointed the young Jawaharlal as Congress president for the Lahore session to be held in December 1929; it came out with the demand for Swaraj or complete independence. Jinnah reacted strongly against it; he condemned "the political hysteria" that it would generate and once again targeted the Mahatma comparing him with "the Bourbons of France", who were "constitutionally incapable of learning and unlearning things". He added that "the Himalayan blunders of the past had failed to open his eyes to the realities of the situation."[11] Jinnah, as subsequent events will unfold, opposed every movement that Gandhi launched — Non-Cooperation (1920-22), the Salt March (1930), Quit India (1942) because in each of these he feared the ousting of the British without the Hindus first conceding the demands that he had been voicing on behalf of the Muslims. He suspected the motive of the Mahatma whom he never forgave for downgrading him and monopolising the limelight, presenting himself as the only saviour who should be fully trusted and unreservedly obeyed. Jinnah had a warped view of the Indian urge for freedom as voiced by the Mahatma; he wanted the British to first give him what he asked for before conceding to the Hindus the freedom they wanted.

SEVEN

Undoing the Past

Jinnah grew weary of warning the Hindus and the Congress that they should be fair to the Muslims; he decided to henceforth concentrate on the Muslims and mobilise them to learn to extract their due. His old strategy had proved futile; it had also isolated him. Never before had he felt so frustrated. Consequently he turned to the British to help him retrieve the situation. One of the staunchest opponents of the all-white Simon Commission, he now started pleading with them to protect the interests of the Muslims. In that he also saw the resurrection of his leadership. The new Viceroy, Lord Irwin, was a liberal with a compassionate and friendly disposition. Jinnah developed a close relationship with him. He wrote to him advising him on how to tackle the political situation and not be alarmed by Gandhi's open defiance of authority as demonstrated by his famous Salt March. The mass resurgence it generated sent shivers through the British establishment; Irwin was badly shaken. Jinnah took advantage of the Viceroy's nervousness and impressed upon him to convene a meeting

of leaders of different political groups in order to thrash out a
solution. Jinnah stressed that this could be fruitful only if it
would "satisfy the nationalists in India subject ofcourse to the
settlement of the Hindu-Muslim question". He wanted
nationalist Muslims also to be included (he became allergic to
them after 1938) and suggested the inclusion of Gandhi's
Muslim lieutenant, Khan Abdul Ghaffar Khan. He exchanged
letters and made frequent contact with the Viceroy to pursue
the matter and eventually won Irwin to his point of view.
Meanwhile Sapru and Jaykar resorted to their usual tactics of
trying to bring the Congress and the Government together and
though they could not succeed, their move delayed the whole
process. Jinnah asked the Viceroy not to be swayed by the
warped logic of the "twins" who thrived on fishing in troubled
waters. He told Irwin that the need of the hour was to arrange
a get-together of leaders to arrive at a consensus to break the
impasse.

As these discussions were on in India, a complete
change took place in the power structure in Britain. The victory
of the Labour Party in the general election had infused new
hope in Jinnah especially as his friend Ramsay MacDonald had
become Prime Minister. Jinnah wrote him a long letter dated
June 19, 1929, wherein he urged him to convene a Round Table
Conference of representative Indian leaders. MacDonald took
two months to reply but his response was warm and friendly.
Encouraged by the attitude of both the Prime Minister and
the Viceroy, Jinnah organised a meeting at Ahmedabad in
November 1929 which was attended among others by the
Patel brothers — Vithalbhai and Vallabhbhai — on behalf of
the Congress. There were prolonged talks lasting several hours.
Jinnah thereafter wrote to Sapru that it had been agreed that
Gandhi, Motilal Nehru, the two Patels, Sapru and Jinnah should

meet and "put our heads together" and then call upon the Viceroy to work out an understanding to resolve the differences. Accordingly a meeting took place between these leaders and the Viceroy on December 23, 1929. Nothing however came of it as Gandhi and Motilal Nehru told Irwin that the Congress would not participate in any Round Table Conference unless the British government first announced the grant of dominion status to India. The Viceroy clarified that the proposed conference of leaders must first come to an agreed settlement between themselves and the same would then be submitted to Parliament for ratification. The cart could not be placed before the horse. He said it was impossible for him or His Majesty's Government to "in any way prejudge the action of the conference or to restrict the liberty of the Parliament".[1]

Notwithstanding the non-cooperative attitude of the Congress, the Viceroy went ahead and announced on October 31, 1929 the convening of the Round Table Conference in London to be presided over by the Prime Minister to discuss the framework of India's Constitution. Jinnah was the first to welcome it. He said in a statement to the press: "I am satisfied that both the declaration and the invitation to a conference are a distinct earnest of the 'bona fides' of His Majesty's Government and of all parties, who have supported it in England. Its guiding note is based on reason and fair play. I sincerely congratulate His Excellency the Viceroy on his great achievement and I am not exaggerating when I say that fortunately we have the Prime Minister and the Secretary of State for India, both of whom with their liberal views sympathise with India's aspirations." So did Irwin, who had by now acquired a clear grasp of Indian affairs. The change in British attitude bolstered Jinnah's confidence for a settlement. He became optimistic about the prospects. He said: "It is now for India to play (its part) and support and strengthen the hands of the Viceroy, who has already established the reputation for a very high sense of integrity and sincerity of purpose in helping the onward progress of our country." He appealed to the Viceroy not to delay the process saying, "Many a good actions are lost by procrastination."[2]

The Congress, however, continued to be in a non-cooperative mood; its rejection of dominion status and call for complete independence at its Lahore session put it on the aggressive path; the bellicose tone adopted by its youthful president, Jawaharlal Nehru had considerably aggravated the situation. It dampened any hope of a settlement with the Government. Jinnah put the whole blame on Gandhi and said that he was "utterly unsuited to modern times and the realities we have to face in India. The proposition has only to be stated to be rejected that independence can be won by non-violent non-cooperation. Why, even before the proceedings of the Congress terminated, the Union Jack was destroyed not very far from the place where Mr. Gandhi was sitting. Does Mr. Gandhi believe that the majority with which he carried the resolutions will enable him to achieve independence without violence? The whole of Mr. Gandhi's political philosophy seems to me a bundle of contradictions impossible for any rational man to follow. I see he is reported to have said, in concluding his speech on the independence resolution: 'What we are going to do heaven only knows, but the Working Committee has taken the longest possible step that can be taken and a step further might throw us in a pit.' All I can say is that heaven help Mr. Gandhi."[3] Despite the rigid stand taken by the Mahatma, the Viceroy pursued his course of consultation and conciliation and convened the proposed Round Table

Conference in the fond expectation that eventually the Congress also might come round.

Jinnah was one of the fifty-eight delegates from British India. The Conference was inaugurated by King George V in St. James Palace on November 12,1930. Jinnah challenged Gandhi's claim that the exercise was bound to end in a fiasco as without the Congress, the Mahatma claimed, no political settlement would be worth the paper on which it was written. Lord Peel warned that any concession to India would only be exploited by leaders like Gandhi who with their enormous influence would wreck whatever would be given. Jinnah replied to this rather arrogantly: "Do you want those parties who have checked, held in abeyance the party that stands for complete independence? Do you want those people to go back with this answer from you — that nothing can be done because there is a strong party which will misuse or wreck the constitution which we will get from you? Is that the answer you want to give? Now let me tell you the tremendous fallacy of that argument and the grave danger. Seventy million of Mussalmans — all, barring a few individuals here and there — have kept aloof from the non-cooperation movement. Thirty-five or forty million of depressed classes have set their face against the non-cooperation movement. Sikhs and Christians have not joined it. And let me tell you that even amongst that party which you characterise as a large party — and I admit that it is an important party — it has not got the support of the bulk of Hindus."[4] It was a clever distortion of facts by which Jinnah intended to fool the British. But the rulers were fully aware that it was not Jinnah and leaders like him but Gandhi and his lieutenants who carried the support of the masses, both Hindu and Muslim, and it was their voice which would finally count.

Jinnah pacified Irwin who seemed to have been much disturbed by the latest development. He assured him that despite Gandhi and the Congress, the rest of India would respond to a positive move. The Viceroy hoped that Jinnah was right. He gave him, on the eve of his departure to London, letters of introduction to four leading British politicians, including Stanley Baldwin, leader of the Conservative Party who subsequently replaced Ramsay MacDonald as Prime Minister. In the letters Irwin spoke highly of Jinnah: "I have seen a good deal of Jinnah from time to time and I have met very few Indians with a more acute intellect or a more independent outlook..."[5] The deliberations at the Conference lasted for ten weeks but no worthwhile progress was made. Hindu and Muslim delegates stuck to their respective demands; the British watched the wordy battles with great relish. Jinnah tried to bring about a communal settlement but failed; without the participation of the Congress the proceedings lacked teeth. The Viceroy was also not happy with the outcome of the conference; no one was able to steer it on to the right lines, including his friend Jinnah in whom he had high hopes. The effect it had in India caused Irwin further depression. Young Nehru criticised Jinnah for his role and said he had "become an anachronism in Indian politics", others accused him of having become "a tool of British imperialism".

Jinnah was disheartened by these attacks; on the conclusion of the First Round Table Conference on January 19,1931 instead of returning to India, he, therefore, remained in London. He took the decision to settle down there and start legal practice before the Privy Council. His experience at the Round Table Conference convinced him that he could no longer play any useful role; no one wanted unity; everyone pushed for his own point of view. Hence the Conference was bogged

down with quarrels and disputes. Apart from the Hindus, the
Muslims also thwarted Jinnah's efforts for consensus. They did
everything to undermine his leadership. The Aga Khan revelled
in the premier position that he had acquired; from New Delhi,
Sir Fazl-i-Husain who was then the most important Executive
Councillor of the Viceroy, prompted his protégé Sir Mohamed
Shafi, whom he had sent as a delegate, to challenge Jinnah at
every stage. He disputed Jinnah's claim that he alone
represented the Muslims and often interrupted him and told
him that he had lost his representative capacity. None of the
other delegates, not even the Aga Khan came to his rescue.
Consequently Jinnah felt dejected and often sulked and
remained silent during the deliberations.

Sir Mirza Ismail who was one of the representatives
of princely India has recorded that at the Conference Jinnah
"was in agreement with no one, not even, in the end with his
own Muslim delegation".[6] Jinnah could not bear the degradation;
he fulminated but could do nothing about it. He remained in
London and bought a large mansion on West Heath Road in
Hampstead where his sister Fatima and his thirteen year old
daughter Dina joined him. He took his chambers in the famous
King's Beach, furnished it tastefully and started his legal
practice. He made a mark in no time. As Lord Jowit has
recorded, "We all had great admiration for his legal skill and
the judgement with which he conducted his cases before the
Privy Council."[7] Apart from his briefs, he went through
newspapers avidly but he rarely read books. During this time
he came across an excellent review of H.C. Armstrong's
biography of Kemal Ataturk, entitled *Grey Wolf: An Intimate
Study of a Dictator*. He bought the book. It so impressed him
that he never ceased talking about it to his daughter and friends
who came to see him. In Ataturk he found his ideal; he was

fascinated by what the Turkish dictator did to reform his co-religionists and to overhaul and modernise their outlook. He wanted to do the same for Indian Muslims. He was no less keen to free them from the clutches of the mullahs and rid them of the stranglehold of orthodoxy. He felt they had to be moulded to live as people in the West did and that unless they shed their obscurantism, their future was doomed. Had he the same power as the Ataturk, he told his sister, he would not have hesitated to follow the example of the Turkish leader to westernise his co-religionists in India.

Undeterred by the failure of the First Round Table Conference, the British government convened the Second Round Table Conference on September 7, 1931; it promised a better outcome as the Viceroy had in the meanwhile managed to conclude a pact with Gandhi who persuaded the Congress to attend it. This roused great expectations because Gandhi himself agreed to participate in the proceedings as the sole representative of the Congress. Jinnah was included by Irwin as one of the Muslim delegates despite opposition from Sir Fazl-i-Husain, his Executive Councillor. To start with, the Conference proceeded on the right lines; the discussions evoked much hope for a settlement. But the controversial communal issue became once again the stumbling block. As the Aga Khan has recorded in his memoirs: "As time went on the hair-splitting became finer and finer, the arguments more and more abstract: a nation could not hand over undisputed power to its provinces; there was no constitutional way of putting a limit on the devices by which a majority could be turned into a minority — fascinating academic issues but with no connection with the real facts and figures of Indian life."[8] Jinnah kept quiet most of the time; he was neither asked to speak; nor did he care to put forth his views. He was sidelined all the time; his past

came in his way. The delegates decided on a new approach;
they felt they had had enough of Jinnah. Jawaharlal Nehru
was trenchant in his criticism. He wrote to Gandhi in London
from India: "If I had to listen to my dear friend Mohammed
Ali Jinnah talking the most mitigated nonsense about his
fourteen points for any length of time, I would have to consider
the desirability of retiring to the South Sea Islands, where there
would be some hope of meeting some people who were
intelligent or ignorant enough not to talk of the fourteen
points.... I marvel at your patience."[9]

Nehru's ire against Jinnah and his "Fourteen Points"
was not quite justified; the Muslim leader was no longer talking
about them. It was really Shafi who had monopolised the
proceedings of the Round Table Conference; he carried the
patronage of the Aga Khan. However they were no more
successful in solving the Hindu-Muslim dispute; even Gandhi's
intervention failed to produce a settlement. On one of his
visits to India, Jinnah mockingly remarked, "We went round
and round in London. We are still going round and round in
India without reaching the straight path that would lead to
freedom."[10]

During his stay in London, while he steered clear of
happenings in India, he could not tear himself away from politics
altogether. He enjoyed appearing and arguing before the Privy
Council but he also felt that he could try his luck for
membership of the House of Commons; he could then succeed
in following in the footsteps of his mentor, Dadabhai Naoroji.
First he sought a Labour Party ticket; having failed to get one,
he approached the Conservatives but he could not succeed
with them either. Labour thought he was too aristocratic while
the Conservatives were not keen on a native Indian. He

abandoned the idea and continued with his legal work; it was familiar ground where he could perform brilliantly and earn more than enough to sustain his luxurious lifestyle which included visiting expensive restaurants and going to the theatre at West End.

But the political itch would not leave him; he could not get out of its clutches. Friends wrote to him from India and told him how much they missed him. He asked them what would he do if he were to return. No one wanted him, he said — neither Hindus nor Muslims. He visited India in connection with some court cases but avoided getting involved in politics. What distressed him most was that even the British did not find him of much use; Sir Fazli had so poisoned the ears of the Viceroy that he began to ignore Jinnah and even dropped him as a delegate to the Third Round Table Conference. That was the last straw — a devastating blow to his ego.

A frustrated and dejected Jinnah, disowned by the Muslims, distrusted by the Hindus, and discarded by the British, decided to reassert himself by changing his way. He threw away the baggage of the past. And with his own hands he dug the grave of Hindu-Muslim unity, to which he had devoted all his years in public life. From a doughty champion of united India he took a vow to start organising the Muslims as a counter-force to the Congress which he believed represented only the Hindus. Consequently he abandoned the idea of staying on in London. He sold his house in Hampstead, packed his belongings, surrendered his chambers and quietly embarked on a new adventure which no one then suspected would ultimately pose the greatest danger to the unity of India. The rage within so overwhelmed him that nothing could sway him from the path he now charted to avenge the ignominy to which he had been subjected. He was hell-bent on showing to Gandhi and the Congress that he and his followers could destroy their dream of a united India. In the past, with the Congress-League Pact, the Delhi Proposals for joint electorate and other such endeavours Jinnah had sought to cement the bond between the two communities. He would now use all his energies to undo that past and dismantle brick by brick the edifice of unity he had worked so hard to build. He devoted himself henceforth to do everything in his power to divide Hindus and Muslims and erect a permanent barrier to keep them apart. Towards that end he utilised the new constitutional reforms enacted by the British through the Government of India Act of 1935. And thus he embarked on mobilising the Muslims to make them a force no one dared ignore.

EIGHT

Preparing for Separation

In the midst of the political darkness that engulfed his public life, Jinnah saw the first ray of hope when he learnt that without his knowledge or consent the Muslim voters of his city had elected him, this time unopposed, to the Central Legislative Assembly. It happened in the month of October 1934 and Jinnah sailed for Bombay in January 1935 to be present at the opening of the Assembly in Delhi. However his participation in the debates of the Assembly was only of peripheral interest to him; the main objective in returning to India was to organise the League which was in a woeful condition and make it an instrument for fulfilling his new mission of aggressive Muslim separatism. In it alone he visualised the restoration of his battered leadership. He made every effort to unite the various Muslim factions. He even extended a hand of friendship to his bitterest enemy Sir Fazl-i-Husain; to placate him he offered him presidentship of the annual session of the League which he had organised in his pocketborough — Bombay. He pleaded with Sir Fazli saying, "your refusal will be the greatest misfortune and a terrible disappointment to me personally", but Sir Fazli cold-shouldered him and declined the invitation. Jinnah then turned to Sir Wazir Hasan, former Chief Judge of the Oudh Chief Court, who readily agreed. The session was held on April 11,1936 in a specially constructed pandal. It attracted a large gathering of over two thousand delegates from various parts of India. The Chairman of the Reception Committee was the financial magnate, Sir Currimbhoy Ibrahim. He declared that it was because of the initiative of Jinnah — "the fearless upholder of the Muslim cause" — that new life was being put into the League. The session was only a moderate success.

In his presidential address, Sir Wazir Hasan said, "I wish to emphasise here and it should always be borne in mind that India is a continent; it should further be borne in mind that the Hindus and the Mussalmans, inhabiting this vast continent, are not communities; but should be considered two nations in many respects."[1] Though it was a passing reference, it reiterated what Jinnah had in mind. It certainly helped him to propagate the new concept of separation and generate the necessary fervour for it among the Muslims. He installed himself as permanent President of the League and remained so until his death in 1948. M.C. Chagla, his confidant for over two decades, has revealed that by this time Jinnah had lost all interest in Hindu-Muslim unity: "I remember a conversation he had with me in the High Court Bar Library about this time. He asked me to work with him to revive the Muslim League. I told him that that was impossible and that what we should really work for was a united party of both Hindus and Muslims, which would function as a centre party between the Congress and the Mahasabha... Jinnah replied that I was an idealist, while he, for his part, must work with such material as he had. It then became clear to me that he had made up his mind to take his stand on a communal platform and to revive his leadership through communal means and methods."[1]

Meanwhile Ramsay MacDonald, the British Prime Minister, announced his Communal Award which granted separate electorate to the Muslims in the central and provincial legislatures. Jinnah welcomed it and saw in it the much needed ground for consolidating the Muslims; he now fully devoted himself to achieve this end. The Congress adopted a neutral stand on the Award; the decision did not bring it any closer to the Muslims. Jinnah used this ambivalence on the part of the Congress to further alienate the Muslims from it.

As for the Government of India Act of 1935 which the British Parliament subsequently enacted, Jinnah made clever use of it. He asked the Muslims "to utilise the Provincial Scheme... for what it is worth", but to oppose its Federal part which, he told them, would perpetuate Hindu domination. On the whole he was not happy with the Act and had quoted his friend Winston Churchill who had characterised it as "the most monstrous monument of sham built by the pigmies".[2] Nevertheless Jinnah urged his League Council to enter the forthcoming electoral battle. The delegates authorised Jinnah to form a Central Election Board which would choose the candidates for the provincial assemblies. The results of the League candidates were far from satisfactory, they won only hundred out of about six hundred reserved seats. Jinnah was no doubt disappointed but he kept his chin up. In fact, in his presidential address to the annual session of the League held in Lucknow on October 15, 1937, he flaunted: "In each and every province where a League Parliamentary Board was established and League parties were constituted, we carried

away about 60 to 70 per cent of the seats that were contested
by the League candidates; and since the elections, I find that
hundreds of district Leagues have been established in almost
every province, from the farthest corner of Madras to the North-
West Frontier Province. Since April last, the Mussalmans of
India have rallied round the League more and more; and I feel
confident that once they understand and realise the policy and
programme of the Muslim League, the entire Mussalman
population of India will rally round the platform and under its
flag."[3] He did not lose any time to target the Congress ministries
which were formed initially in six out of eleven provinces. He
declared that the present leadership of the Congress, especially
during the last ten years, had been responsible for suppressing
the Muslims; they had pursued a policy which, he said, was
exclusively Hindu; their programmes were aimed at
strengthening the hold of the Hindus on the administration;
the Muslims, he pointed out "could not expect any justice or
fair play from them".[4]

Jinnah deprecated the way the Congress discriminated
against the Muslims and lured the newly elected Muslims by
offering them jobs and prevailing upon them to adjure their
party and forswear the policy and programme of the League.
He said, "Any individual Mussalman member who was willing
to unconditionally surrender and sign their pledge was offered
a job as a minister, and was passed off as a Mussalman minister,
although he did not command the confidence or the respect
of an overwhelming majority of the Mussalman representatives
in the legislatures. These men are allowed to move about and
pass off as Muslim ministers for the 'loyal' services they have
rendered to the Congress by surrendering and signing the pledge
unconditionally; and the degree of their reward is the extent
of their perfidy." He then listed the grievances of the Muslims
against Congress ministries: "Hindi is to be the national

language of all India and *Vande Mataram* is to be the national
song and is to be forced upon all. The Congress flag is to be
obeyed and revered by all and sundry. On the very threshold
of what little power and responsibility is given, the majority
community have clearly shown their hand: that Hindustan is
for Hindus. Only the Congress masquerades under the name
of nationalism whereas the Hindu Mahasabha does not mince
words."[5]

Jinnah shrewdly picked up issues which would help
him to work up the communal passion and religious frenzy of
the Muslims. Intoxicated by the little power they enjoyed
under Provincial Autonomy granted by the British, the
Congress governments in the eight provinces — two more were
added subsequently to the earlier six— paid no heed to Jinnah's
warnings; the Congress High Command also ignored these,
with the result that the Congress ministries went about their
task arbitrarily, taking no notice of the grievances of the
Muslims. Jawaharlal Nehru, who was the Congress President,
showed little concern in redressing them and on the contrary
embarked on his ill-conceived plan of mass contact with the
Muslims to undermine the growing strength of the League.
He also announced that there were only two parties in India:
the British and the Congress. The rest did not matter. Jinnah
retorted: "No, Mr. Nehru, there is the third party — the
Mussalmans." The statement electrified the Muslims and
boosted their pride. Jinnah told them: "There are forces which
may bully you, tyrannise over you and intimidate you, and you
may even have to suffer. But it is by going through this crucible
of the fire of persecution which may be thrown at you, the
tyranny that may be exercised over you, the threats and
intimidations that may be given to unnerve you — it is by
resisting, by overcoming, by facing these disadvantages,
hardships and suffering, and maintaining your true convictions

and loyalty, that a nation will emerge, worthy of its past glory and history, and will live to make its future history greater and more glorious not only in India, but in the annals of the world. Eighty millions of Mussalmans in India have nothing to fear. They have their destiny in their hands, and as a well-knit, solid, organised, united force can face any danger and withstand any opposition to its united front and wishes."[6]

Jinnah was one of the cleverest strategists among Indian politicians. He was adept in the art of putting his opponents in the wrong. For instance when B.G. Kher, who was asked by the Governor to form the ministry in the then Bombay Presidency, visited Jinnah and requested support of the League legislators, Jinnah told him to first ask Gandhi to talk to him. On being so informed by Kher, Gandhi wrote a letter to Jinnah on May 22, 1937: "Kher has given me your message. I wish I could do something but I am utterly helpless. My faith in (Hindu-Muslim) unity is as bright as ever. Only I see no daylight out of the impenetrable darkness and in such distress I cry out to God for light."[7] Jinnah was not surprised at this reaction. He told his colleagues that he expected Gandhi to wriggle out of any move to bring the Congress and the League together. The Mahatma, he said, wanted surrender, not cooperation. Jinnah had deliberately distorted Gandhi's intention and misused the letter which was written in good faith. He blamed Gandhi for what he himself was really trying to do— namely to keep the Muslims away from the Congress. He never meant to extend the support of the League which Kher had asked for.

Gandhi's reply provided him with new ammunition to mislead the Muslims and turn them against the Congress. He told his followers that he had done enough of begging the Congress in the past; he would see to it now that the Congress begged of him. And so he began building the League into a mass organisation, something which he had earlier disapproved of. As Jawaharlal Nehru has mentioned in his autobiography: "A few older leaders however dropped out of the Congress and among these a popular and well-known figure was that of Mr. M.A. Jinnah. He felt completely out of his element in the khadi clad crowd demanding speeches in Hindustani. The enthusiasm of the people outside struck him as mob hysteria. There was as much difference between him and the Indian masses as between Saville Row or Bond Street, and the Indian village with its mud huts. He suggested once privately that only matriculates should be taken into the Congress. I do not know if he was serious in making this remarkable suggestion, but it was in harmony with his general outlook."[8]

Jinnah now revised his earlier approach. He had seen the power that Gandhi had acquired by mobilising the uneducated masses. He discarded his western suits for sherwani and pyjama and mixed freely with the ordinary Muslims, warning them of the imminence of Hindu raj. He cried that Islam itself was in danger. His only regret was that he could not speak in Urdu; it was too late for him to learn it. Notwithstanding this handicap he rallied the Muslims, warning them that Hindus would soon dominate them unless they organised themselves under the banner of his League and unitedly stood by him. They embarked on this task in right earnest; in the beginning the response of the Muslims was not very encouraging. Maulana Azad has mentioned in his book *India Wins Freedom* that there would have been no Pakistan if Jawaharlal Nehru had not sabotaged the inclusion of two Leaguers — Chaudhary Khaliquzzaman and Nawab Ismail Khan — in the Congress ministry of U.P. in 1937. Even Nehru's esteemed biographer S. Gopal subscribes to this view.

That is also the line of argument most of us have taken against Nehru but further research into the working of Jinnah's mind reveals that, even if Nehru had agreed to this formula of collaboration, Jinnah would have vetoed it. He desired no settlement with the Congress until he had gathered sufficient popular strength to dictate terms. He was on a single track: no cooperation with the Congress. He would not weaken the League's separatist march.

This view has been confirmed by one of the main actors on the scene, Chaudhary Khaliquzzaman in his book *Pathway to Pakistan*. That was why when he was questioned about such an arrangement in U.P., Jinnah promptly disowned it. So did Nehru. He said he would have been happy if his two friends Khaliquzzaman and Ismail Khan had severed their connections with the League and rejoined the Congress, accepting its secular ideology and programme. The two naturally declined; had they accepted these terms, Jinnah would have expelled them from the organisation and denounced them as traitors. During this time Maulana Azad indulged in a great deal of wishful thinking. He failed to assess Jinnah's changed attitude to the Congress. The fact is that ever since 1935 Jinnah had been feverishly working on only one objective: to show the Congress as a Hindu body and demand the acceptance of the League as the authentic voice of the Muslims. He resisted every move to come to terms with the Congress except on the basis of equality.

During this period Jinnah had warned the Muslims that unless they were united, the Hindus, being the majority community, would subjugate them. He ridiculed Muslims who had thrown in their lot with the Congress. They were traitors to Islam, he asserted, even if they were the best of Muslims; the cause was greater than the individual. As for the rest of the Muslims, whether they were capitalists or paupers, zamindars or tillers of the soil, proprietors or workers and even exploiters, power-brokers or bloodsuckers, if they subscribed to his newly found anti-Congress stand, they were welcomed in his League. Jinnah's main aim was to bring all Muslims, irrespective of sect, class, social position or economic status, under the League banner and mobilise the masses in order to present a united front against the Congress. He concentrated on making the League the only authoritative and sole organisation of the Muslims. He wanted to parley with Gandhi on a basis of equality. And his League to negotiate with the Congress on a one-to-one level.

Jinnah subordinated everything else to this burning passion; to fulfil it he denounced the Congress as anti-Muslim in speech after speech and concentrated on bringing most Muslims under his leadership, irrespective of whether they had opposed him in the past or had been lukewarm in their support of him. He won over Sir Sikander Hayat Khan, premier of Punjab and A.K. Fazl-ul-Haq, premier of Bengal by giving them a free hand in their own provinces under the pact he signed with them at the League session in Lucknow in 1938. He did not hesitate to sacrifice the local League units in Punjab and Bengal, provided the two stalwarts accepted his leadership on an all-India central basis. The poet Iqbal was unhappy at this opportunistic attitude of Jinnah, bringing such known self-seekers under the protection of the League. He wrote to Jinnah that unless he cared for the poor masses, the League would not acquire a popular base. Jinnah ignored Iqbal's plea. To him the poor or the rich, the scrupulous or the unscrupulous, the selfless or the self-centred, were of equal importance; he was in a hurry to become the supreme leader of the Muslims. Towards acquiring this position he was prepared for any compromise or adjustment. That is why when Nehru in letters to him barraged him with social issues and economic problems, Jinnah took no notice of them. He was not interested in any joint action to ameliorate the lot of the poor whether Hindu or Muslim, unless and until the communal triangle had been resolved to his satisfaction. To achieve this he needed time and time seemed to favour him.

The long correspondence between Nehru and Jinnah on differences between Hindus and Muslims was at cross-purposes; the two looked at the main issue of freedom from entirely different angles. Even Jinnah's talks with Rajendra Prasad, Azad, and Subhas Chandra Bose, no less than with Gandhi, brought no result. Jinnah wanted equality in the sharing of power and to achieve it he insisted that unless his League was accepted as the only authoritative and sole representative of the Muslims, no useful purpose would be gained by a dialogue on other issues. He knew that Gandhi and the other Congress leaders were allergic to the acceptance of this condition because they would have let down those Muslims who had always supported the Congress and suffered and sacrificed for it. More importantly it would reduce the Congress from a national to a communal organisation. The stalemate was thus deliberately created by Jinnah because his aim was to make the British equate him with Gandhi and to ensure that all negotiations were held on a tripartite basis — the British, the Congress representing the Hindus and the League representing the Muslims. To bring this about he travelled extensively from one end of India to the other, accepted invitations from all and sundry; he delivered speeches in and out of season, in short, he spared no effort to mobilise the Muslims by whatever means available to him. His mantra was "Islam in danger". He asked Muslims to rise and protect their religion, culture and language by rallying under the banner of the League which inevitably meant the acceptance of his supreme leadership. His charisma acquired irresistible force; regardless of his lack of knowledge of Urdu or the conventions, traditions or even rituals of Islam, he had so mesmerised the Muslims that they endearingly held on to every word he uttered without understanding it and listened to him spellbound and followed him faithfully. They revered him as a messiah who had come to their rescue. No saint could have asked for more.

The Lucknow session of the League in 1938 had consolidated his all-India Muslim leadership. Gandhi was perturbed by the rabidly communal tone of Jinnah; he had felt hurt at the misuse of his letter dated November 5, 1937 in which Gandhi expressed his anguish at his utterances which to the Mahatma appeared like "a declaration of war". Jinnah had replied that it was done "purely in self-defense". After three months Gandhi again wrote to him that "your later pronouncements too confirm the first impression ...(in them) I miss the old nationalist." Jinnah promptly reminded Gandhi that "nationalism is not the monopoly of any single individual..."9 Thus from 1937 onward Jinnah continued to be hostile to the Mahatma. His attitude towards Nehru was no better, though it must be admitted that Nehru was also not particularly polite to him. Jinnah went on harping on Hindu-Muslim differences. Nehru, as Congress President, asked him in a letter dated February 25, 1938, "what the fundamental points of dispute are". Jinnah replied a week later: "I am only amazed at your ignorance. This matter has been tackled since 1925 right upto 1935 by the most prominent leaders in the country and so far no solution has been found."

As for Jinnah's demand that the Congress recognise the League as the most representative body of the Muslims,

Nehru replied on April 6, 1938: "Obviously the Muslim League is an important communal organisation and we deal with it as such. But we have to deal with all organisations and individuals that come within our ken. We do not determine the measure of importance or distinction they possess." He also added, "...This importance does not come from outside recognition but from inherent strength."[10] Jinnah responded instantly: "It seems to me that you cannot even accurately understand my letter...Your tone and language again display the same arrogance and militant spirit, as if the Congress is the sovereign power... I may add that, in my opinion, as I have publicly stated so often that unless the Congress recognises the Muslim League on a footing of complete equality and is prepared as such to negotiate for a Hindu-Muslim settlement, we shall have to wait and depend upon our 'inherent strength' which will 'determine the measure of importance or distinction' it possesses. Having regard to your mentality, it is really difficult for me to make you understand the position any further..."[11] In fact this was the first plank in Jinnah's armour; he was determined to make the League so strong and powerful that both the Congress and the British would have no choice but to recognise it as the only authentic and representative body of Muslims. Even Nehru eventually conceded its importance and distinction.

Jinnah reiterated this in his presidential address to the annual session of the League held in Patna on December 16,1938. At the outset he condoled the death of Kemal Ataturk describing him as "a great hero of the Muslim world" and asked the delegates, "with the example of this great Mussalman in front of them as an inspiration, will the Muslims of India still remain in a quagmire?" Most Muslims would not share this sentiment; they considered Ataturk a renegade and heretic.

He also mourned the passing away of Iqbal whom he called "a personal friend of mine and a singer of the finest poetry in the world." He did not know that Iqbal was a poet-philosopher and not an ordinary writer of songs. He wrote the most soul-stirring poems but he could hardly recite them — much less sing them — as he had in later years developed a bad throat. Not a word about Iqbal's political work, much less about the poet's contribution to the consolidation of the Muslims.

Jinnah then explained how the Congress was a Hindu organisation which claimed to speak on behalf of the Muslims; he said: "The Congress High Command makes the preposterous claim that they are entitled to speak on behalf of the whole of India, that they alone are capable of delivering the goods. Others are asked to accept the gift as from a mighty sovereign. The Congress High Command declares that they will redress the grievances of the Muslims, and they expect the Muslims to accept the declaration. I want to make it plain to all concerned that we Muslims want no gifts. The Muslims want no concessions. We, Muslims of India, have made up our mind to secure our full rights, but we shall have them as rights, not as gifts or concessions. The Congress press may clamour as much as it likes; they may bring out their morning, afternoon, evening and night editions; the Congress leaders may shout as much as they like that the Congress is a national body. But I say it is not true. The Congress is nothing but a Hindu body. That is the truth and the Congress leaders know it. The presence of the few Muslims, the few misled and misguided ones, and the few who are there with ulterior motives, does not, cannot, make it a national body. I challenge anybody to deny that the Congress is not mainly a Hindu body. I ask, does the Congress represent the Muslims?" The gathering responded in one voice, 'No! No!'.[12]

So Jinnah in three years succeeded in mobilising the Muslims by warning them of the threat to Islam and the design of the Congress to impose Hindu raj on them. He painted the Congress as the main instrument of Hindu domination, whose sole object was to subvert the Muslims. Never before was a more disruptive role played by any Muslim leader. Jinnah used the animosity against the Hindus as the easiest way to unite the Muslims. He accused the Congress ministries of carrying out programmes and policies that were anti-Muslim; the compulsory singing of *Vande Mataram* in schools, the preference for Hindi as against Urdu, discrimination in services against the Muslims, depriving them of grants, quotas and licences. Gandhi was alarmed at these charges and offered to get them investigated by the Chief Justice of India Sir Maurice Gwyer; but Jinnah declined and said that he would want a Royal Commission to go into them.

The Viceroy refused because he said there was no prima facie case made out for such a high-powered appointment. It was the responsibility of the governors under the new constitutional framework to safeguard the interests of the minorities and they did not find sufficient ground to interfere with the work of the Congress ministries. Jinnah was however not so much interested in the investigation of his charges as using them to alienate the Muslims from the Congress. In his address to the Ismail College Union, Bombay, in early 1939, he issued a stern warning to the Congress: "Hands off the Muslims. They want nothing to do with you." The break was complete; and hence on September 3, when Britain declared war against Germany and in consequence India was made a party to it without consulting her popular representatives, the Congress ministries resigned in protest. Jinnah heaved a sigh of relief at their exit and announced a

Day of Deliverance. He asked the Muslims to offer thanks to God for being rid of the curse of Congress raj. He exploited to the fullest the exit of the Congress ministers who had provided ample evidence of irritants and misdeeds bordering on communal prejudice. No less a leader of unimpeachable integrity than Sir Tej Bahadur Sapru complained in a letter dated September 16, 1940 to the journalist B. Shiva Rao: "You at Delhi, where there has been no responsible government, probably cannot have any idea of the experience we have had of party dictatorship or of Congress ministries wherever they have existed and particularly in the U.P. and Bihar... one thing I shall say that so long as these people were in power they treated everybody else with undisguised contempt and asserted the weight of their majority in a most unfortunate manner."[13]

I remember attending the mammoth meeting called in Bombay to celebrate the so-called "Deliverance Day". It was jointly addressed by Jinnah and B.R. Ambedkar, the Scheduled Caste leader. Their joint presence and fiery speeches created such mob hysteria that most Hindus were alarmed that they could never live together with Muslims. The venom that was generated aggravated the hostilities between the two communities as never before. That was what Jinnah had aimed at and when he saw the response of the Muslims to his call, he was overjoyed. Ambedkar lent his support by making a scathing attack on Hinduism. He asserted that Islam and Hinduism were irreconcilable. From then on the die was cast to divide the Hindus and the Muslims permanently. To give it intellectual justification, Jinnah propounded his pernicious Two-Nation theory; he propagated it extensively and used it to justify his demand that India must be partitioned and Muslims given a separate homeland.

NINE

Demand for Pakistan

In the early stages of the Second World War (1939-45) Britain faced a life and death struggle as Hitler overran half of Europe. He even entered Paris as conqueror. Gandhi and the Congress were caught on the horns of a dilemma: Should they align with Britain or Germany? They found themselves in a web of ideological contradictions, procrastinating, not deciding what stand to take on the question of India's participation in the war. Jinnah, on the other hand, expressed deep concern for Britain which brought him into more favour with the authorities. He exploited these to gather more and more Muslims on his side, preparing to strike the final blow at the political unity and geographical integrity of India. He carried on a no-holds-barred campaign against the Congress, through the propagation of the Two-Nation theory. He successfully increased the rift between the two communities. He harped upon their differences parrot-like in every speech; he distorted historical facts to convince the world that Hindus and Muslims had nothing in common between them. Having wilfully poisoned the atmosphere of unity, he put forth his demand for the partition of India. It came in the form of a resolution which was moved and supported by some of the tallest Muslim leaders asking for the separation of Muslim-majority areas in the north-west and north-east from the rest of India. These were to be constituted as independent, sovereign states. The venue was Lahore where the annual session of the League was held in 1940; Jinnah, in his presidential address, justified the demand in a language which left little scope for reconciliation.

Unmindful of the common ties which had bound Hindus and Muslims for over a thousand years, Jinnah declared: "It is extremely difficult to appreciate why our Hindu friends fail to understand the real nature of Islam and Hinduism. They are not religions in the strict sense of the word but are, in fact, quite different and distinct social orders, and it is a dream that the Hindus and the Muslims can ever evolve a common nationality, and this misconception of one Indian nation has gone far beyond the limits and is the cause of most of our troubles and will lead India to destruction if we fail to revise our notions in time. The Hindus and the Muslims belong to two different religious philosophies, social customs, literature. They neither intermarry, nor interdine and, indeed, they belong to two different civilisations which are based mainly on conflicting ideas and conceptions. Their aspects on life and of life are different. It is quite clear that Hindus and Mussalmans derive their inspiration from different sources of history. They have different epics, their heroes are different; very often the hero of one is a foe of the other and, likewise, their victories and defeats overlap. To yoke together two such nations under a single state, one as a numerical minority and the other as a majority, must lead to growing discontent and final destruction of any fabric that may be so built up for the government of such a state."[1]

For the first time Gandhi, Nehru and the Congress were alerted to the danger that Jinnah's mischievous move posed to the integrity of the nation; they bestirred themselves to face the challenge that Jinnah and his League had hurled at them. Gandhi appealed to the Muslims that partition would ruin them; he installed Maulana Azad as the next Congress President to explain to them that Jinnah's remedy was worse than the disease. Azad was a Muslim divine, respected all over the world who had spearheaded along with the Ali Brothers the greatest Muslim upsurge during the Khilafat and Non-Cooperation movement. He had enthused them with the power of his pen and the eloquence of his tongue. His appeal, Gandhi felt, would swerve the Muslims from the wrong path.

To begin with Azad rose to the test; in the Ramgarh session of the Congress in 1940, he gave the clarion call to his co-religionists to safeguard the invincible unity of India. He argued: "It was India's historic destiny that many human races and cultures and religions should flow to her, finding a home in her hospitable soil, and many a caravan should rest here....One of the last of these caravans, following the footsteps of its predecessors, was that of the followers of Islam. This came here and settled here for good. This led to a meeting of culture-currents of two different races. Like the Ganga and Jumna, they flowed for a while through separate courses, but nature's immutable law brought them together and joined them in a *sangam*. This fusion was a notable event in history....Eleven hundred years of common history have enriched India with our common achievements. Our languages, our poetry, our literature, our culture, our art, our dress, our manners and customs, the innumerable happenings of our daily life, everything bears the stamp of our joint endeavour. This joint wealth is the heritage of our common nationality and we do not want to leave it and go back to a time when this joint life had not begun....The cast has now been moulded and destiny has set its seal upon it. Whether we like it or not, we have now become an Indian nation, united and indivisible. No fantasy or artificial scheming to separate and divide can break this unity. We must accept the logic of fact and history and engage ourselves in the fashioning of our future destiny."[2]

Gandhi also told the Muslims that what Jinnah advocated in the form of his Two-Nation theory was an untruth; he clarified, "The vast majority of Muslims of India are converts to Islam or are the descendants of converts. They did not become a separate nation as soon as they became converts. A Bengali Muslim speaks the same tongue that a Bengali Hindu does, eats the same food and has the same amusements as his Hindu neighbour. They dress alike. I have often found it difficult to distinguish by outward sign between a Bengali Hindu and a Bengali Muslim. The same phenomenon is observable more or less in the south among the poor, who constitute the masses of India.... Hindus and Muslims of India are not two nations. Those whom God has made one, man will never be able to divide."[3]

The case for unity was not only well argued but it provided a fitting reply to Jinnah's diatribe. The process should have been carried forward with conviction and vigour among the Muslims. The Congress however failed to do so. Its leaders did not take any concrete steps to enlighten the Muslims that the division of the country would be even more disastrous for them than for the Hindus as it would split their community

and leave Muslims in the Hindu-majority provinces in the
lurch. The Congress, like the ostrich, buried its head in the
ground to the growing separatist trends which Jinnah fostered.
After his eloquent peroration, Azad withdrew into a shell
instead of boldly confronting Jinnah by going to the Muslim
masses and awakening them to the dire consequences of such
a dangerous demand. He swallowed even Jinnah's
characterisation of him as a "showboy of the Congress". His
colleagues did not bother to snub Jinnah for insulting their
president. He was pilloried only by the Hindu-owned press
which Jinnah exploited to portray himself as a martyr before
the Muslim public. There was no concerted rational approach
on the part of the Congress to expose Jinnah's game which
threatened to put Hindus and Muslims at loggerheads and thus
to undermine the composite character of the nation.

       Meanwhile Gandhi launched the individual Satyagraha
in 1941 against the British for having involved India in the
war without her consent; it was a half-hearted move, protesting
against denial of free speech which had no impact. Most
Congress leaders were put in jail and were cut off from the
people. The vacuum was fully exploited by Jinnah who went
about campaigning against the Congress and consolidating his
hold on the Muslims. He galvanised them to oppose the
Satyagraha and ridiculed its objective. He said: "I should like
to ask any man with a grain of sense, do you really think that
Gandhi, the supreme leader, commander and general of the
Congress, has started this Satyagraha merely for the purpose
of getting liberty of speech? Don't you really feel that this is
nothing but a weapon of coercion and blackmailing the British
who are in a tight corner, to surrender and concede the Congress
demands?"[4] By so openly daring to oppose the individual
Satyagraha, Jinnah managed to gain considerable goodwill of

the British. His action also helped their war effort. He took advantage of the situation and organised branches of the League in every taluka and district. The Viceroy, Lord Linlithgow assured him that nothing would be done to hamper his onward march to unite the Muslims under his leadership. He was nevertheless nervous about the growing opposition to the war effort that Gandhi and the Congress had generated and the favourable impact that it was having especially on the majority of the Hindus. He advised Churchill that the unrest should be contained by offering some palliative. There was also pressure from President Roosevelt of the United States to come to terms with the Congress.

Churchill sent Sir Stafford Cripps to India to work out some sort of a political settlement. The offer that Sir Stafford brought contained among other things a clause that any province which did not wish to join the proposed federation would be given the choice to opt out. This was a major concession to Jinnah which upset the Congress; there was also no substantial devolution of power. The Congress rejected it on the ground that the offer did not give enough control to the popular representatives. Gandhi went to the extent of observing that it was "a post-dated cheque on a crashing bank". Even Nehru, a friend of Cripps, found him "muddle-headed". Sapru dismissed him as a "third-rate man". Jinnah was ambivalent in his talks with Cripps; he played his cards astutely; he told Cripps that his offer contained the seed of Pakistan but it was vague and not specific. He did not accept or reject it and put the entire blame for turning it down on the Congress and thus alienated the Congress further from the British. Cripps went away disappointed; he had come to India as a friend of Nehru but left as his bitter enemy and blamed him and Gandhi for the failure of his mission. Jinnah on the other hand reaped the harvest of goodwill of both London and New Delhi.

As time passed, Gandhi felt that he had to reassert the authority of the Congress; the Japanese threat of invasion of India seemed imminent; their startling victories in South-East Asia had shaken the British. This was the time to strike and make it clear to the British government that their game of brinkmanship was up; they must now grant immediate transfer of power to the people of India. It should be unreserved and total and not like the bogus offer made in the past. The "August offer" by the Viceroy in 1940 to expand his Executive Council by including popular representatives was a camouflage; under it ultimate power rested with the British. It was therefore rejected outright by the Congress. Similarly the Cripps Offer fell far short of the expectations of the Congress and was also turned down. In both cases transfer of power was half-hearted.

As the Japanese were threatening to invade India, the Congress could not remain a mute spectator to this development; it had to act to restore the people's confidence in its ability to safeguard the frontiers. The British continued to be adamant; Jinnah was deliberately obstructive. So far Gandhi had believed that without Hindu-Muslim unity, Swaraj could not be achieved; now he was convinced that with the British in India no communal settlement was possible. He explained this to a correspondent of *The Hindu*: "Time is a merciless enemy. I have been asking myself why every whole-hearted attempt made by all including myself to reach unity has failed, and failed so completely that I have entirely fallen from grace and am described by some Muslim papers as the greatest enemy of Islam in India. It is a phenomenon I can only account for by the fact that the third power, even without deliberately wishing it, will not allow real unity to take place. Therefore I have reluctantly come to the conclusion that the two communities will come together almost immediately after the British power comes to a final end in India".[5]

Gandhi tried to win over Jinnah several times; but he was not cooperative and so a settlement with him could not be reached. Jinnah did not want the British to quit unless he got what he wanted. He had been in constant touch with Churchill who had grown quite fond of him while his dislike of Gandhi and Nehru had increased. Lord Zetland, the then Secretary of State for India, had revealed in a Cabinet Memo dated January 31, 1940 that Churchill "did not share the anxiety to encourage and promote unity between the Hindu and the Muslim communities. Such unity was, in fact, almost out of the realm of practical politics, while, if it were to be brought about, the immediate result would be that the united communities would join in showing us the door. He regarded the Hindu-Muslim feud as the bulwark of British rule in India."[6] As Prime Minister, Churchill's main concern was to crush the Congress; it was the setback that the Allies had suffered in the war and the Japanese threat in the east which compelled him to send Sir Stafford Cripps on an insincere mission to India. He was happy when the Congress turned down the Cripps Offer; the rejection enabled him to tell the British public as well as American officialdom that Gandhi and the Congress were only interested in sabotaging the war efforts. Their sympathies were more with the Axis than the Allies.

The Congress had to rebut these charges and to counter the campaign of vilification against it both by Churchill abroad and Jinnah at home. It also had to show its popular strength to the world. The Congress was undoubtedly the most important force in India's public life and neither Churchill nor Jinnah could undermine it. To assert its hold on the public, Gandhi decided to strike. A meeting of the All-India Congress

Committee was therefore convened in Bombay on August 8, 1942; it approved the Working Committee's resolution that the British should immediately withdraw from India and in case they failed to do so the country would carry on a mass struggle under Gandhi's leadership to achieve its objective. The Mahatma gave the call to the people to "do or die". Anticipating such a move, the authorities clamped down on the Congress and arrested all its top leaders including Gandhi, Nehru, Patel and its President Azad. The activists in the Congress retaliated in full force and a popular upsurge burst out in raging fury. This came to be known as the Quit India movement and caused much unease to the Government which in turn unleashed a reign of terror against the agitators. Jinnah deplored the movement and hurriedly called a meeting of the Working Committee of the League on August 16 which took stock of the situation and debated for four days the possible consequences to the Muslims. Finally in a strongly worded resolution, the League condemned the Quit India movement as not only anti-British but also anti-Muslim and called upon the Muslims to oppose it and help the Government to suppress it. The Viceroy appreciated the stand of the League and facilitated the installation of League governments in Assam and Sind. An unholy alliance between the two to thwart the popular upsurge was thus formed.

Though most Congress leaders were put behind bars, C. Rajagopalachari did not participate in the movement; he was therefore not arrested. He had earlier advised his colleagues that the Congress should accept the League's demand for self-determination of Muslim-majority areas and come to an amicable settlement with it. He was voted down by the Congress Working Committee, and consequently he resigned from its membership. Nevertheless to pursue his mission he met Jinnah in early November and held prolonged discussions with him with a view to prepare the ground for talks between him and Gandhi for a final solution of the Hindu-Muslim tangle. C.R. then approached the Viceroy and requested him to release Gandhi but Linlithgow flatly refused. He put the entire blame for the violence that had taken place throughout the country in the wake of the Quit India movement on the Apostle of Non-Violence. Gandhi wrote to the Viceroy that it was the Government which had provoked it; he decided to fast for twenty-one days in order to undo the wrong that the authorities had done. His fast began on February 9 and ended on March 3. During the fast, as Gandhi's health began to deteriorate, three members of the Viceroy's Executive Council resigned. There was grave risk to the Mahatma's life but Churchill instructed the Viceroy to remain firm and even asked him to make the necessary arrangements for the funeral rites. On February 19, Sapru called an all-parties conference to urge upon the British to release Gandhi and requested Jinnah to attend and lend his support to save Gandhi's life but Jinnah did not agree. On the contrary he telephoned one of his closest lieutenants, Isphani, directing him that the Muslim League members of the Bengal Legislative Assembly should vote against the resolution demanding the release of the Mahatma, even though Gandhi's life was in danger.

Later Jinnah sarcastically asked Gandhi in a public speech why he did not talk to him instead of pursuing the Viceroy. Jinnah declared that were he to write such a letter, the Government would dare not stop it. Gandhi immediately wrote to him but the Government refused to forward his letter to Jinnah. Linlithgow was inclined to oblige Jinnah but Churchill vetoed it. The League President took the rebuff quietly and wriggled out of the imbroglio by saying that Gandhi

had not denounced the Quit India movement nor accepted
the League's demand for Pakistan and therefore he would not
intervene. This once again proved that though Jinnah was adept
at forensic onslaught, he shied away from confrontation with
the authorities.

He swallowed the slight because he did not want to
lose the goodwill of the British which Churchill had assured
him of. In fact as early as February 1942, his Secretary of State
for India, L.S. Amery had written to the Viceroy, Lord
Linlithgow: "If there are sufficient provinces who want to get
together and form a dominion the dissident provinces should
be free to stand out and either come in after a period of option
or be set up at the end of it as dominions of their own."[7] This
was later incorporated in a guarded manner the Cripps Offer;
hence the process of favouring Jinnah was quietly being
pursued by the British; Jinnah was too shrewd not to see through
the game and instead sulk over a trifling incident which he
knew would have produced no fruitful result.

TEN

Encounter with Gandhi

As the fortunes of the war in Europe started to turn in favour of Britain and the Allies, Churchill's attitude towards India softened, his own Labour ministers and more importantly, the American President Franklin Roosevelt advised him to be more accommodative. Consequently on expiry of the extended term of Lord Linlithgow, he replaced him by Lord Wavell as the Viceroy with the understanding that the new incumbent would adopt a conciliatory approach towards the Congress. In his inaugural address to the Central Legislative Assembly Wavell stressed "the geographical unity of India". It was in a way a sop to the Congress. But it annoyed Jinnah and upset some of the British governors of the provinces who reminded the Viceroy — to quote Sir Henry Twynam of the Central Provinces: "Where would we have been" had Jinnah not opposed the Congress. Francis Mudie of Bihar bluntly told his new master that "Government should make an unequivocal announcement of their unconditional acceptance of Pakistan."[1] Being a soldier by training, Wavell did not want to

cause any turmoil among the armed forces by the threat of
division, specially when fierce fighting on the Eastern Front
was still going on. He did not like Jinnah's obstructive politics
and regretted that "no one seems to have the character to
oppose him".[2] He decided to put Jinnah in his place. Addressing
the Central Legislative Assembly, Wavell declared in
unequivocal terms: "You cannot alter geography. From the
point of view of defence, of relations to the outside world, of
many internal and external economic problems, India is a
natural unit. The two communities, and even two nations can
make arrangements to live together in spite of differing cultures
or religions; history provides many examples."[3]

Although Wavell had no particular liking for Gandhi
either — whose "seditious behaviour" he abhorred — he was
anxious to resolve the political deadlock and bring about some
sort of amicable settlement between the Government, the
Congress and the League. He was alarmed at the continuing
deterioration in the Mahatma's health while in detention. The
first step that Wavell therefore took was to release the
Mahatma on May 5, 1944 after getting clearance from
Churchill. Gandhi rested for a while; he then wrote to Jinnah
who was holidaying in Kashmir that they should meet: "We
will meet whenever you choose. Don't regard me as the enemy
of Islam or of the Muslims of this country."[4] Jinnah replied
that he would meet him on his return to Bombay. For over two
weeks, from September 9 to 26, the two leaders spent hours
together each trying to convince the other but neither
succeeding in the task. They recorded the gist of their talks in
letters; these showed the uncompromising stand of Jinnah on
the most vital question of the division of India. He would not
concede an inch to Gandhi on this score. The Mahatma on the
other hand went to the farthest limit in trying to appease Jinnah

but it was of no avail. Wolpert has observed, "A Congress-League pact at that point would, after all, have taken the wind out of the League's highly successful organising momentum..."[5] Wavell watched anxiously the deliberations of the two leaders and on their failure, recorded in his journal: "Jinnah had an easy task, he merely had to keep on telling Gandhi he was talking nonsense, which was true and he did so rather rudely without having to disclose any of the weaknesses of his own position, or define his Pakistan in any way. I suppose it may increase his prestige with his followers but it cannot add to his reputation with reasonable men."[6]

These talks were the last that Gandhi and Jinnah had; they created much hope not only in India but also in Britain. The press welcomed them, poets wrote in praise of them. Singers applauded them. But the talks failed because Jinnah insisted that Gandhi admit that Hindus and Muslims were two different nations with nothing in common. The Mahatma argued that this was an untruth to which he could not subscribe. He was prepared to concede the right of self-determination to a territorial unit but not to a religious group. As formulated by C.R., the Mahatma told Jinnah he could hold a plebiscite in the Muslim-majority areas provided its non-Muslim citizens were also allowed to vote. Jinnah said that would not be acceptable to him as it would falsify his Two-Nation theory. He wanted division on a religious basis; Gandhi expressed his helplessness to accept that. He told Jinnah: "The more our argument progresses, the more alarming your picture appears to me. It would be alluring, if it were true. But my fear is growing that it is wholly unreal. I find no parallel in history for a body of converts and their descendants claiming to be a nation apart from the parent stock. If India was one nation before the advent of Islam, it remains one in spite of the change of faith of a very large body of her children." The Mahatma asked him whether he was claiming to be a separate nation by right of conquest. It was as absurd a proposition as demanding it on the basis of religion. He added, "You seem to have introduced a new test of nationhood. If I accept it, I would have to subscribe to many more claims and face an insoluble problem."[7]

In his reply, Jinnah explained: "As I have said before, you are a great man and you exercise enormous influence over the Hindus, particularly the masses, and by accepting the road that I am pointing out to you now, you are not prejudicing or harming the interests of the Hindus or of the minorities. On the contrary, Hindus will be the greatest gainers. I am convinced that the true welfare not only of the Muslims but of the rest of India lies in the division of India, as proposed by the Lahore resolution. It is for you to consider whether it is not your policy and your programme in which you have persisted, which has been the principal factor of the 'ruin of whole of India' and of the misery and the degradation of the people to which you refer and which I deplore no less than anyone else. And it is for that very reason that I am pleading before you all these days, although you insist that you are having talks with me only in your own individual capacity, in the hope that you may yet revise your policy and programme."[8]

Gandhi characterised Jinnah's obsession with the Two-Nation theory as a "hallucination"; in his letter dated September 22, he made it clear to Jinnah: "I am unable to accept the proposition that the Muslims of India are a nation distinct from the rest of the inhabitants of India. I cannot be a willing party to a division which does not provide for the simultaneous safeguarding of common interests such as defence, foreign affairs and the like. We seem to be moving in a circle."[9] He asked Jinnah whether his own son Hiralal, who had been converted to Islam, had thus become overnight a member of another nation. Jinnah had no answer. On the failure of talks, the Mahatma replied to a volley of questions by the press: Why did he prolong the talks, they asked, when it was obvious from the beginning that there were fundamental differences between him and Jinnah. Gandhi's reply was typical of him: "Because I possess, by God's grace, inexhaustible patience". He said, "...as long as there was the slightest possibility, I clung to the hope that we shall pull through to the solution." Gandhi reiterated that there was "a large body of Muslims" who did not believe in the Two-Nation theory. One reporter then pointed out that the nationalist Muslims did not like the Mahatma's parleys with Jinnah because they had been put "in a false position".[10] That was not true, Gandhi affirmed. Their stand deserved all respect because it was based on sound principles. He was trying to take Jinnah on the right path; the nationalist Muslims were already treading it.

Nothing irritated Jinnah more than the association of these so-called nationalist Muslims with the Congress; he delighted in referring to them contemptuously. He was particularly harsh on Azad whom Gandhi had installed as President of the Congress. He declined to talk to him or deal with him since according to him, Azad was nothing but a puppet of the Hindus. He condemned all nationalist Muslims as "traitors, cranks, stuntmen or lunatics — an evil from which no society or nation is free." However, such was the awe that Jinnah had created that no one challenged him; he could get away with any atrocious pronouncement.

In all his speeches and negotiations, Jinnah insisted on the acceptance of his two oft-repeated stipulations which he asserted were non-negotiable. One, that his League should be accepted as the only authorised representative body of the Muslims and two, that the division of India on the basis of religion was the only possible solution to the Hindu-Muslim dispute. The first condition was rejected outright by every Congress President from Rajendra Prasad to Nehru, Bose and Azad; they made it clear to Jinnah who was more or less aware that the Congress born in nationalism could not reduce itself to be a vehicle of communalism. It had been nurtured as much by the Muslims as the Hindus; their sacrifices could not be wiped out. As for the second condition, the Congress was committed irrevocably to the unity and integrity of India and it could not, therefore, consent under any circumstance to the division of the country on a religious basis. The Mahatma could concede the right of self-determination to a territorial unit but not to a religious group in a multi-religious society. Not many in the Congress were prepared even for this concession.

Despite the considered opinion of experts that Pakistan could not be in any sense a viable state nor would it solve the Hindu-Muslim problem, on the contrary, it would further complicate the dispute, Jinnah did not deviate from his chosen objective. He was not concerned that the solution he offered would put more than one-third of the Muslims residing in "Hindustan" in the lurch; neither did he reflect on the disastrous economic consequences of partition for the Muslims of the subcontinent. He merely wished to avenge the woeful neglect that he had suffered in public life. Since the advent of Gandhi he struggled hard to avenge his humiliation and succeeded in acquiring a position which equalled that of Gandhi. He reminded an audience in Ahmedabad, the capital of Gandhi's Gujarat, how he was ridiculed and insulted before and how he had risen phoenix-like to dominate the political arena: "I was considered a plague and shunned. But I thrust myself and forced my way through and went from place to place uninvited and unwanted. But now the situation was different."[11] Jinnah was being wooed by the very people who had discarded him earlier; that gave him the greatest satisfaction. He had developed by this time such hostility against the Hindus that when a British journalist asked him whether there were no Hindus he could trust, he replied, "There are none". The Hindu-owned press had repeatedly taunted him that he was an armchair politician who ran away from making the slightest sacrifice for the national cause. In a fit of irritation he told them that they might be enamoured by the antics of Gandhi: "...to obtain leadership, to sit like a goat under the police 'lathi' charge, then to go to jail, then to complain of loss of weight and then to manage release (loud laughter). I don't believe in that sort of struggle, but when the time for suffering comes, I will be the first to get bullet shots in my chest."[12] Jinnah of course saw to it that he had never to face such a situation or undergo any suffering.

One day some Muslim students requested Jinnah to travel in the train by third class as Gandhi did so that the poor Muslims would feel he is one of them. Jinnah lost his temper and told them: "Do not dictate to me what I should do and should not do. It is not your money I am spending. I shall live and act as I choose."[13] Once Gandhi referred affectionately to Jinnah as "brother Jinnah"; Jinnah's response to it was cold and terse: "Brother Gandhi forgets that while he has three votes I have only one". On another occasion when the Mahatma described the League's demand of Pakistan as a sin, Jinnah told the Muslims: "Mind you he calls your demand a sin, not even a crime. He has damned you in this world as well as the next." He was a past master in the art of rebuttal.

Gandhi tried to placate Jinnah but he became even more unresponsive. During the marathon talks, while the

Mahatma continued to be courteous and considerate, Jinnah remained rude and overbearing. He told him: "It is for you to consider whether it is not your policy and your programme in which you have persisted which has been the principal factor of the ruin of India and of the misery and degradation of the people…" Gandhi ignored the rebuke and gently told him that there seemed to be no meeting ground between them. The Mahatma had fervently hoped to bring Jinnah round but failed. Thereafter he never tried again to have any meaningful dialogue with him.

Apart from Gandhi, several friends from abroad who were desirous of bridging the gulf between the two communities, prevailed upon Jinnah not to be so obstructive and ignore the historic reality and economic benefit of preserving the unity of India. One of them was Edward Thompson, an eminent British journalist. He asked Jinnah whether division of India was, in his considered opinion, the right remedy even conceding that every grievance of his against the Hindus was justified. Jinnah did not hesitate for a moment and replied: "Yes, yes, yes. Hindus and Muslims are two different nations who can never live together."

Thompson queried: "Two different nations, Mr. Jinnah, confronting each other in every province, every town, every village of India?"

"Yes," said Jinnah, "two different nations confronting each other in every province, every town, every village of India. It is indeed, unfortunate, but it must be faced. That is why they must be separated. That is the only solution."

"That is a terrible solution, Mr. Jinnah," Thompson said sadly.

"It may be a terrible solution, but it is the only solution," repeated the Quaid-i-Azam doggedly.[14]

ELEVEN

Viceregal Endeavours

S oon after his assumption of the high office of Viceroy, Lord Wavell realised that the British could not hold on to India any longer. The economy had depleted due to the war; British officers had lost interest in their jobs; most of them were preparing to retire and return home; even the Indians in the armed forces could no more be relied on; the tide was turning against the establishment. In such circumstances, it had become increasingly difficult to administer the country. Politically Hindus and Muslims were ranged against one another Jinnah's propagation of the Two-Nation theory had greatly intensified communal feelings. Wavell impressed upon Amery, who had taken over as Secretary of State for India, that a fresh initiative had to be taken to hammer out some kind of political settlement to ease the situation. Amery was responsive but he was not sure about the attitude of Churchill who, he said, "... knew as much of the Indian problem as George III did of the American colonies".[1]

The Viceroy started the process of political consultations by convening a conference at Simla on June 25, 1945 inviting representatives of twenty-one groups and parties. To facilitate the participation of the Congress, he released the members of its Working Committee. His immediate objective was to reconstitute the Executive Council by including leaders who "represented" the main "communities". Wavell suggested that there should be "equal proportions of caste Hindus and Muslims". He assured the conference that it was being done in the hope "that the leaders of Indian parties would agree among themselves on a settlement of the communal issue which is the main stumbling block..." Jinnah put a damper even before the conference met — he informed Wavell that "the League could not participate in an Executive Council in which non-League Muslims were included". At the conference he challenged the national character of the Congress and declared that it represented only the Hindus.

Azad ignored Jinnah's diatribe against him and, on Wavell's request, agreed to submit a list of the representatives of the Congress; this naturally included a Muslim; Jinnah refused to give the names of the representatives of the League until his claim to nominate all the Muslims on the Council was conceded. Wavell rejected his plea and wrote to him: "I fully appreciate your difficulties, but regret that I am unable to give you the guarantee you wish, i.e., that all the Muslim members of the proposed new Council shall necessarily be members of the Muslim League....I have to attempt to form an Executive Council— representative, competent, and generally acceptable.... It will help me greatly if you will let me have names.... I asked for eight, but will certainly accept five if you do not wish to send more."[2]

Jinnah did not relent; he insisted that unless the League was given the sole right to nominate the Muslim members, he would not send the names to the Viceroy. "It is not possible," he wrote, "for us to depart from our fundamental principles." Wavell was equally firm; he told Jinnah he too would not be able to "give way on this point". The British cabinet asked Wavell to once again try and persuade Jinnah to cooperate. Wavell tried but failed. He recorded in his journal: "He even refused to discuss names unless he could be given the absolute right to select all Muslims and some guarantee that any decision which the Muslims opposed in Council could only be passed by a two-thirds majority — in fact a communal veto. I said that these conditions were entirely unacceptable."[3] Disgusted with Jinnah whom he found obstinate, narrow minded and "arrogant", he wrote to Amery: "Jinnah is actuated mainly by fear and distrust of the Congress."[4] He would not cooperate with it under any circumstances, the Viceroy averred. This was in fact in line with what Jinnah had planned right from the time he returned from London; he believed that if he settled with the Congress, it would further the emergence of Hindu raj which he was determined to oppose.

Another obstacle that Jinnah put in the way of arriving at an agreement was to demand 50 per cent representation, parity between Muslim and non-Muslim members. Wavell was amused because he was aware that Muslims constituted only 27 per cent of the Indian population. Jinnah justified his claim by stating: "All other minorities, such as Scheduled Castes, Sikhs and the Christians have the same goal as the Congress.... Their goal and ideology is... of a united India. Ethnically and culturally, they are very closely knitted to Hindu society." In a letter to the Mahatma, Jayakar's comment on Jinnah's statement showed how ridiculous the claim was: "As I read his speech, where he called the Wavell arrangement a snare, it was clear to me that his apprehension (was) that... if he accepted the interim arrangement... in the day to day harmony of working, the acerbities and animosities out of which Pakistan is born and fed, would be gradually smoothened and Muslims would lose the zest for separate existence on discovering that its basis rests not in realities but only in long cherished suspicion." Jayakar summarised Jinnah's two conditions, as prerequisite to his consent, namely (1) assurance about Pakistan and (2) equality of the Muslim vote with all the other interests in India. He observed rather sarcastically, "True to his habit, intensified by frequent successes, he swallows the concessions Muslims have received, viz, parity between caste Hindus and Muslims and now wants parity between Muslims and all other interests put together, i.e., 50 for Muslims, 50 for all the rest of India— a mathematical monstrosity that 27 equals 73... He is in no hurry to attain freedom and would demand for its attainment a price which would almost render it nugatory."[5] Gandhi enjoyed Jayakar's clever analysis; one lawyer trying to have the better of the other, he said. But the numbers game one way or the other was of little interest to him. He was convinced that the Hindu-Muslim tangle could be solved only after the British departed.

Amery wrote to the Viceroy that the best course would be to test the representative character of each party by holding elections to the Central and provincial legislatures. He was of the opinion that once the Congress and the League confronted each other electorally, it might be easier to deal with them. The results would show them their respective popular strength. Though franchise was restricted to less than ten per cent of the adult population, as far as the provincial electorate was concerned, even so, it would help to determine who represented whom. Many voices were raised against such a move; it was feared that it might whip up communal frenzy. At the governors' conference when the Viceroy enquired as to what their reaction was, Governor Glancy of the Punjab struck a note of caution. He said: "Unless the Muslim League could be steered away from the crude version of Pakistan there would be civil war in the Punjab."[6] He warned that the League would make a communal appeal that would vitiate the election campaign. There might even be bloodshed. Some others were also sceptical about the outcome.

The consensus nevertheless was for holding elections; Wavell asked Whitehall for clearance; the matter was referred to Attlee at Downing Street who called the Viceroy for consultation. Wavell left for London on August 20, 1945 to meet the ageing Lord Pethick-Lawrence, a well-known Quaker who had replaced Amery as Secretary of State for India. They discussed the pros and cons of the political stalemate in India. Thereafter Wavell met the India Committee of the Cabinet, chaired by the Prime Minister. All of them seemed hopeful that the Cripps Offer rejected by the Congress and the League could be revived, since there was now a more sympathetic government at Westminster. Wavell tried to dissuade them from indulging in wishful thinking, but most ministers did not agree with his view. They persisted in the hope that the response by the Congress and the League would now be positive. Wavell returned to Delhi wondering whether the British rulers had any real understanding of the state of affairs in India.

Wavell reassessed the situation on his return to Delhi; being the man on the spot, he decided that positive action was called for. Procrastination would be dangerous. Already he had

been warned by his Commander-in-Chief Sir Claude Auchinlek
that the loyalty of Indian soldiers and officers could no longer
be taken for granted; likewise the British civil servants were
apprehensive that they could not rely on their Indian
subordinates as they had in the past. The scenario had changed.
Also time was running out for the British; the Viceroy was
clear in his mind that he could no longer delay the transfer of
power to the popular representatives of India.

   To achieve this objective he took the immediate step
of ordering the elections to the provincial and Central
legislatures. At first the Congress demanded that these should
be on the basis of adult suffrage; but under pressure, it gave
up its objection; Nehru, Patel and especially Azad as Congress
President failed to realise that with the religious frenzy that
Jinnah had whipped up, the League would sweep the polls in
the reserved constituencies; the results would confirm his claim
of being the sole spokesman for his community. The Congress
should have stuck to its demand of adult suffrage and delayed
the process. Unfortunately it was carried away by the
overwhelming support that it undoubtedly enjoyed among non-
Muslims; but it overlooked the fact that Jinnah would gain
the same kind of support among the Muslims. Nehru and
Patel should therefore have insisted that either the prevailing
electoral representation be taken into account for the transfer
of power or that elections be held on the basis of adult
franchise. The results of the provisional elections held in 1937
had shown that the League was not in good shape especially in
the Muslim-majority provinces which were to constitute
Pakistan. In Punjab, it had contested 7 out of 84 Muslim
reserved seats and won only 2. Likewise in Bengal out of 117
Muslim reserved seats, it had won only 38. In Sind out of 133
Muslim reserved seats it had secured only 38. In the North-

West Frontier Province, the League candidates were trounced by those of the Congress which had obtained a clear majority. In the elections to the Central Legislative Assembly which were held only in 1934 when its electorate was less than 1 per cent, the League had returned no official members. Jinnah collected 20-odd independents, grouped them in a party and made himself their leader. As for the Congress, it had won in most of the general constituencies and its representative position was unassailable.

Why then did the Congress leadership succumb to Wavell and agree to the holding of fresh elections on restricted franchise which were bound to strengthen Jinnah's leadership? But that was exactly what happened. Jinnah had used every communal device to win the elections; the reports which the governors sent were alarming. Glancy of Punjab said that "the League made free use of fatwas" to canvass support; the Frontier Governor reported that the Muslim voters were told to choose between Kafirs and Momins. From other centres the official accounts testified that the speakers on behalf of the League candidates warned the Muslim voters that in case the League was defeated Muslims would not be allowed to congregate for prayers on Friday; they would not be able to bury their dead but would be compelled to cremate them. Their madrasas would be shut down. The results of the elections showed the impact of such propaganda; the League candidates won in all the 30 seats reserved for the Muslims in the Central Legislative Assembly. In the elections to the provincial legislatures they also fared as well except in the North-West Frontier Province. Out of 492 Muslim reserved seats in the provincial legislative assemblies, the League won in 428 constituencies as against only 100 that it had captured in the 1937 elections. True, in the general constituencies the Congress candidates did well; but no one had challenged the representative character of the Congress. It gave no special advantage to it. It was Jinnah who wanted the seal of approval on his claim that his League was the authentic representative body of the Muslims. And he managed to get it. On the basis of the previous statistics, such a claim would not have been valid. Thus by consenting to participate in such elections, the Congress lost in the final count and Jinnah emerged the real winner.

Soon after the declaration of the results, Attlee announced in the two Houses of Parliament at Westminster that Britain would hand over power to Indian representatives at the latest by June 1948. To expedite the transfer, he sent a powerful Cabinet Mission, consisting of three of his senior ministers, Lord Pethick-Lawrence, Sir Stafford Cripps and A.V. Alexander to India to work out a constitutional settlement in consultation with the representatives of the major political parties, in particular the Congress and the League. Before starting on their fateful journey, Francis Turnbull, secretary to Lord Pethick-Lawrence, prepared a note for the Mission wherein he explained that "the division of India will be born in bitter antagonism and it will certainly be rash to assume that this will not be reflected in the efforts necessary to regulate the machinery of communication and economic intercourse between the Pakistan states and the rest of India." He expressed the view that "the splitting up of India will be the reverse of beneficial so far as the livelihood of the people is concerned".[7]

The Mission reached Delhi in the last week of March 1946. Its members, all seasoned politicians, were bombarded with statements which somehow baffled them. Before the official talks, they held preliminary discussions with Gandhi and Nehru on the one side and Jinnah on the other. They had come to save the unity of India, if possible. That was why their dialogue with Jinnah was crucial. He was firm on his demand for a separate homeland for the Muslims. He told the British ministers that the only solution to break the political impasse was to divide the country and make the Muslim-majority provinces, as outlined in the Lahore Resolution, a separate sovereign state.

The Mission asked Jinnah: "Do you realise that the Pakistan you are demanding will leave substantial Hindus under Muslim domination?"

Jinnah replied: "That will be so; but I will leave many more Muslims under Hindu domination in Hindustan."

Surprised at this reply the Mission said: "How does it then resolve Hindu-Muslim discord? It will only perpetuate the hostilities."

Jinnah persisted: "I will free at least two-third Muslims from Hindu domination."

The Mission told him: "And you will put more than that number of Hindus under Muslim domination. That is no solution."

Jinnah was adamant. He asserted: "That is the only solution if you don't want civil war."

The Mission was nonplussed at his stand and asked: "But should you adopt such a callous attitude towards the minorities in the two states, they will be in worse condition than the Muslims in united India — also the Muslims in divided India will be the worst sufferers."

Jinnah replied: "Their best protection will be the establishment of two strong states, neither of which will dare misbehave towards each other's minorities."

The Mission enquired: "You mean to say that these minorities will be hostages."

Jinnah said: "Exactly. If one state mistreats its minorities, the other state will retaliate against its minorities. It will be tit for tat."

The Mission was aghast at this reply and remarked: "That is a horrible concept which did not work even in medieval times."

Jinnah stood his ground and asserted: "Fear is the most potent weapon; I am sure the rulers in either state will be wise enough to conduct themselves properly. They will be afraid of retaliation against their co-religionists."

The Mission reminded Jinnah that the world had much advanced and that it would never accept the theory of hostages as propounded by him. The Mission entreated him not to destroy the unity of India which the British had worked so hard to build.

Jinnah told them bluntly: "I wish I could fulfil your wish; but Hindus and the Congress have made it impossible for me to do so. I am sorry."[8]

The Mission had not realised before their arrival that the task they faced was so formidable. The Congress was in a conciliatory mood; but the League had adopted an aggressive tone. Some of its leaders were openly talking of civil war. This was witnessed at the convention of the victorious Muslim legislators that their Quaid-i-Azam had called, soon after the results of the recent elections. I.I. Chundrigar of Bombay, who subsequently became Prime Minister of Pakistan, asked the Mission to hand over India to the Muslims from whom they had taken it just a few centuries ago. Other leaders like Khizar Hyat Khan and Muhammad Ismail talked of Jihad. The most frightening threat was uttered by the well-known stooge of the British Sir Feroz Khan Noon who thundered that if the Muslims were driven to a fight then, to quote his words: "The havoc which they will cause will put to shame what Ghengiz Khan and Halaku did."[9] Such bravado inflamed further the communal passion and made settlement between the two communities well-nigh impossible. Surprisingly, Jinnah, the acclaimed gentleman, allowed such uncivilised and provocative outbursts which seemed to be the precursor of the change in his attitude — from the constitutionalist to the rabble-rouser.

TWELVE

Failure of Negotiations

Attlee in his statement had made it clear that while "the minorities should be able to live free from fear" they could not be allowed "to place their veto on the advance of the majority". Jinnah reacted sharply against it and told the Foreign Editor of London's now defunct *News Chronicle* that the British were guilty of "a flagrant breach of faith" and further that "there was no such country as India", adding "I am not an Indian at all".[1] On arrival the Mission held talks with no less than 472 leaders, representing different groups and parties. The more they talked, the more confused the Mission became. Most of their time was of course taken in discussions with the Congress and League leaders, trying to reconcile their differences and persuade them to agree on the formation of some kind of union to which power could be transferred. But Jinnah was not in a mood for any compromise. Lord Alexander has described the League President's behaviour in his diary dated April 16, 1946: "I have never seen a man with such a mind twisting and turning to avoid as far as possible direct answers. I came to the conclusion that he is playing this game, which is one of life and death for millions of people, very largely from the point of view of scoring a triumph in a legal negotiation by first making large demands and secondly insisting that he should make no offer reducing that demand but should wait for the other side always to say how much they would advance towards granting that demand."[2]

Though discouraged by the preliminary reaction, the Mission pursued its efforts to thrash out a settlement; it convened a meeting of the Congress and the League "bigwigs" at Simla on May 5, 1943. The basis of their discussion was a new proposal, formulated by the British Cabinet. It stated: "A Union Government dealing with the following subjects: Foreign Affairs, Defence and Communications. There will be two groups of provinces, the one of predominantly Hindu provinces, the other of predominantly Muslim provinces dealing with all other subjects which the provinces in the respective groups desire to be dealt with in common. The Provincial Governments will deal with all other subjects and will have all the residuary sovereign rights."[3] Once again Jinnah, took a non-compromising attitude; he told the Mission that the basis of any agreement had to be division. And he stuck to it from start to finish. He showed his contempt for Congress President Azad by refusing to shake hands with him. Patel warned him that if he misbehaved again the Congress would refuse to sit with him at the same table. He took the rebuke in his stride but showed no sign of repentance. Pethick-Lawrence intervened and restored calm; but as talks proceeded, it became clear that the gulf was far too wide to be bridged.

Tired, exhausted and frustrated, the Mission went to Kashmir for some rest and stayed there from April 17 to 23, 1946. On their return they announced their own plan on May

16, which came to be known as the Cabinet Mission's Plan. At the outset it clarified that "the setting up of a separate sovereign state of Pakistan on the lines claimed by the Muslim League would not solve the communal minority problem; nor can we see any justification for including within a sovereign Pakistan those districts of the Punjab and of Bengal and Assam in which the population is predominantly non-Muslim. Every argument that can be used in favour of Pakistan, can equally in our view be used in favour of the exclusion of the non-Muslim areas from Pakistan. This point would particularly affect the position of the Sikhs."[4] The Mission was also not in favour of creating a truncated Pakistan by partitioning Bengal and Punjab as, "there are mighty administrative, military and economic considerations" against it. Further, they pointed out that "there is the geographical fact that the two halves of the proposed Pakistan State would be separated by some seven hundred miles",[5] which would work against it both in war and peace.

The Mission emphasised that the unity of India must be preserved but conceded that in view of the Muslim fear of Hindu domination, the Union would have to be restricted to the exercise of only three subjects: Defence, Foreign Affairs and Communications; it would have an executive and a legislature, but the representation on it would be in proportion to the population as reflected in various provinces. However to meet the Muslim aspirations there would be below the Union or federation, a sub-federation of three Groups: Group A would consist of Hindu-majority provinces and Groups B and C would consist of the Muslim-majority provinces in the north-west and north-east. In Group C Assam was added despite the fact that it did not have a Muslim majority. Most of the powers of governance and legislation were vested in these Groups. This was done to appease Jinnah and in effect to give him the essence of Pakistan. Below the Groups were to be the provinces with limited autonomy, with the choice given to each of them to opt out, if they so decide, but only after a lapse of ten years.

This was a complicated framework but it was a genuine effort on the part of the Mission to preserve a united India with enough scope in it for the fulfilment of separatist Muslim aspirations. This was a long-term scheme but along with it there was a short-term scheme for the immediate formation of an interim government which would consist of five caste Hindus, five Muslims, one Sikh, one Christian, one Schedule Caste and one European. The short-term scheme was made integral to the long-term one. The parties had to accept both. After some initial hesitation Gandhi welcomed the scheme: "Whatever the wrong done to India by British rule, if the statement of the Mission was genuine, as he believed it was in discharge of an obligation that they had declared the British owed to India, namely to get off India's back, it contained the seed to convert this land of sorrow into a land without sorrow and suffering." [6]

Jinnah was recuperating from an illness in Srinagar; he issued a statement from there saying the reaction of the Muslims against the Cabinet Mission's Plan was very strong. He said he would have to consult his colleagues and his Council before announcing the decision of the League. He bid for time which the Mission was not prepared to give him. They bluntly told this to his lieutenant Liaquat Ali Khan and pointed out that they had to decide on the course of action without further delay.

Gandhi also raised some doubt about the grouping of provinces but Cripps explained to him that there was no scope for negotiation as far as the contents of their Plan were concerned and that these were "in their final form" and should be accepted or rejected as a whole. Jinnah realised for the first time that the British meant to quit India whether there was agreement between the Congress and the League or not. He told Woodrow Wyatt, Private Secretary to Cripps, confidentially that the British in their own interest should divide India into Hindustan and Pakistan and "remain as the binding force in the Indian Centre for some 15 years and deal with defence and foreign affairs for Pakistan and Hindustan consulting the Prime Minister of each state."[7]

Despite the rumblings within both the Congress and the League camps, the Mission became hopeful that they might succeed in getting the two parties to agree to their Plan. On May 28, 1946, Pethick-Lawrence wired his Prime Minister: "What is going to happen I don't know. Gandhi is provokingly enigmatic and blows hot and cold. Azad, Nehru and Jinnah I think all want a settlement. But already we are up against the second hurdle.... Azad and Nehru and the Congress generally are willing to waive any formal or legal change in the interim constitution, but they want almost absolute power in reality and they want something to be able to say about it to their people. Jinnah not only does not want the Viceroy to relinquish his authority but he positively wants him to retain it. The Viceroy is now I think convinced that he must go to the limit of what is possible in satisfying the Congress.... I have not...abandoned hope that we may surmount this difficulty and that both Congress and Muslim League may express a grudging acquiescence in our Plan sufficient to enable us to go ahead with summoning the Constituent Assembly...on or before June 15th. There are many people who would welcome our positively getting on with the job."[8]

Both the Congress and the League debated on the pros and cons of the Mission's statement and ultimately accepted it with reservations. Neither was sincere in wanting to implement it in toto; the Congress insisted on a strong Centre and was therefore averse to the grouping of provinces which were entrusted with most of the powers; the League, on the other hand, saw in these groupings the fulfilment of their communal aspirations. Jinnah was also distressed that in the set-up at the Centre, there would be no parity for the League with the Congress. Nevertheless he accepted the long-term statement in the hope that it would considerably curb the Hindu domination at the Centre. However as far as the interim government was concerned, he refused to compromise on his two demands: (1) that there should be parity between the representatives of the Congress and the League; and (2) that he should have the sole right to nominate the Muslim members. On both these points the Mission did not yield.

The trouble arose however after the acceptance of the Plan by the Congress among some of its followers who did not like (1) the inclusion of the North-West Frontier, a Congress stronghold in Group B which would be dominated by the League; and (2) the inclusion of Assam in Group C which was not a Muslim-majority province. The Mission had to make some such adjustment while grouping the provinces to satisfy the League. Both Gandhi and the Congress Working Committee appreciated this; that was why their initial response was quite positive. They did not seem to be concerned about the inclusion of the Frontier province; but the local Congress leaders of Assam headed by their icon, Gopinath Bardolai, created such a commotion that the attitude of not only Gandhi but that of Nehru and Patel also changed; they opposed Assam's inclusion in Group C. This countermanded the grouping provision which was an essential feature of the Cabinet Mission's Plan; it was obvious that on that basis alone Jinnah and his League had given their acceptance; they were able to convince their followers that the grouping of provinces in the north-west and north-east would provide to the Muslims enough scope for eventually transforming these into Pakistan. There was therefore a hidden motive behind Jinnah's acceptance; likewise the Congress attitude was also not sincere; it started quibbling about the grouping. Both the parties had resorted to dubious games; neither was sincere in their acceptance of the Plan. Only Azad was positive. He said: "The acceptance of the Cabinet Mission's Plan by both the Congress and the League was a glorious event in the history of the Freedom Movement in India. It meant that the difficult question of Indian freedom had been settled by negotiation and agreement and not by methods of violence and conflict. It also seemed that communal difficulties had been finally left behind. Throughout the country there was a sense of jubilation and all the people were united in their demand of freedom..."[9]

However as soon as Nehru took over as Congress President from Azad, in his first press conference on July 10, 1946 in Bombay, he changed the hopeful atmosphere by declaring, "We are not bound by a single thing except that we have decided for the moment to go into the Constituent Assembly." He elaborated it more precisely in his concluding address to the AICC meeting: "The big probability is, from any approach to the question, there will be no grouping. Obviously, section A will decide against grouping. Speaking in betting language, there is a four to one chance of the North West Frontier Province deciding against grouping. Then Group B collapses. It is highly likely that Bengal and Assam will decide against grouping, although I would not like to say what the initial decision may be since it is evenly balanced. But I can say with every assurance and conviction that there is going to be finally no grouping there, because Assam will not tolerate it under any circumstances whatever. Thus you see this grouping business, approached from any point of view, does not get us on at all."[10]

This was certainly uncalled for; even Patel felt that it was an emotional outburst bordering on insanity which could have been avoided by the newly elected Congress President. He should have exercised circumspection; there were moments in history when much was gained by silence. In League circles it caused consternation. Jinnah was furious; he felt betrayed. He made it clear to the Mission that he could not trust the Congress anymore. As Leonard Mosley has observed in his book *The Last Days of the British Raj*: "Did Nehru realise what he was saying? He was telling the world that once in power, Congress would use its strength at the Centre to alter the Cabinet Mission Plan as it thought fit. The Muslim League (as had Congress) had accepted the Plan as a cut and dried scheme.... It was a compromise plan which obviously could not afterwards be altered in favour of one side or another."[11]

Azad was distressed; he has explained his anguish in his autobiography *India Wins Freedom*: "I was extremely perturbed by this new development. I saw that the scheme for which I worked so hard was being destroyed through our own action. I felt that a meeting of the Working Committee must be held immediately to review the situation. The Working Committee accordingly met on August 8. I pointed out if we wanted to save the situation, we must make it clear that the view of the Congress was expressed by the resolution passed by the AICC, and that no individual, not even the Congress President, could change it. The Working Committee felt that it faced a dilemma. On the one side, the prestige of the Congress President was at stake. On the other, the settlement which we had so painfully achieved was in danger. To repudiate the President's statement would weaken the organisation, but to give up the Cabinet Mission Plan would ruin the country. I must place on record that Jawaharlal's statement was wrong. It is not correct to say that Congress was free to modify the Plan as it pleased..."[12]

At Azad's insistence the Congress Working Committee passed a resolution assuring the League that the Congress was in principle not against grouping; its objection was confined to the contention that a province should not be forced into entering a group. This could have hardly satisfied Jinnah; he protested to Pethick-Lawrence who was in London. The Secretary of State for India clarified in a statement: "We saw both parties shortly before we left India and they said to us quite categorically that it was their intention to go into the Assembly with the object of making it work. But having agreed to the statement of May 16, and the Constituent Assembly elected in accordance with that statement, they cannot, of course, go outside the terms of what has been agreed. To do so would not be fair to other parties who come in and it is on the basis of that agreed procedure that His Majesty's Government have said that they will accept the decisions of the Constituent Assembly."[13]

Jinnah was waiting for such an opportunity to get out of the acceptance. He was able to prove to the British that his obduracy was entirely because of the duplicity of the Congress; the Muslims were always hoodwinked by the Congress; the words of their leaders could never be trusted; they agreed to one thing and went back on it as soon as it did not suit them. Jinnah called a meeting of the Council of the League which not only endorsed his withdrawal of the acceptance of the Cabinet Mission's Plan but called upon the Muslims to take to the streets and resort to Direct Action to achieve the objective of Pakistan. It was a clarion call for civil war; in its resolution it put the entire blame on the Congress. It stated: "Whereas Muslim India has exhausted, without success, all efforts to find a peaceful solution of the Indian problem by compromise and constitutional means; and whereas the Congress is bent upon setting up Caste-Hindu Raj in India with the connivance of the British; and whereas recent events have shown that power politics and not justice and fair play are the deciding factors in Indian affairs; and whereas it has become abundantly clear that the Muslims of India would not rest contented with anything less than the immediate establishment of an independent and fully sovereign state of Pakistan ... the time has come for the Muslim nation to resort to Direct Action to achieve Pakistan to assert their just rights, to vindicate their honour and to get rid of the present British slavery and the contemplated future Caste-Hindu domination." [14]

In calling for Direct Action on August 16, 1946, Jinnah had lost his balance; he himself did not know what was meant by it. On being questioned he said, "I am not going to discuss ethics"; but his chief lieutenant Liaquat Ali Khan clarified that it meant "action against law". The League also inserted the following advertisement in the press which was clearly a provocative call for violence:

Today is Direct Action Day
Today Muslims of India dedicate anew
their lives and all
they possess to the cause of freedom
Today let every Muslim swear in the
name of Allah to resist aggression

Direct Action is now their only course
Because they offered peace but peace was spurned
They honoured their word but were betrayed
They claimed Liberty but are offered Thraldom
Now Might alone can secure their Right. [15]

Jinnah had got so frustrated that he abandoned the constitutional methods by which he always swore. To a foreign journalist he described Direct Action as "mass illegal movement". He asked his followers to take out their pistols and remember that "today we have said goodbye to constitutional methods".[16]

The result was widespread communal rioting in several parts of India; it caused death and destruction of thousands of innocent Hindus and Muslims, particularly in Calcutta which witnessed the worst massacres – brutal and senseless – in the annals of the country described in our history books as the Great Calcutta Killings; I fail to understand what was great about this ghastly occurrence. What did Jinnah gain by calling for Direct Action? Suhrawardy as Prime Minister of Bengal encouraged the goons of the underworld to unleash unmitigated terror in Calcutta; he prevented his police from intervening; there was no law and order. Its repercussions were felt immediately in neighbouring Bihar where Hindus indulged in a virtual genocide of Muslims. Being better armed, better equipped and better organised, the Hindus succeeded in inflicting on the Muslims the worst form of butchery. Statistics revealed that many more Muslims were killed than Hindus. Gandhi rushed to their rescue. Had he not stopped the process of murder and looting, many more Muslims would have died. Jinnah never visited Bihar; he saw from Delhi how his call for Direct Action had boomeranged on the Muslims and how thousands of innocent Muslims lost their all. Patel mockingly remarked, "It has served Jinnah right". But, as subsequent events proved, Jinnah was not bothered; he asked for his pound of flesh and was determined to take it whatever the cost. Shylock in Shakespeare's *Merchant of Venice* was prevented by the laws of Venice from shedding even a drop of blood before obtaining his pound of flesh:

Portia warned Shylock before he started to cut it:

> Tarry a little; there is something else.
> This bond doth give thee here no jot of blood;
> The words expressly are "a pound of flesh"
> Take then thy bond, take thou thy pound of flesh;
> But, in the cutting it, if thou dost shed
> One drop of Christian blood, thy lands and goods
> Are, by the laws of Venice, confiscate
> Unto the state of Venice.[17]

Alas there was no such embargo which could have prevented Jinnah from cutting portions from the body of India without shedding blood; in fact it was mercilessly amputated with no thought for the grievous consequences.

THIRTEEN

Surrender to Partition

Wavell was horrified at the spectacle of communal violence that he witnessed during his visit to some of the riot-affected areas. He decided that he must put into effect, without further delay, the formation of the interim government which was the short-term part of the Cabinet Mission's Plan. The Congress claimed that it had accepted the long-term scheme and therefore was entitled to be invited to form the interim government; the League could not be called upon to join as it had rejected the plan and embarked on what it euphemistically called Direct Action; this also disqualified it from being entrusted with power. However, Wavell was convinced that without the participation of the League, law and order could not be brought under control. Though the short-term part was integral to the long-term Plan, which the League had rejected, the Viceroy believed that it was so because of the duplicity of the Congress which tried to wriggle out of the provision regarding grouping of provinces — an integral part of the Cabinet Mission's Plan. He told

Gandhi and Nehru bluntly in his meeting with them on August 27, 1946 that their attitude towards the League had not been fair. Had they unreservedly accepted the provision of "grouping of provinces", he was confident the League would not have taken the step it did. Wavell was keen that India must have a coalition government of the Congress and the League at that critical juncture. He said: "As a result of the killings in Calcutta, India is on the verge of civil war. It is my duty to prevent it. I can not prevent it if I allow the Congress to form a Government which excludes the Muslims. They will then decide that Direct Action is the only way and we shall have the massacre of Bengal all over again."

Jinnah was not prepared to join the interim government unless two of his conditions were fulfilled: one, parity with the Congress at the Centre and two, the League to have the sole right to nominate Muslim members. He could not allow his Leaguers to sit with the "Muslim quislings"; Wavell expressed his inability to accept his demands. Meanwhile Attlee instructed the Viceroy not to lose any more time and install the interim government, if necessary without the participation of the League representatives. Wavell went ahead and constituted the interim government with Nehru as Vice-President and most of the members belonging to the Congress. They took office on September 2, 1946.

Jinnah was angry at this move; he asked his followers to fly black flags from housetops to mark their protest. Soon it dawned on him that staying out of power would hurt the League. He sent word to Wavell that the League would reconsider its decision not to join the government. Pleased with the unexpected development the Viceroy prevailed upon Nehru to extend in the larger interest of the nation a hand of friendship to Jinnah. The Nawab of Bhopal, who was the Chancellor of the Chamber of Princes, arranged a meeting between Nehru and Jinnah. The two leaders met on October 5, 1946 and exchanged views. The next day Nehru wrote to Jinnah: "I have consulted some of my colleagues about the matters discussed by us yesterday.... We all agreed that nothing could be happier and better for the country than that these two organisations [Congress and the League] should meet again as before, as friends having no mental reservations and bent on resolving all their differences by mutual consultation, and never desiring or allowing the intervention of the British Government through the Viceroy or some other.... We would therefore welcome the decision of the League to join the interim Government for it to work as a united team on behalf of India as a whole."[1]

At first Jinnah was responsive; but later he became suspicious when Nehru asked that the Viceroy's role be eliminated. He suspected that there was a subtle design to subordinate the League and make Congress the dominant partner. For that Jinnah was not ready. Hence he instructed his nominees who joined the interim government on October 27, 1946 to be obstructive and not cooperative. Liaquat Ali Khan declared himself leader of the separate Muslim League group in the council of ministers as against Nehru who was already designated Vice-President, and in effect the Prime Minister; the Viceroy continued to be the head; the interim government was, in effect, his Executive Council and all the members were equal. Jinnah refused to accept the interim government as a cabinet nor did he agree that ministers would be collectively accountable.

In a sarcastic note Jinnah wrote: "If Nehru can only come down to earth and think coolly and calmly he must understand that he is neither the Prime Minister nor is it a Nehru Government. He is only the member for External Affairs and the Commonwealth Department."[2] On Nehru's insistence that it was, in effect, a cabinet, Jinnah retorted, "Little things please little minds. You cannot turn a donkey into an elephant by calling it an elephant." His ministers were no less aggressive; one of them, Ghazanfar Ali Khan said that they had entered the interim government "to fight for our cherished goal of Pakistan", while one of the closest associates of Jinnah, Ispahani declared, "League's participation in the new Government only means that the struggle for Pakistan will now be carried on within as well as outside the Government."[3] On October 29, 1946 when the Central Legislative Assembly met, the treasury benches appeared sullen and grim. The League ministers sat separately from their Congress colleagues. Far from exhibiting collective responsibility the government, for all practical purposes, was a house divided against itself. It could not, in all honesty, carry on the affairs of state. A few days later *Dawn*, the Muslim League organ, splashed on its front page an interview by Jinnah given to a foreign journal in which he declared that the only solution was division of India into Hindustan and Pakistan. The Muslim League ministers were there, he said, to fight for Pakistan. In reply to a question, he said it was best that the interim government be disbanded.

The first blow against mutual cooperation was struck by Liaquat Ali Khan who had taken over as Finance Minister. In his budget he imposed heavy taxation on businessmen with an income of more than one lakh rupees. This adversely affected the Hindus; he also proposed an income-tax investigation commission to look into the evasion of taxes by businessmen and industrialists from their war contracts. This again was aimed at Hindus in particular. Patel and C.R.

vehemently opposed these measures and for weeks the governmental machinery stood at a standstill, gripped by crisis after crisis. To make matters worse Jinnah convened a meeting of the League Council on January 29, 1947 calling upon the British government to scrap the Cabinet Mission's Plan. Nehru and Patel, in consequence, demanded the withdrawal of the League ministers from the government and announced that in case the Viceroy failed to do so, the Congress ministers would withdraw from the government.

Attlee was alarmed at the developments; he asked Wavell to come to London and also invited Nehru and Jinnah with some of their colleagues in a last-ditch effort to salvage the situation. They arrived in London on December 3, 1946 and had several meetings with Attlee and his ministers. Both sides remained adamant; neither was prepared for any adjustment or accommodation. Hence no consensus could be reached on the controversial points. Neither Nehru nor Jinnah would climb down; each firmly stood his ground, particularly on the question of the grouping of provinces. Jinnah was encouraged by a secret meeting he had with Churchill who promised that he would not allow the Muslims to be put under Hindu raj. The meeting was held on December 11, 1946; it was also attended by Lord Simon and other Tory leaders. They assured Jinnah that he could rely on their unflinching support. Churchill took Jinnah aside and told him that he "greatly valued our talk", assured him of his friendship and asked him to keep in touch with him. He gave him a secret address which Jinnah could use "without attracting attention in India. I shall always sign myself 'Gilliatt' (my secretary's name). Perhaps you will let me know to what address I can telegraph to you and how you will sign yourself."[4] The next day Churchill challenged the Labour government declaring that he and his colleagues in the opposition would not allow India to be handed over to the Congress and thus betray the Muslims and the princes who had always stood by the British.

Attlee was badgered from all sides; he gave up hope of bringing about an amicable settlement between the Congress and the League. The parting of ways between Hindus and Muslims had become inevitable. Also the law and order situation in India was on the verge of collapse. The British Prime Minister had to take a firm decision to stem the decline. He decided to act quickly and told the House of Commons: "After months of hard work by the Cabinet Mission, a great measure of agreement was obtained as to the method by which a constitution should be worked out. This was embodied in their statements of May last. His Majesty's Government therein agreed to recommend to Parliament a constitution worked out in accordance with the proposals made therein by a fully representative Constituent Assembly. But if it should appear that such a constitution will not have been worked out by a fully representative Assembly before the time mentioned ... His Majesty's Government will have to consider to whom the powers of the Central Government in British India should be handed over, on due date, whether as a whole to some form of Central Government for British India, or in some areas to the existing provincial Government, or in such other way as may seem most reasonable and in the best interests of the Indian people."[5]

Meanwhile the British press and the public had begun to worry about happenings in India; they were not certain that their government "was acting in the best possible manner". The Conservatives had so far cooperated with the Labour government in the handling of the Indian problem; but with reports of rioting on a big scale and the constant political infighting, they were becoming apprehensive of the future. Churchill demanded a full discussion in Parliament. He said, "His Majesty's opposition have shown over all these long months great forbearance and restraint in not raising a debate upon India, but I must give the Leader of the House notice that we feel a debate must now take place. Matters are assuming so grave an aspect that it is necessary that the nation at large shall have its attention concentrated upon them." Attlee agreed and the debate was initiated by Cripps in the House of Commons. It lasted two days. The only member who openly supported the League's demand for Pakistan was the Labour MP Zilliacus, well-known for his communist leanings. He wanted Pakistan to be not only conceded to the Muslims but also the new dominion made a member of the United Nations on the same lines as Ukraine, by copying the Soviet example.

Churchill vent his full fury against "the policy of scuttle" pursued by the Labour government. He said, "I warned the House as long ago as 1931 ... that if we were to wash our hands of all responsibility, a ferocious civil war would speedily break out between the Muslims and Hindus. But this, like other warnings, fell upon deaf and unregarding ears. Indeed, it is certain that more people have lost their lives or have been wounded in India by violence since the interim Government under Mr. Nehru was installed in office four months ago by the Viceroy, than in the previous 90 years. This is only a foretaste of what may come. It may be only the first few heavy drops before the thunderstorm breaks upon us. These frightful slaughters over wide regions and in obscure uncounted villages have, in the main, fallen upon Muslim minorities. I must record my own belief...that any attempt to establish the reign of a Hindu numerical majority in India will never be achieved without a civil war, proceeding, not perhaps at first on the fronts of armies or organised forces, but in thousands of separate and isolated places. This war will, before it is decided, lead through unaccountable agonies to an awful abridgement of the Indian population....The Muslims, numbering 90 million,...comprise the majority of the fighting elements in India...the word 'minority' has no relevance or sense when applied to masses of human beings numbered in many scores of millions."[6] Attlee had also become apprehensive of what his Cabinet note dated February 5, 1947 had warned him of: "civil war.... Perhaps it was Mr. Jinnah's intention to bring it about.... In the long run the extent to which the League would be able to cause serious trouble would depend on whether their atrocities caused the Indian Army to disintegrate."[7]

The Prime Minister decided to act firmly without any loss of time. He was convinced that Wavell was unable to handle the rapidly deteriorating situation; a new man, with a different outlook and background, was needed to overcome it. He consulted the King and chose Lord Mountbatten to replace Wavell. He made the announcement in Parliament. King George VI noted in his diary: "Attlee told me that Lord Wavell's plan for our leaving India savours too much of a military retreat, he does not realise it is a political problem and not a military one. Wavell has done very good work up to now but Attlee doubts whether he has the finesse to negotiate the next step when we must keep the two Indian parties friendly to us all the time."[8]

Lord Mountbatten arrived in Delhi on March 22, 1947 with more powers than any Viceroy was ever given in the past. He was also suitably briefed by his British friends. He came determined to close the British chapter without jeopardising Britain's long-term interests. Nehru welcomed the change in the viceroyalty; but Jinnah was sceptical. He had heard of

Mountbatten's friendship with Nehru. He also did not like
Wavell being removed at a time when he had just begun to be
helpful to the League. He was doubtful whether the new
Viceroy would appreciate his stand on partition; even in the
case of Wavell it had taken a good deal of time and persuasion
on Jinnah's part to bring him round so as to modify his attitude.
Mountbatten was reported to be in a hurry. All along Jinnah
had relied on the support of the British; if he were not to get
it, his objective could not be achieved. He therefore approached
the future with trepidation; he was worried the new Viceroy
would let him down.

FOURTEEN

Creation of Pakistan

Mountbatten went into parleys first with Nehru, Patel and Liaquat, who were ministers, followed by a long and intimate talk with Gandhi. Armed with their views he met Jinnah; the encounter has been picturesquely captured in the following passage by the authors of the classic, *Freedom at Midnight*:

> Mountbatten and Jinnah held six critical meetings during the first fortnight of April 1947. They were the vital conversations — not quite ten hours in length — which ultimately determined the resolution of the Indian dilemma. Mountbatten went into them armed with "the most enormous conceit in my ability to persuade people to do the right thing, not because I am persuasive so much as because I have the knack of being able to present the facts in their most favourable light." As he would later recall, he "tried every trick I could play, used every appeal I could imagine", to shake Jinnah's resolve to have partition.

Nothing would. There was no argument that could move him from his consuming determination to realize the impossible dream of Pakistan.

Jinnah owed his commanding position to two things. He had made himself absolute dictator of the Moslem League. There were men below him who might have been prepared to negotiate a compromise but, so long as Mohammed Ali Jinnah was alive, they would hold their silence. Second, more important, was the memory of the blood spilled in the streets of Calcutta a year before.

Mountbatten and Jinnah did agree on one point at the outset — the need for speed. India, Jinnah declared, had gone beyond the stage at which a compromise solution was possible. There was only one solution, a speedy "surgical operation". Otherwise, he warned, India would perish.

When Mountbatten expressed concern lest partition might produce bloodshed and violence, Jinnah reassured him. Once his "surgical operation" had taken place, all troubles would cease and India's two halves would live in harmony and happiness. It was, Jinnah told Mountbatten, like a court case he'd handled between two brothers embittered by the shares assigned them under their father's will. Yet, two years after the court had adjudicated their dispute, they were the greatest friends. That, he promised the Viceroy, would be the case in India.

The Moslems of India, Jinnah insisted, were a nation with a "distinctive culture and civilization, language and literature, art and architecture, laws and moral codes, customs and calendar, history and traditions".

"India has never been a true nation," Jinnah asserted. "It only looks that way on the map. The cows I want to eat, the Hindu stops me from killing. Every time a Hindu shakes hands with me he has to wash his hands. The only thing the Moslem has in common with the Hindu is his slavery to the British."

Their arguments became, the Viceroy would later recall, an "amusing and rather tragic game of round and round the mulberry bush"; Jinnah, the March Hare of *Alice in Wonderland,* never conceding a point; Mountbatten, the determined advocate of unity, driving at Jinnah from every angle, until he was afraid lest, as he noted at the time, "I drove the old gentleman quite mad."

For Jinnah, the division he proposed was the natural course. That division, however, would have to produce a viable state and that, Jinnah argued, meant that two of India's great provinces, the Punjab and Bengal, would have to go into his Pakistan, despite the fact that each contained enormous Hindu populations.

Mountbatten could not agree. The basis of Jinnah's argument for Pakistan was that India's Moslem minority should not be ruled by its Hindu majority. How then justify taking the Hindu minorities of Bengal and the Punjab into a Moslem state? If Jinnah insisted on dividing India to get his Islamic state, then the very logic he'd used to get it would compel

Mountbatten to divide the Punjab and Bengal as part of the bargain.

Jinnah protested. That would give him an economically unviable, "moth-eaten Pakistan". Mountbatten, who didn't want to give him any Pakistan at all, told the Moslem leader, that if he felt the nation he was to receive was as "moth-eaten" as all that, he'd prefer he didn't take it.

"Ah," Jinnah would counter, "Your Excellency doesn't understand. A man is a Punjabi or a Bengali before he is Hindu or Moslem. They share a common history, language, culture and economy. You must not divide them. You will cause endless bloodshed and trouble."

"Mr. Jinnah, I entirely agree."

"You do?"

"Of course," Mountbatten would continue. "A man is not only a Punjabi or Bengali before he is a Hindu or a Moslem, he is an Indian before all else. You have presented the unanswerable argument for Indian unity."

"But you don't understand at all." Jinnah would counter, and the discussions would start around the mulberry bush again.

Mountbatten was stunned by the rigidity of Jinnah's position. "I never would have believed," he later recalled, "that an intelligent man, well-educated, trained in the Inns of Court was capable of simply closing his mind as Jinnah did. It wasn't that he didn't see the point. He did, but a kind of shutter came down. He was the evil genius in the whole thing. The others could be persuaded, but not Jinnah. While he was alive nothing could be done."

The climax to their talks came on 10th April less than three weeks after Mountbatten's arrival in India. For two hours he begged, cajoled, argued, and pleaded with Jinnah to keep India united. With all the eloquence he could command, he painted a picture of the greatness India could achieve, 400 million people of different races and creeds, bound together by a Central Union Government, with all the economic strength that would accrue to them from increased industrialization, playing a great part in world affairs as the most progressive, single entity in the Far East. Surely, Mr. Jinnah did not want to destroy all that, to condemn the subcontinent to the existence of a third-rate power?

Jinnah remained unmoved. He was, Mountbatten sadly concluded, a psychopathic case, hell bent on this Pakistan.[1]

The question that arises is: why did Mountbatten, so convinced that partition would be a disaster and the man asking for it a "psychopathic", work so tenaciously to make it possible? The subtle way in which he went about using all his charm, on the contrary, to convince Nehru and Patel that partition was the only solution makes most intriguing reading. He had with him the report of the Constitutional Advisor to the Government of India, Sir Reginald Coupland, who had conclusively proved that partition would ruin not only Hindus but also Muslims. He had observed: "I have no doubt that partition will be a festering sore in the body politic of South

Asia. It is an unnatural solution of the Hindu-Muslim problem.
The comparison of it to Europe, which Jinnah often makes, is
not relevant. Europe's division in several national states was
largely due to physical factors; but even then it led to frequent
wars. The last one has been most diabolical. On the other hand
nature has fashioned India into not only a geographical but
also an economic unity — one unit supporting the other."
Coupland elaborated: "Look at the peninsular map of India!
On two sides it has the sea, on the third the greatest mountain
in the world. Except for Cochin, which is an island, and
Kathiawar, which is a peninsula, it has been endowed with
one long, unbroken seaboard. And across the land it has one
substantial natural frontier, the Vindhya mountains." The
Advisor added, "Which country has been blessed with such
unifying features, and yet India seems bent upon its
dismemberment. It will anger nature and cause nothing but
trouble all around."[2]

For the next few weeks Mountbatten used all his
resources, energy and tact to expedite the process of dividing
India; though convinced, as he told everyone he talked to,
that division would be the worst calamity that the country
would have to face, still he did not lift his royal finger to prevent
it. The Bengal leaders Suhrawardy and Sarat Bose assured him
that if he could bring round Nehru and Patel to unreserved
acceptance of the Cabinet Mission's Plan, the unity of India
could still be saved. The foremost Muslim League leader of
Bengal, Khwaja Nazimuddin who had the ear of Jinnah,
informed the new Viceroy that Jinnah was in a chastened
mood. He was most upset at the prospect of Punjab and Bengal
being partitioned. He would therefore not be averse to some
sort of a union. To all such pleas Mountbatten turned a deaf
ear. On the contrary he used the two persons closest to Nehru

and Patel — V.K. Krishna Menon and V.P. Menon respectively — and through them tried to convince their leaders that this was the best solution in view of the permanent hostility that existed between Hindus and Muslims. Mountbatten knew that Gandhi would never agree to partition; the best way to make him acquiesce in it would be to get round Nehru and Patel. How the Viceroy achieved this, he himself has explained; it is a sad reflection on the whole episode: "Don't forget Krishna Menon and V.P. Menon were my... spies is the wrong word; they were my contacts, my links. And so, I'd got this feeling, right the way through and was able to nip it in the bud. And if I hadn't these links, I shouldn't have known in time. It would have been very difficult."[3]

Mountbatten also dangled the bait of the division of Bengal and Punjab before the two leaders and assured them that with it Pakistan would be politically so insecure, economically so weak and militarily so unsafe that it would pose no threat to India. It might even rejoin the Indian Union. Krishna Menon was the first to be taken in by it, followed by V.P. Menon. The former influenced Nehru and the latter, Patel; but it took them some time before they could convince their mentors to accept the so-called "Balkanisation Plan" which Mountbatten had worked out in consultation with his chief of staff and other officials.

The Viceroy used a clever method to achieve this; he invited Nehru for a holiday to Simla. One night he showed Nehru a map of divided India with not only the proposed Pakistan regions but also some of the major princely states, each as an independent unit. Nehru lost his temper. He could not bear to see India so fractured. Mountbatten was not surprised at Nehru's reaction. He mollified him by telling him that he was only showing him how various interests were trying to take away parts of the country and disrupt its unity. He would not allow this to happen. However some form of Pakistan would have to be conceded, he urged. Without that, transfer of power could not be possible. Nehru listened to him without responding; he brooded over it; he was being consistently persuaded by Krishna Menon to give in to Mountbatten. Reluctantly Nehru accepted the proposed division and the formation of a fragmented Pakistan, with only half of Bengal and Punjab. Likewise V.P. Menon prevailed upon Patel; the Iron Man took time but finally acquiesced in it when he realised there was no alternative to what Mountbatten had offered. The Viceroy had won; he felt exhilarated when both Nehru and Patel at last gave their consent to the Balkanisation Plan.

The Viceroy then confronted Jinnah and told him bluntly that the only Pakistan he would get was a truncated one, with its two major provinces Punjab and Bengal divided into half. Jinnah was heartbroken; he pleaded that at least Calcutta be given to him; it was, he said, the heart of Bengal. Not possible, the Viceroy said; its majority was Hindu and it was located in the midst of Hindu-majority areas. Then Jinnah begged him to keep Bengal united and independent. Mountbatten appreciated the suggestion but pointed out that it did not fit into his Two-Nation theory. Jinnah was puzzled and asked for time to reconsider the question. The Viceroy reacted harshly and told him sternly that the Congress-League hostilities had already paralysed the administration and he was not in a position to delay the matter as it would result in chaos and disorder. Jinnah understood that his game of procrastination was over. He had no option but to accept whatever was being offered — a state which was a geographical absurdity, with its two wings separated by hundreds of miles of Hindu-dominated territory. He was nevertheless satisfied that at least he would have a kingdom of his own which he would be able to rule without being at the mercy of the Hindus. And so finally the die was cast. Mountbatten, so armed, rushed to London to obtain clearance of his plan by the British cabinet. He got it without any difficulty. Attlee lauded his effort; Churchill hugged him warmly. The "bulldog" was pleased that his pupil had managed to shatter Gandhi's dream of ruling over the whole of India.

On his return to Delhi Mountbatten did not lose time to ask Gandhi to meet him; he had, so far, deliberately kept the Mahatma out of the negotiations; even Nehru and Patel, Gandhi's closest and most trusted lieutenants did not take him into confidence. They were all apprehensive of his reaction; he had repeatedly declared: "Vivisect me before you vivisect India." Hence no sooner the Mahatma got wind that a sinister plan was being hatched in the corridors of power than he rushed to Delhi and asked Azad if he would stand by him or let him down as Nehru and Patel had done. Azad told him with tears in his eyes that he was deeply distressed by the way Nehru had surrendered. "You", he told Gandhi, "are the only hope left to save India. If you stand against partition, we may yet save the situation. If you, however, acquiesce in it, I am afraid India is lost." Gandhi replied, "What a question to ask? If the Congress wishes to accept partition, it will be over my dead body. So long as I am alive, I will never agree..."[4]

Once again Mountbatten played his Machiavellian game; he saw the Mahatma and pleaded with him to give his blessings to the new plan; he explained, it was nothing more than what Gandhi himself had offered Jinnah under the C.R. formula. The Mahatma told him that there was a world of

difference between the two formulae: "You have given in to
religious division," Gandhi said, "I had never accepted it." They
argued at length but Mountbatten did not relent. Gandhi
returned to Bhangi Colony downcast and dejected. What
troubled him most was the acceptance of the "Balkanisation
plan" by his two lieutenants whom he had relied on all through
the freedom struggle. They were his right hand and left hand.
He wondered, therefore, how he would fight both the British
and Jinnah. He had often told the British that he would not
mind even a civil war if that was the price he had to pay to
make them quit India. But if he were to resist now India might
well be plunged into a communal civil war, would he then be
able to control it, he wondered. He had always propagated
Hindu-Muslim unity; how would he be able to take a partisan
stand now and be involved in a violent confrontation between
the two communities. Hindus and Muslims would slaughter
each other and India's sacred soil would be soaked in blood.
Could he be a party to it; would it not violate his mission of
non-violence? A civil war between the two communities would
undo all that he had stood for. The vivisection of his beloved
country was no doubt a sin; but how could he protect India's
unity unless he abandoned non-violence and allowed the
massive genocide and the colossal carnage that would follow?
Would he be able to safeguard India's territorial integrity on
the corpses of her people? These forebodings tormented him.
For the first time in his life he did not heed his inner voice; he
felt helpless to carry on any more with his life-long mission.

Apart from the pain and anguish that Nehru and Patel
caused Gandhi, they betrayed not only Muslims like Azad
and Ghaffar Khan but also leading socialists like Jayaprakash
Narayan and Ram Manohar Lohia who resisted partition until
the last. There was, in fact, a large body of members of the

All-India Congress Committee who were taken aback by the decision announced by the Viceroy on June 2, 1947 after he obtained the approval of the British cabinet. It was formally endorsed by the Congress and the League at Simla at a meeting convened by Mountbatten on June 3. Subsequently a meeting of the Congress Working Committee was called to ratify it; the irony was that this crucial meeting was presided over by its newly elected President, J.B. Kripalani, a Sindhi whose home province was to go to Pakistan. There were many dejected and depressed faces of those who had suffered so long during various phases of the freedom struggle launched by the Mahatma. Though freedom was achieved, it came with partition and it brought joy to no one. The tragic scene at the meeting is best described by Ram Manohar Lohia who attended the historic meeting as a member. He has written in his book *Guilty Men of India's Partition*:

Maulana Azad sat in a chair throughout the two days of this meeting in a corner of the very small room which packed us all, puffed away at his endless cigarettes, and spoke not a word. He may have been pained. But it is silly of him to try to make out as though he were the only one opposed to partition. Not only did he keep unbrokenly silent at this meeting, he also continued in office as a minister of partitioned India for an entire decade and more. I may concede, and even understand, that he was unhappy at the partition and tried to oppose it in his own way at informal or tete-a-tete meetings. But this was an opposition that did not object to the service of the thing opposed — a strange combination of opposition and service in a conscience which was greatly wise or equally elastic. It might be interesting to explore

Maulana Azad's conscience, for I sometimes suspect that wisdom and elasticity go together.

Acharya Kripalani was a pathetic figure at this meeting. He was president of the Congress party at that time. He sat drowsily and reclined at this meeting. At some point in the debate, Mahatma Gandhi referred to the exhausted Congress president and I shook his arm in deep annoyance. He volunteered the information that he was suffering from a bad headache. His opposition to partition must have been sincere, for it was also personal. But the disease of old age and exhaustion had come over this fighting organisation of freedom in its moment of greatest distress.

Khan Abdul Ghaffar Khan spoke a bare two sentences. He expressed his sorrow over the fact that his colleagues had accepted the scheme of partition. As a small mercy, he wanted them to find out if the proposed plebiscite in the North-West Frontier could include the alternative of independence alongside of the two other choices of accession to India or Pakistan. He spoke not a word more at any stage; he must have been so pained.

Mr. Jayaprakash Narayan spoke some brief but definitive remarks against partition in a single stretch and was silent for the rest of the meeting. What made him do that? Was he disgusted at the way the Working Committee was going about the business of partitioning the country? Or, did he consider it prudent to keep quiet in the face of a leadership so stubbornly united for acceptance of the partition? His character is probably a mixture of healthful responses at some stage and prudence for most of the time, a very irritating mixture, no doubt, which has often made me very angry with him.

My own opposition to partition was persistent and vocal, but it could not have been serious enough and I now recollect some false notes. In any event, my opposition could not have moved mountains. It could only have been on record as the healthful opposition of a fighter for freedom without much influence. Nevertheless, the absence of serious opposition to partition even from a man like me, who had absolutely no selfish axes to grind showed the depths of weakness and fear to which our people and I, as an ordinary one among them, had fallen. I may have occasion to reveal some of the aspects of my opposition. What is of significance is Mahatma Gandhi's intervention at this meeting.

I should like especially to bring out two points that Gandhiji made at this meeting. He turned to Mr. Nehru and Sardar Patel in mild complaint that they had not informed him of the scheme of partition before committing themselves to it. Before Gandhiji could make out his point fully, Mr. Nehru intervened with some passion to say that he had kept him fully informed. On Mahatma Gandhi's repeating that he did not know of the scheme of partition, Mr. Nehru slightly altered his earlier observation. He said that Noakhali was so far away and that, while he may not have described the details of the scheme, he had broadly written of partition to Gandhiji.

I will accept Mahatma Gandhi's version of the case, and not Mr. Nehru's and who will not? One does not have to dismiss Mr. Nehru as a liar. All that is at issue here is whether Mahatma Gandhi knew of the scheme of partition before Mr. Nehru and Sardar Patel had committed themselves to it. It would not do for Mr. Nehru to publish vague letters which he might have written to Mahatma Gandhi doling out hypothetical and insubstantial information. That was definitely a hole-and-corner aspect of this business. Mr. Nehru and Sardar Patel had obviously between themselves decided that it would be best not to scare Gandhiji away before the deed was definitely resolved upon.[5]

After the mournful passage of the tragic resolution, one member came to the Mahatma and joyfully declared, "Bapu, is it not wonderful that our non-violent army has at last thrown out the British." Gandhi looked at him sadly and replied, "Yes, but in so doing it has also thrown out its general..."

Why did Nehru and Patel go back on their commitment which they had repeatedly sworn to stand by? Could they not have accepted the grouping of provinces in the Cabinet Mission's Plan, however distasteful it was to them? True it would have deprived them of overall control on a strong Centre but at worst they would have had to suffer it until the British left the shores of India, which Attlee had solemnly promised on the floor of Britain's Parliament. The firm date given by him was the end of June 1948. Once the third party had quit, the Congress which had an overwhelming and decisive majority in the Constituent Assembly, would have been in a dominant position. Moreover, as it turned out, even Jinnah, the greatest obstacle to the unity of India, would have passed away; he was in the last stage of cancer (he died in September 1948). What was the reason to insist on such a disastrous short-sighted solution which dismembered the whole fabric of united India? Even if the League were to be obstructive during the interim period, it would not have been in a position to force the division — Lohia's explanation is that the ageing, tired, power-hungry Congress leaders in a riotous situation had become so impatient to get hold of the reins of office that they agreed to partition, to rule over the country's dismembered parts. Lohia discounted the reason advanced by many that without partition"India could not have achieved stability nor progress." History has proved him right.

Another explanation given in support of partition is that the Congress did not possess the strength and temperament to cope with the civil war that might have broken out between the Hindus and the Muslims. Gandhi would not have been able to deal with it because of his complete involvement in non-violence. Patel and Nehru could have stood the ground but refused to do so. They lacked the iron will which, for instance, a leader like Abraham Lincoln possessed. It is said that the two situations were incomparable but nothing can be further from the truth; on the eve of the civil war in America in 1860, relations between the people in the north and the south were much worse than between Hindus and Muslims in India in the 1940s. To start with, in America the civil war began on the question of slavery of the blacks whom the north wanted to free; but as the war intensified this became secondary to the main issue of preservation of the Union. Lincoln was absolutely uncompromising on it; he was often pressured by various vested interests in the north to agree to the separation of the south which in any case was then the backwaters of America; even his cabinet wanted him to concede separation. But Lincoln

was unbending; he declared that regardless of the price that
the north would have to pay, he would not permit the Union
to be dismembered.

He admonished the hesitant Senator Trumball: "The
tug has to come and better now than any time hereafter." He
wrote to another waverer, Washburne, "Hold firm, as with a
chain of steel." To the American public he pointed out: "A
house divided against itself can not stand." He also pointedly
asked "in a free government would the minority have the right
to break up the government, whenever they chose. If we fail it
will go to prove the incapacity of the people to govern
themselves." For over four years he conducted the civil war
against heavy odds. He had to contend with his own colleagues
in the cabinet; even some of the commanders of the armed
forces were replaced because he found them not sufficiently
committed; as his biographer Prof. Benjamin P. Thomas has
pointed out: "Recruiting officers were found murdered. Lonely
countrysides were terrorised. Union agents reported a maze of
plots and conspiracies, one to seize prison camps and arm
Confederate prisoners; another, inspired by Confederate agents
in Canada, to set up a Northwestern Confederacy. These
seditionists were known as Copperheads, because of their
practice of cutting the head of the Goddess of Liberty from a
copper penny to wear in their coat lapels, and from the
venomous snake of that name."[6]

Even foreign powers, including Britain, showed more
sympathy to the south than the north. But nothing could deter
Lincoln from pursuing the course that he had chosen; gradually
support for his stand increased; the Governor of Kansas
assured him, "This union must, will, and should be perpetuated,
not a star shall be dimmed or a stripe erased from its banner."[7]
In the civil war, millions of Americans on either side died.

Lincoln was killed by an assassin's bullet. But the Union was preserved, with the result that America is today the mightiest superpower in the world. Had Lincoln taken a soft line and agreed to the separation of the southern states from the north, it would have resulted in the emergence of independent states in the same way as in Latin America which is always in a mess. Unfortunately at a critical juncture in India's history there was no Lincoln with the vision, foresight and determination, who could have staved off the dismemberment. Nehru and Patel lost nerve; they could not muster courage to face the possibility of a civil war between the Hindus and the Muslims. Or if Lohia is to be believed, the lure of power deluded them. Jinnah's bluff worked and the country was divided.

Though Jinnah was at first rather upset at getting what he called, "a moth-eaten Pakistan", he was later overjoyed at the fact that he had founded a state where his will was to prevail. Neither the truncated form nor its two wings, separated by hundreds of miles of Hindu territory, seemed to bother him much. Nehru asked Mountbatten to continue as Governor-General of the new Dominion of India. Mountbatten accepted in the belief that Jinnah would also make the same offer and consequently he would be able to serve during the transition period as a link between the two newly created dominions. He got a shock when Jinnah appointed himself Governor-General of Pakistan. Ismay reminded him that under the British parliamentary system, all power vested in the Prime Minister, the Governor-General was only a titular head. Jinnah corrected him. In Pakistan, he said, as Governor-General he would rule; the Prime Minister would be his subordinate. Such was the arrogance of power which had seized Jinnah. His ego knew no bounds.

He kept by his bedside, Beverley Nichols' *Verdict on India*, wherein the author has observed: "The most important man in Asia is sixty-seven, tall, thin, and elegant, with a monocle on a grey silk cord, and a stiff white collar which he wears in the hottest weather. He suggests a gentleman of Spain, a diplomat of the old school; one used to see his like sitting in the window of the St. James's Club, sipping Contrexeville while he read *Le Temps,* which was propped against a Queen Anne toast rack stacked with toast Melba."

Nichols added: "I have called Mr. Jinnah the most important man in Asia. That was to ensure that you kept him spotlit in your mind. Like all superlatives the description is open to argument, but it is not really so far from the truth. India is likely to be the world's greatest problem for some years to come, and Mr. Jinnah is in a position of unique strategic importance. He can sway the battle this way or that as he chooses. His 100 million Muslims will march to the left, to the right, to the front, to the rear at his bidding, *and at nobody else's* ... that is the point."[8]

The passage had so pleased him that he had underlined it, he read it often. It boosted his ego.

Some of the League leaders of the Hindu-majority provinces saw him on the eve of his departure to Karachi which was to be the capital of the Dominion of Pakistan. Anxiously they asked him what was in store for them. He said they would have to look after themselves. They protested that they needed better protection and should not be left to the mercy of the Hindus. After all, they pointed out, it was because of them that Pakistan had been won. Looking sternly at them, Jinnah said, "You are mistaken; the whole world knows that it is I who single-handedly has brought Pakistan into existence. I am its sole creator. No one else can take credit for it."

FIFTEEN

The Grim Aftermath

To give constitutional shape to the ill-fated Mountbatten Plan of June 2, 1947, the British Parliament passed the India Independence Act. Its preamble endorsed Jinnah's Two-Nation theory by describing the two dominions as two nations; Gandhi immediately objected; but there was not even a murmur of disapproval or unfavourable comment from Nehru or Patel. Jinnah was naturally happy. His stand had been vindicated by the mother of parliaments.

After the passage of the bill by both Houses of Parliament and Royal assent, Mountbatten embarked on putting into practice its various provisions. He was in a hurry to carry out the operation to divide India. Having had no administrative experience and little knowledge of the ground realities of the Indian situation, he started to plan the whole intricate and complex process of partition as if it were a military operation. He was completely oblivious of the human factor and almost callous of the brutal consequences which had already begun to show their ugly, inhuman face. As days passed these happenings shocked the civilised world. Never in history was such a dreadful spectacle of slaughter, rape and terror witnessed. The Viceroy was warned by the authorities on the spot that hustling would have a deadly effect; the British Governors of Punjab and Bengal, the two provinces which were to be divided on the basis of Hindu-majority and Muslim-majority districts, were shaken. Even Nehru and Patel were worried; they had never imagined that their decision to agree to partition would bring such suffering to the people on either side of the border. But Mountbatten seemed least bothered; he assured everyone that everything would be alright. Unperturbed, he preponed, without proper preparations, the transfer of power from the British to the proposed dominions; it was to be on August 15, 1947 — barely 90 days later. He fixed the date so early because he said it was on that date that he had won the decisive battle against the Japanese as Commander of the Eastern Front; this would be another victorious feather in his royal cap. He put everyone in the government on their toes but the situation deteriorated so fast that neither the police nor the army could control it. He felt on top of the world despite the fact that several parts of India were plunged into a bloodbath.

Azad has given a graphic account of how Mountbatten went through such a huge operation, supremely unconcerned of its possible inhuman fallout: "I also asked Lord Mountbatten to take into consideration the likely consequences of partition of the country. Even without partition of the country, there had been riots in Calcutta, Noakhali, Bihar, Bombay and the Punjab. Hindus attacked Muslims and Muslims had attacked Hindus. If the country was divided in such an atmosphere, there would be rivers of blood flowing in different parts of the country and the British would be responsible for the carnage.

Without a moment's hesitation Lord Mountbatten replied, 'At least on this question I shall give you complete assurance. I shall see to it that there is no bloodshed and riot. I am a soldier and not a civilian. Once partition is accepted on principle, I shall issue orders to see that there are no communal disturbances anywhere in the country. If there should be the slightest agitation, I shall adopt the sternest measures to nip the trouble in the bud. I shall not use even the armed police. I will order the Army and Air Force to act and I will use tanks and aeroplanes to suppress anybody who wants to create trouble.' The whole world knows what was the sequel to Lord Mountbatten's brave declaration. When partition actually took place, rivers of blood flowed in large parts of the country. Innocent men, women and children were massacred. The Indian Army was divided and nothing effective was done to stop the murder of innocent Hindus and Muslims."[1]

The result was that more than a million Hindus and Muslims died in the most gruesome manner and hundreds of thousands of women were raped and an equal number of children either massacred or orphaned; over fifteen million were uprooted from their hearths and homes; they fled, leaving behind everything in search of safer destinations across the border. What a price India had to pay for its freedom! The British true to their imperial design left their premier colony bleeding. They had ruled by dividing Hindus and Muslims; they left, dividing their richest possession, but after depleting it. As Trevor Royle observes poignantly in his graphic account of *The Last Days of the Raj:* "Modern times have seen sufficient examples of man's inhumanity to man for us not to quail at such descriptions; the Nazi concentration camps, civil war in Biafra, the wars in Vietnam, the Lebanon are all sharp reminders of our capacity to lose our reason in mindless violence....

Friends or neighbours of long standing turned on one another simply because one was Hindu, the other Muslim: logic and common humanity found themselves being replaced by fear, panic and hatred. For a while it seemed as if the whole world had gone mad as stories began to emerge of the wholesale slaughter of refugees, of trainloads of men, women and children meeting ghastly ends, of the burning alive of communities in their homes and places of worship, of death, destruction and rape."[2]

Churchill gloated over what he mockingly described as the "ferocity of cannibals". No one was bothered about the plight and agony of the people in the affected areas except Gandhi who first went to Noakhali in East Bengal where the Hindus were being murdered; Jinnah stayed in Delhi enjoying the triumphant culmination of his mad scheme. He did not go to Patna where the Hindus were killing Muslims, nor to Bombay where they were facing a similar fate. In all these riot-affected places it was only the Mahatma who rushed there and gave relief and succour to both Hindus and Muslims.

Jinnah was, no doubt, anguished at the massacre of the Muslims; but unlike Gandhi, he did nothing to save the riot-stricken people, nor went to console them. He remained in his palatial bungalow in Delhi while the poor, helpless Muslims were being butchered. One day a Muslim officer of the Indian Civil Service came to see him with a document which contained a plan to eliminate the Muslims in a particular Hindu-majority province. The officer was the secretary to the Chief Minister of that province. The document came accidentally into his hands and he surreptitiously took it to Jinnah who read it, but instead of getting worried, he admonished the officer: "You have been guilty of violating the confidence of your boss. You should not have brought this confidential document to me. Instead, if you were deeply concerned about it, you should have taken it to your boss and expressed your honest views about it. Now take this back and do not ever do such a thing again."[3] In an ordinary situation, his rebuke could well have been appreciated; but when his own co-religionists were to face such a carnage because of his politics, his cool reaction even if technically correct, seemed strange and heartless. The officer was Ali Arshad who migrated to Pakistan and became Foreign Secretary (1972-74) and later Ambassador to America (1986-87).

On August 15, while Nehru made his "tryst with destiny" speech before the Constituent Assembly, Gandhi was engaged in restoring communal harmony and peace in faraway Bengal. He refused to join in the celebrations of freedom even though he was the architect of it; he was prevailed upon by the beleaguered League Premier of Bengal, H.S. Suhrawardy to come to Calcutta where Hindus and Muslims had run amok, indulging in the worst kinds of atrocities. Nehru and Patel were aghast that the Mahatma responded to the call of "that butcher" and went on a fast unto death to stop the brutalities; within a week Gandhi transformed the city of sorrow into one of peace. Mountbatten admitted that what thousands of his soldiers could not do, the "one-man boundary" force of Gandhi had achieved. Later in Delhi, the capital, hostilities degenerated to such an alarming extent that Gandhi had to rush there to bring solace and comfort to its harassed citizens; once again he had to undertake a fast unto death to stop the killings. But he could not rebuild the mutual trust among Hindus and Muslims which partition had so wantonly destroyed. Temporarily he was able to change the environment but the barriers that the division had built were so strong that these could not be easily demolished. Eventually a mad man, a Hindu, thought the best way to perpetuate the communal divide was to assassinate the only one who had worked ceaselessly to preserve the unity of the country; the man who had inflamed these passions and caused the division was spared. Jinnah went about his task without losing much sleep over the tragic aftermath; he died peacefully in Karachi a year later.

On January 30, 1948 three bullets silenced forever the apostle of communal peace and harmony; it robbed the country of its greatest treasure and most abiding moral force. The whole world mourned the death of the Mahatma but not Jinnah whose arrogance had so corrupted his outlook that he was unable to come out of the clutches of hate. His co-religionists who followed him realised too late that their future was endangered. The Muslims who remained behind in India found themselves in the lurch. Azad tried to wipe their tears. He could not help reminding them of how he had warned them that by following Jinnah they were ruining themselves. In his inimitable style, while addressing them from the Jama Masjid in Delhi on October 23, 1947, the Maulana cried in anguish: "The uneasiness on your faces and the desolation in your hearts that I see today, remind me of the events of the past few years. Do you remember I hailed you, you cut off my tongue. I picked up my pen, you severed my hand. I wanted to move forward, you cut off my legs. I tried to turn over, and you injured my back. When the bitter political games of the last seven years were at their peak, I tried to wake you up at every danger signal. You not only did not heed my call but revived all the past traditions of neglect and denial. As a result, the same perils surround you today, their onset had diverted you from the righteous path."[4]

The Muslims of pre-partition India had scorned Azad when he had cautioned them of the fate their Quaid-i-Azam was driving them to; they flocked to him and followed him blindly. They hailed him as their saviour and humiliated their real benefactor, Azad. Now, dejected and forlorn, they beseeched the same Azad to rescue them but he told them frankly: "Today, mine is no more than an inert existence or a forlorn cry. I am an orphan in my own motherland. My sensitivities are blunted, my heart is heavy. Think for one moment, what course did you adopt? Where have you reached, and where do you stand now? Haven't your senses become torpid? Aren't you living in a constant state of fear? This fear is of your own creation, a fruit of your own deeds."[5]

Reminiscing about the past and the blunders that the Muslims had committed by listening to Jinnah, the Maulana said: "It was not long ago when I warned you that the two-nation theory was a death-knell to a meaningful, dignified life; forsake it. I told you that the pillars upon which you were leaning would inevitably crumble. To all this you turned a deaf ear. You did not realise that fleet-footed time would not change its course to suit your convenience. Time sped along. And now you have discovered that the so-called anchors of your faith have set you adrift, to be kicked around by fate."[6]

He reminded them of the plight in which Jinnah and his associates had put them: "The chessboard of British gamesmanship has been overturned. Those pawns called 'leaders' whom you had created, you had installed them on the pedestal, have disappeared overnight....But what I have to say today needs to be direct and to the point. The Partition of India was a fundamental mistake. The manner in which religious differences were incited, inevitably, led to the devastation that we have seen with our own eyes....There is no use recounting the events of the past seven years, nor will it serve any good. Yet, it must be stated that the debacle of Indian Muslims is the result of the colossal blunders committed by the Muslim League's misguided leadership. These consequences however were no surprise to me; I had anticipated them from the very start."[7]

The Hindu communalists — even the liberals and radicals among them — protested half-heartedly against the dismemberment of the motherland but most of them, in their heart of hearts, were pleased that they had got rid of the bulk of the Muslims. Of course they abused Jinnah for what he had done but strangely they also poured venom on Gandhi who had struggled to preserve a united India. They blamed him for working for Hindu-Muslim unity. They were for the transfer of population but that was neither physically feasible nor would the British have agreed to it; it would also have been condemned by the international community as it would have violated the UN charter of human rights. However, the after-effects of Jinnah's Two-Nation theory continued to vitiate inter-communal relations. Bal Thackeray, for instance, even today constantly cries himself hoarse asking the Government of India to dump the Muslims into the Arabian Sea. Fortunately India's heritage of broad humanism has so far frustrated his evil design. No one can predict what will happen in the future, with both countries armed with nuclear weapons.

The casual manner in which Nehru and Patel took such a momentous decision, bypassing the Mahatma, is captured in a passage by Mountbatten's press adviser, Alan Campbell-Johnson in his *Mission with Mountbatten*: "Nehru and Vallabhbhai Patel, the two big Congressmen in the Interim Government, accepted Partition on the understanding that by conceding Pakistan to Jinnah they will hear no more of him and eliminate his nuisance value, or, as Nehru put it privately — by 'cutting off the head we will get rid of the headache'."[8] They cut off the head alright; but the headache persists to this day.

Later both the leaders realised that they had committed a great blunder. Nehru confessed: "When we decided on partition I do not think any of us ever thought that there would be this terror of mutual killing after partition. It was in a sense to avoid that that we decided on partition. So we paid a double price for it. First, you might say politically, ideologically; second, the actual thing happened what we tried to avoid." Similar was the remorse of Patel who admitted that they were so blinded by the happenings around them that they could not see the wrong they were doing to India. The Sardar had fondly hoped that the separated parts would soon realise their folly and ask for reunion. That alas was wishful thinking. Generations to come shall continue to pay the price for the ill-fated and ill-conceived decision of these leaders. As an Urdu poet has said, "Moments commit mistakes but centuries have to suffer." In Pakistan also, many of Jinnah's lieutenants like Chaudhary Khaliquzzaman and H.S. Suhrawardy publicly confessed that Muslims had been the worst sufferers of partition.

It was Nehru's vacillation that let him down at the crucial moment in his life. How else can his behaviour be explained. Lincoln along with Gandhi had been his inspiration. As Shashi Tharoor has revealed in his weekly column in *The Indian Express*, "On his desk, Jawaharlal Nehru kept two totems – a gold statuette of Mahatma Gandhi and a bronze cast of the hand of Abraham Lincoln which he would occasionally touch for comfort. The two objects reflected the range of his sources of inspiration: he often spoke of his wish to confront problems with the heart of the Mahatma and the hand of Lincoln."[9] In accepting partition, he let down both his mentors. Also had Patel, the Iron Man, not developed cold feet as a reaction to Jinnah's obstructive tactics and agreed with Nehru, unity would still have been saved. Patel was apprehensive that Muslims might have continued to be troublesome even in undivided India. He did not realise that even if they had, they could not have been a threat to its security which after partition Pakistan certainly has become. In obtaining temporary relief, the two titans who were charged with the destiny of millions of their fellow citizens lost sight of the long-range view. Had they stood firm and not been swayed by Mountbatten, the history of India would not have taken such an unfortunate turn.

SIXTEEN

Authoritarian Misrule

In the midst of the holocaust all around with gruesome tales of plunder, rape and killings in several parts of the subcontinent, Indian Muslims like the rest of their countrymen were stunned. Meanwhile the Quaid-i-Azam unmindful of these sufferings which had been inflicted equally on his co-religionists, arrived in Karachi to take charge of his newly formed kingdom. He was proud of his singular achievement. Margaret Bourke-White, ace photographer of the well-known American journals *Time* and *Life*, found Jinnah on his arrival in Karachi gripped with "a fever of ecstasy. Jinnah's deep-sunk eyes were pinpoints of excitement. His whole manner indicated that an almost overwhelming exultation was racing through his veins". On Bourke-White congratulating him on creating the world's largest Islamic nation, Jinnah corrected her: "Oh, it is not just the largest Islamic nation. Pakistan is the fifth largest nation in the world." Bourke-White commented, "The note of personal triumph was so unmistakable that I wondered how much thought he gave to the human cost: more Muslim lives had been sacrificed to create the new Muslim homeland than America, for example, had lost during the entire Second World War."[1] Or during the civil war between the north and the south of America. Jinnah had also used Islam to obtain immediate recognition from the Muslim world for his Pakistan. He was however determined in accordance with his western training and anglicised outlook not to turn Pakistan into an Islamic state. It would be governed in the same way as the British had run its abandoned colony. He made this clear at the earliest opportunity.

It came about a few days before the inauguration of Pakistan when Sikandar Mirza, an ICS officer, who later became the head of the new state, enquired of Jinnah: "What kind of polity are you going to have? Are you going to have an Islamic state?" Jinnah replied, "Nonsense. I am going to have a modern state."[2]

Inaugurating the Constituent Assembly on August 11, 1947, he told its members in no uncertain terms: "You may belong to any religion or caste or creed — that has nothing to do with the business of the state.... We are starting with this fundamental principle, that we are all citizens of one state." He elaborated that a citizen of Pakistan "no matter to what community he belongs, no matter what is his colour, caste or creed is first, second and last a citizen of this state with equal rights, privileges and obligations..." He added without any reservation: "In course of time all these angularities of the majority and minority communities ... will vanish."[3] This unequivocal statement not only knocked down the very basis of the Two-Nation theory and struck at the root of his own thesis for the creation of Pakistan but also rejected the idea of the state being made Islamic. He had no doubt exploited Islam to achieve Pakistan; as for his involvement in his religion there was no trace of it in practice. During the inaugural celebrations on the birth of Pakistan on August 14, 1947, he invited Lord and Lady Mountbatten as chief guests to a special luncheon when Jinnah was cautioned that it was the month of Ramadan and it would be sacrilege to do so. The luncheon party was then changed to dinner. This has been commented upon by Mountbatten himself in his recollection of the event.

A few days later when a group of leading Ulama waited on him and asked him to apply the Shariah to the functioning of the new state, he told them sternly: "Whose Shariah? Hanafis? Hambalis? Sha'afis? Ma'alikis? Ja'afris? I don't want to get involved. The moment I enter this field, the ulama will take over for they claim to be the experts and I certainly don't propose to hand over the field to the ulama. I am aware of their criticism but I don't propose to fall into their trap."[4] This was conveyed to all his colleagues in the hierarchy of the Muslim League; surprisingly none objected to it. Jinnah wanted in fact to dissolve the Muslim League and transform it into the Pakistan National League. Tariq Ali reveals this in his book *Can Pakistan Survive?*: "The speech (of Jinnah advocating secularism) has been strongly criticised (usually in private, since Jinnah is above public criticism in Pakistan) by religious divines, confessional sects and right-wing political parties because of its opposition to the creation of an 'Islamic state'. The criticisms are not without logic. If Pakistan was the culmination of the struggle for a 'Muslim nation', then clearly secularism was a somewhat inappropriate ideology for it. A 'Muslim nation' should have a 'Muslim constitution'. An additional point could also be made regarding the speech: if its aspirations could be implemented in Pakistan, then surely they could equally have been put into practice in a united India. In reality, if the subcontinent had not been divided on a religious basis, the

Muslims would actually have been a stronger force. Jinnah's addiction to constitutionalism was creditable, but it merely brought to the fore the confused character of the campaign which had preceded the formation of the new state. Soon after partition, Jinnah seriously considered the possibility of declaring the Muslim League a secular party and changing its name to the Pakistan National League. His intention, however, was prematurely revealed by the then left-wing daily, *The Pakistan Times,* and the resulting hue and cry from reactionary elements compelled him to shelve the proposal."[5]

Jinnah was indeed worried about the future of the Muslim League; with partition, its all-India character had lost its meaning. It had to be divided; with a wrench in his heart, after almost four months of soul-searching, he convened a meeting of the Governing Council which met in Karachi on December 14-15, 1947. More than half of the members — 160 out of 300 — came from divided India. Though Jinnah presided, he told his devotees that the League would have to be split and the Indian part would have to function independently without his leadership. The separation was permanent and he was extremely sorry about it. One of the Indian members shouted: "We never thought this would be our fate; you have divided brother and brother. And left us completely in the lurch."

Jinnah replied, "But that was inevitable; it could not have been avoided."

Another member from India interjected, "But you never warned us about it; you said we would be rid of Hindu domination; you have chained us to them forever."

There were shouts and counter-shouts leading to a commotion. Maulana Jamal Mian protested that what Jinnah had given to the Muslims was not even an Islamic state. He said: "Pakistan could hardly take pride in calling itself a 'Muslim state'. He found many un-Islamic things in the state from top to bottom ….The behaviour of the ministers is not like that of Muslims. The poor cannot enter the houses of the ministers; the needy and the lowly cannot see them. Only the courtiers can enter, those who possess large bungalows can enter. The name of Islam has been disgraced enough."[6] Jinnah tried to pacify the agitators and soothe their frayed nerves. He took pains to assure them that as time passed everything would be alright. There was no need, he said, to be so pessimistic. "God willing we shall overcome our difficulties. Have patience and have faith in yourself."

Jinnah did not allow any change in the application of the laws which the British had introduced in India; in fact he wanted to transform Pakistan into another Turkey on the lines of his hero Kemal Ataturk. Like him he planned to completely westernise Pakistanis. He cherished the British style of life and always lived by it. In his day-to-day life, he enjoyed his bacon and eggs for breakfast, ham sandwiches for lunch and two or three pegs of whisky before dinner. Though he wore sherwani and the black cap (which came to be known as the Jinnah cap) for public appearances in the evening of his life, he was always more at home in his Saville Row suit and hat. Similarly his outlook and thinking were deeply influenced by western ideas and principles. He had neither read Ghazali nor Rumi nor any of the other classical thinkers of Islam. Nor any of the works of Iqbal, translated into the English. His ignorance of Islamic teachings can best be illustrated by an incident that took place during Eid prayers in Karachi. A close associate of Jinnah, Qazi Isa suggested to him that while addressing the Eid congregation he should recite a Quranic verse. Jinnah readily agreed and learnt one by heart. As soon as he finished his address he turned to the Qazi and asked him whether he had recited the verse correctly.

Excitedly the Qazi exclaimed, "Alhamdo Lillah."
"What does that mean?" Jinnah asked.
Isa said, "It means Allah be praised."
"Damn you," Jinnah shouted, "I did not ask you about Allah but about me."
The Qazi coolly assured him, "You, my Quaid, are always right."

One evening, Maulana Hasrat Mohani went to see him without prior appointment. Jinnah was in his room and was as usual sipping whisky. He asked for the Maulana to be ushered in. Mohani, with his deep orthodox Islamic background was taken aback to see Quaid-i-Azam drinking. Despite the anger seething within him, he composed himself. Jinnah saw the Maulana's face change colour. To humour him, he asked him whether he would like to taste the forbidden drink. "No, thank you, Sir," replied the Maulana, "I have to answer my Allah." Jinnah sensed his discomfiture: "Maulana Saheb, I am a better Muslim than you are. Unlike me you have no faith in the mercy and benevolence of God." Mohani spent a few minutes with his leader, acquainting him with the problems which troubled him and quietly went away, wondering whether all the sacrifices that pious Muslims like him had made in following Jinnah in the pursuit of Pakistan had really been worth it. He felt betrayed with what he personally witnessed that evening.

Maulana Maududi, the founder of Jamat-i-Islami, had much earlier lamented the lack of any kind of religious involvement on Jinnah's part; even when he was being hailed as the saviour, Maududi had objected to the title of Quaid-i-Azam conferred on him by the generality of the Muslims of

166   THE MAN WHO DIVIDED INDIA

undivided India. The Maulana had pointed out: "One cannot discover even a hint of Islam in the ideas, ideals and the political style (of Jinnah).... From the most trivial to the most crucial problems, he shows no knowledge of the Quranic point of view nor does he care or consider it necessary to seek it. All his knowledge comes from the western laws and sources."[7]

Even in his will which was disclosed after his death, Jinnah did not respect the injunction of the Prophet which classical jurists have sanctified as a mandatory part of the Shariah; it has been universally accepted that a Muslim cannot by will dispose of all his assets; he can do so only to the extent of one-third. Two-thirds of his estate has to be left to his heirs who automatically step into their respective share after his death. In Mulla's *Principles of Mahomedan Law*, edited by the former Chief Justice of India, M. Hidayatullah, it is explained by the author on the authority of *Sahi Bukhari*, thus: "This limit derives sanction from a tradition reported by Abee Vekass. It is said that the Prophet paid a visit to Abee Vekass who had no heirs except a daughter, and he asked the Prophet whether he could dispose of the whole of his property by will to which the Prophet replied saying that he could not dispose of the whole, not even two-thirds, nor one-half, but only one-third: *Hedaya*, 671."[8] Jinnah, despite having been well-versed in the principles of Mahomedan Law, did not adhere to the limitation of one-third but as under Hindu Law authorised and directed the executors to distribute his assets to various relations and parties as specifically mentioned by him in his will.

Jinnah continued to be Governor-General of Pakistan for over a year. He was invariably troubled by many state problems. His health too was in bad shape. He had become a skeleton. He could no longer direct the affairs of state in the manner he wanted. He had lost the energy and his will had considerably weakened. He felt dejected with what he saw before his eyes; all that he had obtained after such hard struggle turning into a mess and his newly created beloved country harbouring evils like corruption, nepotism and fanaticism. He was disillusioned by the performance of his trusted colleague, Liaquat Ali Khan. He lamented to M.A. Khuhro, Chief Minister of Sind, that he was sorely disappointed in his Prime Minister. He had proved to be just "mediocre". Jinnah had also started suspecting Liaquat's loyalty. Likewise he was unhappy with the Chief Minister of Punjab, the Nawab of Mamdot who had no control on administration nor any idea of dealing with problems. He called the Governor, an Englishman by the name Mudie, and ordered him to sack Mamdot and appoint Mian Mumtaz Daulatana in his place. Mudie called the Mian and offered him the job but he refused. He told Jinnah that had he accepted the chief ministership "Mamdot would have just cut my throat". Quaid-i-Azam could not believe his ears; he was shocked to learn that his Pakistan was almost being taken over by a mafia.

There were many such instances which made Jinnah realise that his so-called lieutenants of the past whom he had patronised, turned out to be self-seekers who would not even mind resorting to murder to usurp power; they lacked character and would even conspire against their Quaid-i-Azam if need be. Someone who was in his complete confidence warned him that many politicians had no scruples whatsoever; they were capable of instigating the army to overthrow him. Alarmed at such a possibility, he decided to visit Quetta much against the advice of his doctors. Jinnah addressed the officers of the Staff College on June 14, 1947. He expressed, indirectly, his anxiety on this score: "You, along with other forces of Pakistan, are the custodians of the life, property and honour of the people of Pakistan. The Defence Forces are the most vital of all Pakistan Services and correspondingly a very heavy responsibility and burden lies on your shoulders.... I want you to remember and if you have time enough you should study the Government of India Act, as adapted for use in Pakistan, which is our present Constitution, that the executive authority flows from the Head of the Government of Pakistan, who is the Governor-General, and, therefore, any command or orders that may come to you cannot come without the sanction of the Executive Head."[9]

Apart from reminding them that no one else mattered in Pakistan but him, he told them that there was no need to modify the existing administrative set-up and warned them that they should not listen to the mullahs who had no idea about how to run a state. If they were to be followed, Jinnah said, there would be nothing but chaos everywhere and Pakistan would be thrown back into the Middle Ages.

Apart from the intrigues and incompetence of those whom he had put in charge of administration, what shocked Jinnah was the growing linguistic trouble in East Pakistan. He had been cautioned by several experts before partition that it would be difficult for him to manage both the western and the eastern wings separated by seven hundred miles of foreign territory and inhabited by people different in their habits, customs and lifestyle. But he had such confidence in the supremacy of his leadership that he believed that he would be able to put everything right. Now he became aware that neither he nor the bond of Islam would be able to knit together two such diverse peoples. The gulf in every respect — political, economic and social — was so wide that even Islamic brotherhood could not keep them together. He received the biggest setback when the Bengalis in the eastern wing rose en masse against his Government's decision to make Urdu the only official language of the dominion. They demanded that as they constituted more than half the population of the new state, their language, Bengali, should also be made an official language. The situation was so explosive that despite his ill-health Jinnah rushed to Dacca to pacify the agitated Bengalis. He arrived in the capital of the eastern wing on March 21, 1948 to a cold reception. There were no shouts of "Quaid-i-Azam Zindabad". He had been told that the Islamic bond would be strong enough to silence the opposition; he was, however, taken aback to find that language was proving to be a much more powerful link than religion. More than three lakh people had gathered to hear him, hoping he would concede their demand, but Jinnah was in an aggressive mood. He was not prepared to tolerate such open defiance of his authority. Hence he declared in unequivocal terms that "the official language of Pakistan shall be Urdu and no other language."

The public reacted angrily; they heckled him. There was pandemonium. Jinnah lost his calm and admonished the unruly crowd: "Anyone who tries to mislead you is really the enemy of Pakistan. Without one state language, no nation can remain tied up solidly together and function. Look at the history of other countries. Therefore, so far as the state language is concerned, Pakistan's language shall be Urdu....I tell you once again, do not fall into the trap of those who are the enemies of Pakistan. Unfortunately you have fifth-columnists and I am sorry to say they are Muslims — who are financed by outsiders... you must have patience."[10] Jinnah returned to Karachi from Dacca, his first and only visit to turbulent East Pakistan exhausted, depressed and forlorn; he confided to his sister Fatima, "I am sorry the game is lost. I backed the wrong horse."

As Jinnah struggled with death in Quetta, his doctors advised that he be shifted to Karachi, then the capital of Pakistan; he undertook the journey on August 13, 1948, six weeks before he passed away on September 28. His sister Fatima suggested he wear kurta-pyjama for the plane journey in order to be comfortable, but Jinnah though frail and very sick, insisted on wearing "a brand new suit with a tie to match and a handkerchief in his vanity pocket". She helped him to put on his pump shoes and his favourite hat. A gentleman to his fingertips even during his last days, Jinnah could not bring himself to dress in any other way. His style of living, mode of dressing, day-to-day habits, even his thinking were too deep-rooted to change. In death, of course, he was clothed in Islamic attire and blessed with Islamic rituals. His mausoleum in Karachi has become a centre of pilgrimage for the faithful.

SEVENTEEN

The Struggle to Survive

Jinnah died a disheartened man. He had no doubt won Pakistan — even if "mauled, mutilated and moth-eaten" to use his words; but he could not run it as he wanted. It turned out to be a hybrid — neither secular nor Islamic. In his lifetime the ulama protested that the whole *raison d'etre* for its formation was being destroyed. They were silenced by the Quaid-i-Azam but they could not contain their anger when they found that even after his death, the Muslim Leaguers, occupying seats of power, only paid lip service to the objective; none of them took any steps to implement it. They did not want to disturb the status quo. For instance, though Liaquat Ali Khan unlike Jinnah was a practising Muslim, steeped in Islamic traditions, he made only a feeble attempt to give a kind of Islamic garb to the new state. He was not ready to go all the way. In fact he clarified right at the outset that "people are the real recipients of power. This naturally eliminates any danger of the establishment of a theocracy."[1] Nevertheless in order to temper the turbulent gust of fanaticism which partition had generated, he was careful not to upset the *Islam passands*. Also he had neither the charisma nor the necessary hold on the people to control or curb the demand for Islamisation. He therefore held a series of discussions with different groups of ulama who only confused and confounded him with their varying suggestions. Every sect pressed for a specific framework; there were so many contradictory assertions that consensus eluded him. He was not unhappy about the outcome as he was not ready to turn Pakistan into the theocracy that they demanded.

To pacify the agitated ulama and to respect the sentiments of the millions of Muslims who were led to believe that Pakistan would be an Islamic state, Liaquat came out with a tame "Objectives Resolution" and got it passed unanimously by the Constituent Assembly. It stated that sovereignty over the whole world vested in Allah and further that all laws would be in conformity with the Quran and the Sunnah. It was a vague and general statement; in the words of Prof. Leonard Binder, "it was merely a deposit on account, to be accepted as an indication of good faith. The ulama desired to enshrine the principle of the supremacy of the Shariah while the politicians, or most of them, found this principle acceptable so long as it was not clearly defined."[2]

The rest of the provisions, which were secular, were clear and precise; they were more in conformity with British-made rather than Islamic laws. Except for the ulama and the mullahs in the mosques, there was hardly any pressure on the Constituent Assembly to bring into effect a real Islamic jurisprudence, much less an Islamic state. Most politicians were busy trying to line their pocket; they were averse to upsetting the prevalent set-up. There was not only an unseemly scramble for power but also for material gain — *nafsa, nafsi,* the "I" syndrome was their motto. There was no doubt some talk of an Islamic society to be ushered in but as G.M. Sayed, the foremost Sindhi champion of Pakistan and a trusted lieutenant of Jinnah, observed, "Do not forget also that Islamic society actually in existence is that in which the religious head is an ignorant mullah, the spiritual head an immoral pir, the political guide a power-intoxicated feudal landlord ... their cry of 'Islam in danger' became a cloak for dark deeds and reactionary moves, complacency and tyranny. Such is the extent to which mockery can be made of Islam in these days of capitalist subterfuge and commercialised politics."[3]

Nothing concrete emerged out of the speeches made during the extensive debates on the "Objectives Resolution". The politicians extolled the virtues of Islam but took care to see that the state was not made Islamic; that would have taken away power from their hands and left the field open to the ulama. Most of them relying on the declarations of the Quaid-i-Azam frankly expressed their fears; they asserted, as desired by their supreme leader, that Pakistan would not be a theocracy. The ulama on the other hand demanded that the whole fight for Pakistan was on religious grounds and they alone should be entrusted with the task of shaping its polity. Their leader Maulana Shabbir Ahmad Usmani who had singlehandedly broken the hold of the Congress on the Muslim religious elite in undivided India, and brought them under the umbrella of the Muslim League, told the Constituent Assembly with unqualified frankness: "They want the mullah to devote his attention to reforming the society while they are left free to spoil the society day in and day out. If the term 'unsuitable environment' is interpreted to mean that the environment of those ruling over us is unsuitable, then the community will have to reconsider who should govern this country...it is also said that the mullah wants power…I say when people aspire for power for worldly ends, what is the harm if the mullah also aspires for power to set up a truly Islamic state. The mullah does not want to rule, he only wants the rulers to be somewhat like the mullah…."[4]

After passing the "Objectives Resolution", the Constituent Assembly entrusted the task of defining its implications, particularly the running of the state, to the Basic Principles' Committee; it was asked to formulate the fundamentals of a federal constitution in the light of Islamic norms. The Committee was to be assisted by the Board of Islamic Teaching (Taalimat-i-Islami). They were composed mostly of ulama who differed so vehemently on even major issues that it became difficult to arrive at a consensus. For long, members of the Committee grappled with the various points of view but could only come out with a tame, confused report. It was presented to the Constituent Assembly on September 7, 1950; its recommendations were not very different from many of the articles in the Government of India Act. Sardar Shaukat Hyat Khan, a young influential Muslim Leaguer remarked, "If Mr. Churchill had been the leader of this House (which God forbid), he would have drawn up just such a Constitution."[5] The general reaction was most unfavourable; some of the prominent Muslim Leaguers described the product as "most undemocratic, unIslamic and most reactionary". The strongest protest came from East Pakistan which saw in it a sinister design to subjugate its people. As *The Pakistan Observer*, the influential daily published from Dacca wrote: "The citizens of Dacca, mostly East Bengalis, were rudely shocked when local dailies carried to them the full text of the Basic Principles Committee Report with regard to the future constitution of Pakistan; they were from all walks of life, high officials, professors, teachers, lawyers, students, medical men, police personnel etc. Their first reaction was that of bewilderment."[6] In the result the Constituent Assembly in its meeting on November 21, 1951 decided to shelve the consideration of the report and referred it to the public for their comments and suggestions.

Meanwhile Liaquat Ali Khan, the first Prime Minister of Pakistan, was assassinated within three years of its formation. His death dealt a blow to the process of stabilisation. His successor Khwaja Nazimuddin, former chief minister of undivided Bengal, presented a revised draft of the report of the Basic Principles Committee to the Constituent Assembly on December 22, 1954. It recommended parity between the two wings which upset the Punjabis. Surprisingly the whole tenor of discussion shifted from Islamisation to sharing of power between Bengalis and Punjabis. Some sort of compromise was however worked out which dealt mainly with allocation of seats and powers in the provincial and federal legislatures. It was approved by the Constituent Assembly on September 21, 1954. Its Islamic principles were of a general nature and by and large mollified the ulama; though only ten provisions pertained to Islamic injunctions such as prohibiting drinking liquor, gambling, *riba* or taking of interest, prostitution, and organising of *zakat* and *auqaf* and promotion of Islamic moral standards; 266 provisions were of a secular nature concerning the composition and powers of the provincial and federal legislative, executive and judicial set-up; they were copied from the Government of India Act of 1935.

In the proposed constitution the pattern of governance was not too different from what had been left behind by the British. The enforceable and mandatory provisions were all secular; the Islamic ones were directives, not enforceable in law. These could not form the basis of the establishment of an Islamic state; nor did the members of the Constituent Assembly desire that any radical change in the administrative arrangement, as inherited from the British, be brought about. In March 1956 the Constitution, almost nine years after the creation of Pakistan, was adopted by the Constituent Assembly. It embodied a secular rather than religious pattern. To give it an Islamic character, it provided that the head of state be a Muslim; the ulama wanted that it be qualified by adding "pious" to it but that was not agreed upon. Their specific recommendation was "that the Mussalmans elect the wisest and most God-fearing person from amongst themselves as their head to discharge these duties and responsibilities on their behalf and in consultation with pious and sagacious members of the *millat* enjoying their confidence."[7]

Had this been accepted, all those who subsequently became heads of state, with the exception of one, would have been disqualified. The republic was no doubt named Islamic but it was a façade; Suhrawardy rightly commented, "You are deluding the people here calling this an Islamic state."[8] For two years this Constitution remained in force but the administration continued on old lines; no step was taken to Islamise it. On the ulama protesting that the rulers had forgotten Islam, Iskandur Mirza, the Governor-General, as head of state, told them: "We cannot run wild with Islam."[9] Maulana Ataullah Shah Bokhari accused the Muslim League members of the Constituent Assembly of being *be-imaan* (heretics) who would be damned in afterlife. He said what they were creating was not Pakistan but — Khakistan "the land of dust". Others called it "*napak-istan* — the impure land".[10]

One offshoot of the adoption of the Constitution was the demand by some ulama particularly the Ahraras, that the Ahmadis — a sect of Muslims founded by Ghulam Ahmad of Quadian, who did not accept the finality of Muhammad's prophethood, be declared non-Muslim. On the Government refusing to accept the demand, riots broke out in Lahore and other parts of Punjab. The army was called in to suppress them. Thereafter a commission headed by the Chief Justice of Pakistan, Justice Mohammad Munir was appointed to go into the question of who was a Muslim; it took the evidence of the leading ulama, representing different schools of thought, to define the qualifications and requirements of a Muslim. Its findings were eye-opening. According to Justice Munir every sect considered the other as kafir or heretic. Sunnis declared that Shias were kafirs because they claimed that Hazrat Ali shared the prophethood with Prophet Muhammad. On the other hand Shias regarded Sunnis as kafirs because they were associates in the murder of Hazrat Ali and his sons. To quote Justice Munir: "The net result of all this is that neither Shias nor Sunnis nor Deobandis nor Ahl-i-Hadith nor Barelvis are Muslims and any change from one view to the other must be accomplished in an Islamic state with the penalty of death if the government of the state is in the hands of the party which considers the other party to be kafirs. And it does not require much imagination to judge of the consequences of this doctrine when it is remembered that no two ulama have agreed before us as to the definition of a Muslim."[11]

According to the perception of most ulama, in a truly Islamic state there would be no equality for non-Muslims. Justice Munir asked Maulana Maududi: "If we have this form of government in Pakistan (treating non-Muslims as *zimmis*), will you permit Hindus to have their constitution on the basis

of their religion?" Maududi replied: "Certainly. I should have
no objection even if the Muslims of India are treated in that
form of government as shudras and malichas and Manu's laws
are applied to them depriving them of all share in the
government and the rights of a citizen." [12]

The men in charge of the affairs of Pakistan, whether
politicians, bureaucrats or army commanders, were hardly
practising Muslims; they were the products of Anglo-Saxon
training; their administrative approach was so oriented. Their
living and thinking was also anglicised. They enjoyed the pelfs
and perks that a secular state gave them; most of their time
was spent at lunch and dinner parties and intriguing against
one another. All of them were busy making money. They
disliked the Islamic fundamentalists and distrusted their
mentors, clamouring for the establishment of an Islamic state.
They saw to it that the status quo was maintained. They clung
to the British mode of administration. Ayaz Amir has pointed
out in his scintillating article in *Dawn*, "Britishness was on the
surface — all form and little substance". He elaborates it
picturesquely: "The British experience has been reduced to a
set of ephemera: turbaned waiters, leather sofas, chota pegs
(or rather, since we like our whisky, burra pegs) tweed coats,
cricket (now increasingly golf)..."[13] And in order to sustain
themselves in this artificial westernised set-up they resorted
to more and more intrigue.

This caused the replacement of one government by
another. Consequently there was no stability; corruption
became rampant, the economy was shattered, administration
decayed. At this time, according to the noted Pakistani scholar,
Golam W. Choudhury: "An attempt was made to introduce a
modified version of the presidential system in 1954-55 by the
Governor-General Ghulam Mohammad who had no faith in

the democratic process, and whose model was not the presidential system but the 'viceregal' system of the British period. The British constitutional expert, Sir Ivor Jennings, was commissioned to draft a system of government for Pakistan in which, to quote his words, the American idea of an executive for four years was grafted onto a British system of representation. Sir Ivor Jenning's draft constitution of 1955 not only tried to draft the American system with the British one but also proposed serious limitations on the powers of the legislature in money matters which is unknown in either the American or British system."[14]

Unlike in India, there was neither a dependable leadership nor a reliable system which could contain the slide. On Liaquat's death, to placate the turbulent East Pakistanis, Khwaja Nazimuddin was appointed Prime Minister. But he was too weak to control the situation; the politicians in West Pakistan, especially the Punjabis, openly defied him. The civil servants had scant respect for him. After some time Governor-General Ghulam Mohammad dismissed him. He did not know how to react; it was rumoured that he appealed to the Queen of England to save him on the ground that he enjoyed majority support in the National Assembly. He had yet to shed his loyalty to the British who had gone away for good. There was of course no response from Her Majesty. In his place the Governor-General nominated an obscure Bengali politician, Mohamed Ali Bogra, as Prime Minister. He was then serving as Pakistan's Ambassador in Washington. In order to strengthen his position, Bogra made the Assembly amend the Constitution depriving the Governor-General of the power to dismiss the Prime Minister. Ghulam Mohammad threatened to suspend the Constitution. However better counsel prevailed and a truce between him and the Prime Minister was brought about.

This did not put a stop to intrigues. One set of
politicians jockeyed for position by siding with the Prime
Minister and the other aligned itself with the Governor-
General. Bogra was a simpleton with little experience of
political manoeuvrings; Ghulam Mohammad, though ailing,
was wily and adept in manipulation. As time passed he was
able to subdue Bogra and split the Muslim League which had
control over the Assembly. On October 24, 1954 he dissolved
the Constituent Assembly which had not only outlived its utility
but had become a beehive of conspiracies. He continued Bogra
as a stop-gap Prime Minister and as a sop to the East Pakistanis
but as soon as he was able to enlist the support of Suhrawardy,
he threw out Bogra and appointed Chaudhary Mohammad Ali
as Prime Minister who produced a new constitution to give
legitimacy to the changing development. He then manoeuvred
to have Ghulam Mohammad deposed and in his place he
arranged to elect Iskander Mirza as first President of the
Republic. Ayub Khan who had by then become an important
member of the cabinet has described how Iskander Mirza turned
the tables on those who chose him: "Shrewd as he was, he
could see how the constitution could be used to promote
political intrigues and bargaining. No one knew any longer who
belonged to which political party; it was all a question of
swapping labels: a Muslim Leaguer today, a Republican
tomorrow; and yesterday's 'traitors' were tomorrow's chief
ministers, indistinguishable as Tweedledum and Tweedledee!"[15]

One of the first acts of the new President was to sack
Chaudhary Mohammad Ali and appoint Suhrawardy as Prime
Minister who helped Mirza to maintain the existing
constitutional arrangement. In East Pakistan Fazlul Haq who
was then its Governor dismissed the cabinet of Ataur Rahman
Khan. Upset with this action, Mirza dismissed Fazlul Haq

himself and appointed Abu Hussain Sarkar as Chief Minister. However within twelve hours he was also dismissed and Ataur Rahman Khan was brought back as Chief Minister. There were fist-fights among members of the Assembly; chaos prevailed; the Speaker was declared of "unsound mind" and removed; the hapless Deputy Speaker being a nonentity was beaten to death on the floor of the House. The President played such diabolical games that he was able to expose every politician and discredit all of them. He then decided to entrust the administration to the army. He called Ayub Khan and asked him to take over. The historic event has been illustrated by Ayub in these words: "I arrived in Karachi on 5 October. Yahya, Hamid, and one or two other officers had preceded me. I went to see General Iskander Mirza. He was sitting on the lawn, brooding, bitter and desperate. I asked him, 'Have you made up your mind, sir?' 'Yes,' he replied. 'Do you think it is absolutely necessary?' 'It is absolutely necessary,' he said firmly. My reaction was that it was very unfortunate that such a desperate stage had been reached, necessitating drastic action. And it was not pleasant to get involved in it, but there was no escape. It was the last bid to save the country."[16]

And thus an end was put to civilian rule which was replaced by that of the army. For the first time martial law was imposed in Pakistan. Ayub Khan became the supreme arbiter of the state which Jinnah had founded with the solemn assurance to the Muslims that it would be more democratic than India. Ayub painted a grim picture of the rot the existing system of governance had caused to Pakistan. In a broadcast to the people on October 8, 1958 he said: "Ever since the death of the Quaid-i-Azam and Mr. Liaquat Ali Khan, politicians started a free-for-all type of fighting in which no holds were barred. They waged a ceaseless and bitter war against each other regardless of the ill effects on the country, just to whet their appetites and satisfy their base motives. There has been no limit to the depth of their baseness, chicanery, deceit, and degradation. Having nothing constructive to offer, they used provincial feelings, sectarian, religious and racial differences to set a Pakistani against a Pakistani. They could see no good in anybody else. All that mattered was self-interest. In this mad rush for power and acquisition, the country and people could go to the dogs as far as they were concerned." [17]

How the system worked to the detriment of the newly formed state is recapitulated by the General in his memoirs: "The period between Liaquat Ali Khan's death and 1958 was distressing. Not only was the central government at loggerheads with the provinces, but a great deal of intrigue and dog-fighting was going on within the central government itself. A civil servant who had become Finance Minister at the time of Independence elevated himself to the position of Governor-General. Another turned himself overnight from Secretary to Government (a civil service post) to Minister for Finance. All it required was rewriting the designation on the name-plates outside their offices. The politicians were naturally dependent on permanent services, but the more powerful among the services had developed political ambitions of their own. Everyone seemed to have a group of his own and his sole occupation was to grind his own axe regardless of whether the country was ground to pieces in the process." [18]

Most of these persons who had controlled the affairs of the new state in the first decade of its existence were the chosen lieutenants of the Quaid-i-Azam; they had backed him all through in his relentless pursuit to bring in an Islamic dispensation so as to free the Muslims of undivided India from the iron clutches of the Hindus. Facts have proved that they were all self-seekers, hungry for power , with no interest in the welfare of the poor and downtrodden or in the establishment of an order which could be in accordance with the canons and traditions of Islam. They brought nothing but misery to the people of Pakistan. They ruined its economy; they unleashed corruption; they encouraged nepotism; in short they defied every principle of the Shariah and disgraced the fair name of Islam. Ever since the formation of Pakistan they had exhibited such greed for power that there would be few examples of it in the annals of mankind. Ayub was fully justified in taking over the administration but instead of using it for the betterment and uplift of the people he succumbed to the temptations that power offered him. He utilised every lever of it for personal aggrandisement, enriching himself and his family. In the end the saviour turned out to be an arch exploiter as subsequent events would indicate.

In order to give democratic semblance to his arbitrary rule, Ayub Khan presented an ingeniously drafted constitution to the people. It was based on the recommendations of a Commission appointed and briefed by him. It declared that parliamentary democracy, as practised in most countries, was unsuited for Pakistan. It cited Jinnah who had condemned it, and pointed out that even in the founder's lifetime "when the enthusiasm of the people for building up a new country was at the highest, personal rivalry started among the members of the party in power." The Commission also rejected the wholesale application of the presidential system based on adult suffrage; that would lead to mob rule. And recommended instead Basic Democracy with restricted franchise and indirect election, the electors being members of local bodies. Nor did it favour the establishment of an Islamic state; it averred that "the bringing of the laws into conformity with the Quran and the Sunnah does not by itself make a good Muslim".[19]

Ayub Khan announced the salient features of the new Constitution through his broadcast on March 1, 1962. It replaced parliamentary democracy by basic democracy. He rejected the ulama's plea to make Islam the state religion. The only concession he made to orthodox sentiment was the provision for the setting up of an Advisory Council of Islamic Ideology which would not enjoy any control over the President or the Legislature "who will be elected by the people" and who would be responsible "for making laws and giving decisions". He stated that he could not allow the ulama to be the final arbiters of the destiny of the people and declared, "this was a position which neither the people nor I were prepared to accept, opposed as it was to the fundamental democratic principle that all authority must vest in the people."[20] He explained that by introducing basic democracy under which indirect election was provided, there would be no scope for intrigue and power politics. Instead of the mob, elected representatives would choose the President.

However, his scheme failed miserably; it hardly enthused the people; in fact one of the reasons for the rebellion in East Pakistan was its authoritarian nature which eventually caused the ouster of Ayub Khan and his handing over power to General Mohamad Yahya Khan, who held general elections on the basis of one-man one-vote; it gave Mujibur Rehman's Awami League of East Pakistan a majority in the national assembly. This was resented by Zulfiqar Ali Bhutto whose Pakistan People's Party had obtained the majority of seats in West Pakistan. The Punjabis were not prepared to play second fiddle to the Bengalis. The result was political deadlock. Yahya therefore promulgated a Legal Framework Order which enjoined that since Pakistan was created in the name of Islam, the constitution must adhere to Islamic ideology. This was a clever move to subordinate the forces of Bengali nationalism which propagated the predominance of language over religion. In order to suppress the revolt in East Pakistan, Yahya resorted to the worst form of repression and the army indulged in the genocide of Bengali agitators who resisted the onslaught and with the help of India seceded from Pakistan and became the free, separate state of Bangladesh. The conflict exhibited the ironic spectacle of Muslims killing Muslims; West Pakistani personnel behaved in the most inhuman manner, committing atrocities and sadism to defend their hold on East Pakistan. There could have been no greater betrayal of the so-called Islamic brotherhood which Jinnah had so relentlessly and stubbornly proclaimed; it negated the whole basis for the formation of Pakistan.

Eighteen

The Fanatical Fringe

G eneral Yahya Khan handed over power to Zulfiqar Ali Bhutto who assumed dictatorial powers and tried to rebuild the divided state, comprising now only West Pakistan. In order to gain popular support, he resorted to gimmicks like banning gambling and the sale of liquor and declaring Friday as the weekly holiday instead of Sunday, and the Ahmadis a non-Muslim minority. In the general election held in 1977 though his party had won, the public accused him of rigging and rose en masse against him. He had to quit office and hand over the reins to the Commander-in-Chief, General Muhammad Zia-ul-Haq; he put Bhutto on trial for murder and obtained from the Supreme Court a judicial order to hang him. Being a practising, orthodox Muslim, aligned to the Jamaat-i-Islami, Zia introduced various measures in his long rule of eleven years to transform Pakistan into an Islamic state. He used this device to contain the growing popular upsurge for the restoration of democracy. He was a clever administrator who managed to appease the fundamentalists without overhauling the existing set-up. He carried on the administration quietly without ruffling too many feathers.

One of the leaders of the opposition, Field Marshal Mohammad Asghar Khan has described Zia's move to Islamise the state thus: "Zia-ul-Haq exploited religion to the full to impress the people with his love for and devotion to Islam. This found expression in a greater use of the media for religious programmes, introduction of *zakat* and *ushr* and opening of profit and loss counters in banks. Greater emphasis was also laid on the ritualistic aspects of religion. Severe punishments were ordered for those not observing the sanctity of the holy month of Ramadan. These measures undoubtedly provided an Islamic veneer to an otherwise un-Islamic military regime. For no regime that is repressive in character and fails to guarantee human rights and liberty can even be remotely Islamic. No society which is based on the exploitation of man, in which the rich are encouraged to get richer and the poor are daily becoming poorer, can be Islamic. A system that allows the rulers to spend the people's hard earned wealth without giving them or their chosen representatives an opportunity to question the ruler's actions cannot be considered to be in keeping with the teachings of this great religion. In a country, where the majority are living below subsistence level, where 85 per cent of the people cannot get clean water to drink, the lavish expenditure of the rulers on themselves is a far cry from the Islamic concept of equality."[1]

I.A. Rehman, Director of the Human Rights Commission of Pakistan has been more specific about how the common people suffered under the Zia regime: "The HRCP was started in 1986 during Zia-ul-Haq's martial law regime. This was one of the most brutal regimes in the history of

Pakistan. It stamped down ruthlessly upon the rights of the people. People could be arrested at will. There were public hangings and whippings."[2] Air Chief Marshal Nur Khan has condemned every military rule. He has written: "There is not one general who has left a good name for himself. There were disasters after disasters and the Army always pretended nothing had happened. They were protecting lies. They claim to be fighting for Islam but the rank-and-file believes the leadership had been dishonest."[3] The only enquiry into the behaviour of these generals and their cohorts, the brigadiers and colonels, was carried out by Chief Justice Hamoodur Rahman of Pakistan. His report which was made public in 1999 after a lapse of more than a decade disclosed:"Due to corruption arising out of the performance of martial law duties, lust for wine and women, and greed for lands and houses, a large number of senior army officers, particularly those occupying the highest positions, had not only lost the will to fight but also the professional competence necessary for taking the vital and critical decisions demanded of them for the successful prosecution of the war." Further the Commission found that "these perversions led to the army brass wilfully subverting public life in Pakistan. In furtherance of their common purpose they did actually try to influence political parties by threats, inducements and even bribes to support their designs."[4]

Zia was killed in an aircraft explosion on August 17, 1988 and with his passing away the prospect of the formation of a civilian government brightened. Bhutto's daughter Benazir returned from exile in London and was cheered and mobbed by the crowd wherever she went; she won a landslide victory in the election to the National Assembly. President Ghulam Ishaq Khan who had succeeded Zia, invited her to form the government; initially the ulama objected to a woman being appointed as head of government under the Shariah. This, they averred, would not be acceptable. However the President ignored the protest and installed Benazir as Prime Minister. Her regime brought no relief to the people; her husband Asif Zardari indulged in such large-scale corruption that Benazir was ousted. She returned to power after a short interval winning the election once more. But again she was thrown out in a palace coup engineered by her own hand-picked President, Farooq Leghari. It was alleged that she and Zardari had amassed large private fortunes estimated at one billion US dollars. In the election that followed, the Muslim League won a two-third majority in the National Assembly; its leader Nawaz Sharif formed the government. He ruled like an autocrat spending billions of dollars on a nuclear programme. Like Benazir, Sharif and his family also enriched themselves by corrupt practices and lived lavishly. He also interfered with the top generals with the result that the army staged a coup and its Commander-in-Chief General Parvez Musharraf took over as Chief Executive. He put Sharif behind bars on a murder charge; Sharif was sentenced to imprisonment for life by the court in the latter half of 2000; the Saudis then intervened and helped strike a deal between Sharif and Musharraf whereby the former Prime Minister and his family were pardoned and sent to Saudi Arabia where they now live in exile. Meanwhile his party started disintegrating.

Tariq Ali describes how Nawaz Sharif was overthrown by Musharraf: "Nawaz Sharif, his brother, Shahbaz and their father, Muhammad, strong believers in globalisation and neo-liberal economics, helped create an enterprise culture in which they genuinely believed that everything was for sale, including politicians, civil servants and, yes, generals. There were widespread rumours that, in order to buy time and make yet more money, the Sharif family had provided sackfuls of general-friendly dollars to bolster their support in the army. A section of the army high command was enraged by this civilian interference. The immediate cause of the latest coup was Sharif's decision to sack the army chief, General Musharraf, while he was on an official visit to Sri Lanka, and appoint the head of Inter Services Intelligence (ISI), General Ziauddin, in his place. Just as Pakistan TV was showing Sharif appointing and congratulating the new army chief, the former chief pulled the plug out and the country's TV screens went blank. Ziauddin, as the ISI boss, was the main supplier of the Taliban army in Afghanistan. He was sympathetic to the fundamentalist cause and loathed by officers who value the secular side of the army and enjoy drinking whisky to the tune of bagpipes at regimental dinners."[5]

However the changes in government, whether these came about as a result of an army takeover or popular elections made no difference to the administrative set-up. It has been described aptly by the distinguished Pakistani journalist B.S. Jafri in *Dawn* thus: "Whoever is under the impression that what has followed the drop-scene on the Zia dictatorship has been the restoration or revival of the political culture in Pakistan is either of feeble mind or just pretending to be clever. Put in front of the mind's eye all those characters that have been the government in post-Zia Pakistan. Is any of these protagonists an honourable person?" Jafri has graphically described what the civilian leaders from Benazir Bhutto to Nawaz Sharif gave to the people of Pakistan, to whom Jinnah had assured social justice, political fair play and economic reforms. He writes: "What we have today around us is a caboodle known for bank loan defaults, massive tax evasion, pilferage of power, theft of irrigation canal water, running slave camps, patronising highwaymen, dacoits, drug traffickers, smugglers, killing their women in the name of honour, building palaces and pleasure hideouts, buying jewellery worth millions of dollars, riding the most expensive sports cars, acquiring palatial estates in foreign countries, transferring millions of dollars to foreign banks, taking hefty cuts on government contracts, playing polo on imported ponies, absconding from their country to escape the nemesis. It is an endless list of gross misdemeanour and felony."[6] Ayaz Amir endorses the analysis: "Is there anything to choose between the jokers of the Muslim League and the PPP? The common factor between both parties is gangsterism and corruption. Shahbaz Sharif resembled nothing so much as a Mafioso don. What does Asif Zardari look like? In any Godfather sequel he can easily get a part."[7]

General Musharraf has shown no particular inclination to transform Pakistan into either a proper secular or a real Islamic state. Like his predecessors all he has done is to concentrate power in his hands. The abrupt manner in which on the eve of his visit to India, he installed himself as the President by removing the incumbent Rafiq Tarar, shocked the world; America officially denounced the move, but Musharraf was unmindful of all criticism. He came to Delhi in July 2001 on the invitation of Prime Minister Vajpayee, and conducted himself as the master of all that he surveyed. He dominated the summit at Agra, thanks to the media, but it was all show and no substance. He harped on Kashmir knowing very well that Vajpayee could not gift him the valley; that was the hidden meaning behind his insistence on the solution of the so-called "core issue". Instead of cementing the bond of friendship between India and Pakistan, he further disrupted it.

Likewise he has deluded the people of Pakistan by only paying lip service to Islam; like Ayub he has no interest in Islamising the polity. In fact when he took over the reins of office as Chief Executive he declared that instead of following the ulama he would rather follow the Turkish revolutionary leader Kemal Ataturk. The declaration infuriated the ulama; the chief of the Jamaat-i-Islami Qazi Hussain Ahmad warned him while addressing a public meeting in Peshawar: "How can Ataturk, who destroyed the Islamic ideology be the ideal of a Pakistani ruler? Those who are giving such senseless statements to make God angry and America happy should learn a lesson from Nawaz Sharif."[8]

All in all, in fifty years and more, Islam has been surreptitiously sidetracked in the affairs of state — even Zia played around with the Shariah but did not change the basic Anglo-Saxon structure of the state. All along the politicians, the bureaucrats and the army commanders who ran the government enjoyed the fruits of power while the people were kept under tight control in the name of fake secularism on the one hand and fostering fanaticism on the other. Ninety per cent of Pakistan's population is Sunni and the rest is Shia. Sunnis are broadly divided into Deobandis who are orthodox and aligned to Saudi Arabia, and Barelvis who are believers in synthetic Islam and revere saints and sufis. There is no love lost between the two. Deobandis regard Barelvis as heretics and vice versa. Both condemn Shias as traitors to Islam and attack their mosques, they have killed many of their members while at prayer. Shias of late have retaliated in a similar manner; they are backed by Shiite Iran. Hundreds have died in the clashes between Sunnis and Shias.

To continue this senseless confrontation both sections have organised themselves, arming their followers with guns, arms and ammunition. Sunnis have set up a network of madrasas throughout Pakistan where aggressive training is given to young pupils who are motivated for jihad. Since board and lodging are provided free, children of poor families are attracted to these madrasas. Apart from orthodox religious indoctrination, the entrants are trained in the use of sophisticated hand weapons and firearms and in the planting of bombs; the ISI provides the teachers and the equipment and their officers give vigorous military training for terrorist action and motivate the trainees to even sacrifice their lives in the cause of jihad which has been launched to turn Afghanistan into a worn-out, stern theocracy and to free Kashmir from the occupation of kafirs and bring it within the orbit of militant Islam.

According to very recent statistics, there are 2,500 such madrasas in different parts of Pakistan and they produce 2,25,000 fighters annually, ready to kill and die for Islam, either in religious conflicts within Pakistan or in the wars in Afghanistan or for subversive activities in Kashmir. The ideological indoctrination is provided by the Jamia Dawat-ul-Islam, established in 1989. It rejects democracy as an evil imported by the west and trains students militarily for suicide missions, though they term it *shahadat* or martyrdom, as suicide is prohibited in Islam. The students are called *fidayoon* or devotees ready to sacrifice their lives for Islam. Many get killed but there is no dearth of new recruits. They come mostly from Punjab, the Frontier and even Sind. They are instructed to infiltrate into the enemy camps and if killed are told that their place in paradise is assured. These young men are not only from the madrasas but also from the other educational institutions. Their mentors continue to be the two retired lieutenant-generals, Hamid Gul and Javed Nasir — they were the original evil geniuses who introduced the cult of terrorism in Pakistan through the ISI.

One of the most virulent groups, inspired by the teachings of the Jamia, is Lakshari-e-Toiba (Soldiers of

Madina); it is organised and trained by the ISI. They have branches in the UK and USA which function to recruit Muslim youth to solicit funds in the name of jihad against the enemies of Islam. The Lakshar has a membership of 50,000 militants and is mostly engaged in terrorist activities in Kashmir; they are fully backed by the ISI and trained and equipped by its personnel. Though it has foreign members, the bulk comes from the local Pakistanis, aided by Kashmiris. Its associate Jaish-i-Mohammed is headed by Maulana Masood Azhar whom the Government of India released in the wake of the hijacking of Indian Airlines flight IC 814. It is managed by three hundred Afghan commandos. Its activities are complemented by Al-Umar Mujahideen which is led by Mushtaq Zardar who was also freed by the Government of India along with Azhar. Harkatul Mujahideen, which was originally named Harkatul Ansar, is also the creation of the ISI; it was mostly engaged in aiding Talibans in Afghanistan. It is funded by the Saudi billionaire Osama bin Laden who has a considerable following in Pakistan. He donates substantial funds to most of the madrasas in Pakistan. It is said that if the Musharraf regime nabs him and hands him over to America, as demanded by the latter, it may lead to bloody confrontation. One of the leading religious leaders of Pakistan Maulana Fazlur Rehman has already warned Musharraf that he and his people "will kill all American and European citizens in the country if the government tried to capture Bin Laden."[9] Then there is the Hizbul Mujahideen, led by the thickly-bearded Salahuddin. It is the largest militant outfit and manages to get considerable local following. It is unashamedly pro-Pakistan and functions at the behest of the authorities.

What these terrorists calling themselves mujahids and exploiting Islam are doing is patently un-Islamic; such murderous activities were condemned by Maulana Maududi in very strong terms since they violate the Quranic injunction which equates murder without a just cause with murder of the entire human race. The innocent men, women and children who are targeted and killed by the mujahids have done nothing wrong. In the history of Islam there is only one instance of the perpetration of such heinous crimes by a sect of Shias known as Nazaris, an offshoot of Ismailis. Their criminal actions covered the period from 1090 to 1256; they were called Assassins. Their leader was the notorious Hasan al-Sabbah. They infiltrated the ranks of their adversaries often in the guise of dervishes and religious teachers and then surreptitiously killed their benefactors. Their weapon was the knife; they would first kill their victim and then kill themselves. They mostly targeted leaders; for instance they murdered the famous Saljuq Vizier Nizam al-Mulk as well as his brother and son whom they regarded as enemies of Islam. They also fatally attacked the two Abbasid Caliphs and hundreds, if not thousands of others. In Syria, they put to death several of the Crusaders and also Conrad of Montferrat, King of Jerusalem. Saladin, hero of the Crusades, narrowly escaped death at their hands. The Assassins were indoctrinated by the use of hashish and other drugs; they caused much political destabilisation by organising a series of murders of important persons. They lived in castles in northern Persia and Syria that were almost impregnable to siege. Many of their enemies thus sought compromise with them to avoid a fatal dagger stroke; they so terrorised people that they agreed to either flee or surrender. Al-Ghazali, the eminent philosopher and theologian, wrote polemics against them and warned the Muslims that if they did not confront and finish the Assassins, they would bring disgrace to Islam. Likewise Fakhr ad-Din Razi also denounced them; but they silenced him by gifting him a bag of gold. The

Assassins were eventually trounced by the Mongols under Halaku and Ghengiz Khan whose battalions hounded them out and destroyed every trace of their existence.

It is strange that the same phenomenon in a more murderous form has now appeared in the Muslim world; their perpetrators call themselves mujahids and proclaim jihad against whomsoever they find convenient to do away with. They have twisted and distorted the whole concept of jihad as propounded in the Quran. There is a vast literature on this subject and tomes have been written as to who and when a Muslim is required to resort to jihad. The word itself makes no reference to warring; it means "to strive, or exert oneself". Classical jurists have classified many forms of jihad; but broadly it has been divided into two. One, al-jihadul akbar, "the greater jihad" which means exerting oneself against temptations and evil: two, al-jihadul asghar or "lesser jihad" which means fighting in the path of God. The interpretation that the preachers of madrasas have given in recent times is at complete variance with the Quranic text. In fact when the Prophet was asked under what circumstances a Muslim has to undertake jihad, he replied: "Every prophet sent by God to a nation (umma) before me has had disciples and followers who followed his ways (Sunnah) and obeyed his commands. But after them came successors who preached what they did not practise and practised what they are not commanded. Whoever strives (jahada) against them with one's hand is a believer, whoever strives against them with one's tongue is a believer, whoever strives against them with one's heart is a believer."[10] In the present context those who strive against the band of misguided mujahids of today will be the true mujahids.

The Assassins in the past were no less misguided; but they operated differently. They targeted leaders; the present mujahids go after innocent civilians and soldiers. Their aim is to create an atmosphere of terror with a view to fulfil their misguided and nefarious mission. Though they have so far concentrated in countries abroad, their ultimate aim seems to be to take over Pakistan by spreading their tentacles over its people. They have become adept in misrepresenting Islamic tenets and traditions. They are not very different from the Talibans in Afghanistan. By whipping up religious emotions, these misguided mujahids are luring the simple, ordinary Muslims and making them believe that a new and better life awaits them. Under it the clerics will rule; strict rules of Shariah as misinterpreted by them would be enforced, civil liberties curtailed and women confined to homes. They are aided in the pursuit of their oppressive designs by the ISI.

Khaleel Ahmed, consulting editor of the well-known Pakistani weekly, *Friday Times*, has observed:"The Talibanisation of the state dates back to the days when Pakistan began handling the Afghan jihad against the Soviets. That the army was the first party affected by this process is proved by the reverse indoctrination experienced by the officers of the ISI. At least two former heads of the ISI, Gen. Hamid Gul and Gen. Javed Nasir, today stand at the head of the Islamic movement in Pakistan and enjoy leverage over governments by reason of their contacts with the militia on the one hand and the army on the other. Both favour an Islamic revolution which will wean Pakistan away from its perceived cultural and political alignment with the West in general and the US in particular. They represent also the intense anti-Indian orientation of the army and the common people."[11]

It was fondly hoped by some intellectuals in Pakistan that General Musharraf with his admiration for the Turkish reformist leader Kemal Ataturk would rein in the militants who were becoming a nuisance, striding about in towns and villages with their Kalashnikovs and AK-47s, imposing on the people discarded customs and traditions in the name of Islam and depriving the young as well as the old of the freedom to enjoy life; but as Irfan Husain writing in *Dawn* points out: "Initially, the fundamentalist groups were forced on the backfoot by the prospect of a hostile military command. But all too soon, the Chief Executive distanced himself from any Kemalist notions he may have entertained in the face of a strident attack from the Jamaat chief, Qazi Hussain Ahmad. The final surrender to the force of darkness came when General Musharraf retracted his pledge to make the much-criticised blasphemy law less draconian. Having seen and demonstrated that the army is a paper tiger, the bigots are bent on implementing their agenda to drag us back to the dark ages. Knowing full well that they stand no chance in winning an election (as proved yet again in the recent partial local body polls), they are confident that they can press ahead with the army's tacit support."[12]

Apart from the civil disturbances and terrorist activities that these mujahids, aided by the ISI, cause in Kashmir, they are also becoming increasingly active in Bangladesh. They have a two-pronged objective to harass India: one to supply arms and ammunition to the insurgents in the north-eastern regions of India, and two to spread their wings within Bangladesh and train its youth to terrorise and destabilise its polity. To achieve this objective they whip up religious frenzy, especially against the Awami League which has been struggling to establish friendly relations with India. They propagate the same obnoxious Two-Nation theory and stress that Bangladesh, with its overwhelming Muslim population, should refrain from getting close to the idolatrous Hindu India which they tell them, will swallow their country and exterminate the Muslims. They no doubt face a formidable task. The soil of Bangladesh for such fanaticism is not fertile; its people have had long fraternal relations with the Hindus; the Pakistani atrocities during their freedom struggle are still fresh in their minds. But Islam can be exploited by these mujahids; its hold on the innocent, God-fearing Muslims can override all other factors. Vigilance is therefore needed to defeat their evil designs. Unfortunately the mujahids have found many supporters among the leaders and party workers of the former Prime Minister, Begum Khalida Zia who constantly raises the anti-India bogey to oust Hasina Wajed and her Awami League from power.

Moreover, these mujahids have managed, with the support of the ISI, to infiltrate the network of madrasas where the young Bangladeshis are taught to live and die for their religion and to rid their land of every link with India. They are striving to Islamise Bangladesh and make it the vehicle of hate against the neighbouring Hindus. They receive political support from Khalida Zia's Bangla Nationalist Party (BNP); they also get financial assistance from some large commercial houses like the Beximo Group which is closely associated among others with Syed Iskander who is the brother of Khalida Zia. Several other pro-Pakistan establishments like Habib Bank and Ibnesina and religious organisations like the Jamaat-i-Islami and Jamaat-i-Tulba provide them substantial help in one form or the other.

Unfortunately the economy of Bangladesh, hard hit by the partition has not recovered; it remains in a shambles. It has been sustained by either imports or smuggling of goods from West Bengal which is certainly not good for it. This has given a handle to the pro-Pakistan mujahids to insinuate, as

Nasim Haider has done by stating in *Impact International* that pro-India "quislings" were active in propagating that "the best choice for Bangladesh is to abandon its pretence of independence and join the Indian Union as a province." Such mischievous tactics can prove explosive; but the progressive forces, spearheaded by the Awami League, are alert. They have successfully thwarted these attempts. The mujahideen may nevertheless embark on terrorist activities to destabilise public life in Bangladesh. They are waiting for the right moment to strike. The notorious gangster Abdul Kazim alias Tunda who hails from Chittagong has already sent the red signal awaiting popular response. The recent mutilation and killing of BSF jawans on the Indo-Bangladesh border was obviously the result of a sinister plot hatched by the pro-Pakistan Lt. General Fazlur Rehman, the Director-General of Bangladesh Rifles who has no love lost for the Awami League of Shaikh Hasina Wajed. He and the likes of him in the police and the army will welcome the ouster of secular elements from the establishment in the forthcoming election. Bangladesh is however strongly committed to communal harmony and cannot be led astray even by the mujahids who are aided and abetted by ISI personnel and anti-India agents. Nevertheless India needs to do some introspection; demanding eternal gratitude for its role in the liberation of Bangladesh can sometimes be irritating. More concrete measures are required to cement the ties of friendship. Mahfuz Anam, editor of *The Daily Star,* Dhaka, has rightly observed: "...for India there are only two neighbours — Pakistan and China, the rest of us are mere geographic entities deserving very little attention and understanding."[13] He complained that neither the Government of India nor the Indian media has any time for Bangladesh which can be the most effective counter to Pakistan.

NINETEEN

Victims of Partition

O f the Muslims in undivided India, three segments have been hit the hardest by partition; they are (1) the Muslims who remained in India and now number almost 140 million; (2) the Mohajirs who migrated mainly from East Punjab and the Hindu-majority provinces of India; and (3) the Biharis, comprising Muslim immigrants from Bihar and parts of UP and Rajasthan who went to East Bengal after partition and because of their alignment with the Pakistan forces during the war of liberation in 1971, are now unwanted in Bangladesh; ever since, they have been subjected to harassment and ill-treatment at the hands of Bangladeshis. Each one of the three segments has a separate identity, historical background and emotional attachment but all of them, numbering over 300 million, have been the victims of the aftermath of partition.

Let us first deal with the Indian Muslims; their story is heart-rending. I have detailed their plight in my book *The Widening Divide*, published by Penguin India. Suffice to say that in their religious frenzy and the fear of Hindu domination indoctrinated in them by Jinnah, they became blind to the possible consequences of partition. The Muslims of Bombay, UP and Bihar were the first to respond to the call of Jinnah for partition and enthusiastically supported the movement for Pakistan. They became its vanguard. They were so fanatically charged by Jinnah's slogan of "Islam in danger" and frightened by the bogey of Hindu domination, constantly raised by him that they were easily misled. They failed to ask themselves: How could the creation of a state in the faraway North-West — consisting of half of Punjab, Sind, the Frontier and Baluchistan and still further in the North-East — consisting of half of Bengal and a part of Assam — provide any security to the rest of the Muslims living in Hindu-dominated regions and spread over cities, towns and villages? No sooner did this realisation dawn on them than they asked Jinnah on the eve of the formation of Pakistan: "What is to happen to us who are being left behind?" He assured them that if any harm came to them, Pakistan would retaliate against the Hindus under its control. But he could not have been serious about that for he must have known that after the hate campaign he had unleashed against the Hindus, few of them would have dared to stay on in his Pakistan. And they did not; they fled in the most excruciating circumstances — many died on the way, the rest reached India with nothing. The Hindus from East Bengal did not migrate to India because the Bengali Muslims had behaved better towards them; they had a stronger cultural affinity with the Bengali Hindus. Later on the agitation for the status of the Bengali language, which had been the common heritage of both Muslims and Hindus, and its secular character under the leadership of Shaikh Mujibur Rehman and Maulana Bhashani reassured the Hindus of their safety and security. It was the bond of inter-communal harmony and not Jinnah's so-called doctrine of hostages which prevented the large-scale migration of Hindus from East Pakistan.

The condition of Indian Muslims was no better; though the number of those who migrated to Pakistan was not as great, their plight was equally miserable. In fact those who remained in India suffered terrible hardships. The Mahatma had to undertake "fasts unto death" to protect them. However as the years rolled on there was a perceptible change in the attitude of both the Hindus and the authorities. This was mainly because of the impact of the teachings of Gandhi and his emphasis on broad humanism as embodied in India's national heritage and the categorical stand taken by Nehru to protect and preserve the secular character of the new state. Indian Muslims nevertheless could not escape the fallout of Jinnah's Two-Nation theory and the resultant partition. It took considerable time for them to gain some kind of acceptability among the Hindus. The influx of Hindu refugees from West Pakistan had stirred the deepest sentiments of their co-religionists; this in turn caused great resentment, pain and anger among the local Hindus and these got so embedded in their psyche that to this day they harbour distrust and ill-feeling against Muslims.

On the formation of Pakistan, many Muslims in their enthusiasm visited the newborn state; when they returned they found they had lost their nationality and in consequence forfeited all their assets under the newly enacted Evacuee Property Law. On the other side the door on their entry was shut by the government of Pakistan which banned all further migration. An Urdu verse aptly describes their ambivalence:

Na Khuda hee mila, na visaal-e-Sanam
Na idhar kay rahey, na udhar kay rahey
They met neither Allah, nor the idol
They could remain — neither here nor there

For a long time after partition, Indian Muslims had to go through this agony which they had brought upon themselves. It darkened their future. Azad had repeatedly warned them that Jinnah and the League were taking them on a suicidal path; but they did not heed the advice. Later, they came to him with their tales of woe. He told them: "The Partition of India was a fundamental mistake. The manner in which religious differences were incited, inevitably, led to the devastation that we have seen with our own eyes....There is no use recounting the events of the past seven years, nor will it serve any good. Yet, it must be stated that the debacle of Indian Muslims is the result of the colossal blunders committed by the Muslim League's misguided leadership."[1]

Nehru tried his best to protect the legitimate rights and interests of the Indian Muslims; they were also guaranteed equality of treatment by the Constitution, but the whole atmosphere had become vitiated; they encountered hostility everywhere; with no work, life became miserable. Opportunities were deliberately denied. This was indeed the most trying time for them. To add to their misery, Pakistan started aggressive action against India to annex Kashmir; this intensified the prevailing illwill among Hindus against Indian Muslims. The result was that they were discriminated against in every sector; they could neither find employment nor get the necessary wherewithal for business or industry. Apart from Hindu politicians, civil servants too had developed prejudices against them. The doors of the private and the public sector were closed to them. They were denied the grant of licences, quotas and permits by the Government, whether state or Union. The younger generation which had nothing to do with the movement for Pakistan had to mainly bear the brunt of the hardship and deprivation. Most of them could not even go to schools or colleges because their parents were unable to afford to educate them. I have translated into the English an Urdu poem which reflected the prevalent mood among the Muslims:

> I am a Muslim, I cannot help my tears;
> I have gone through thirty long years,
> Suffering pangs of hunger, day after day
> And unbearable humiliation all the way.
> I faced riots, bullets, sword and dagger,
> They burnt my home, mother and sister;
> When I complained, they put me in a cell.
> There are no jobs, life is one big hell.
> Under the benign sky of my beloved land,
> I am reduced to starve with outstretched hand.
> Weary and worn out, I search for solace,
> I wander crestfallen from place to place,
> I have no home, so no ration card
> And thus no vote, no identity card;
> With nothing to offer, I cannot marry
> I have remained a bachelor, desolate and solitary;
> If only my father had had the foresight
> To remain a bachelor too, to save me this plight.

Things, however, gradually changed; the wounds began to heal; the hatred lessened with the passage of time. Secular Hindus became more sympathetic; Muslims also became more confident and self-reliant. On the assumption of office by Indira Gandhi as Prime Minister some concrete steps were taken to ameliorate their condition; unfortunately the Muslim leadership was not of much help; instead of concentrating on the real issues of education and employment, it whipped up religious frenzy on petty issues and widened the divide between Hindus and Muslims. It seemed unconcerned that in every field Muslims had reached a nadir; whether it was education from primary to post-graduate level or professional courses, or business or industry. The Muslims had also lost politically; their representation came down everywhere; it slipped in every sector — from local bodies to provincial legislatures and in the two Houses of Parliament as well. The fall was continuous and steady. Political parties issued manifestos to better their lot in order to get their votes, but in practice no one really cared.

The decline of the Muslims was such that their uplift became a Herculean task. However, out of adversity, a new awakening started to stir them. They were so jolted out of their slumber and despondency that they began to exert themselves. They realised that crumbs and crutches would take them nowhere; they had to stand on their own feet and learn to develop their own inner strength; to prosper they had to compete and win. The Muslim youth, in particular, has now taken to hard work, equipping themselves with new skills; consequently many of them have been able to win laurels. This change in the outlook of the new generation, which has unfortunately gone unnoticed by the media, augurs well for their future. There is no talk any more of their appeasement; those who propagated it are now adopting a truly realistic approach and are indeed keen to help the Muslims attain self-reliance.

The condition of Mohajirs in Pakistan has grown from bad to worse; in the initial stage of migration they had a fairly acceptable status. Most of them managed to get the assets of the Hindus who had left for India allotted to them; many of these Muslim migrants were absorbed in various departments of the Pakistan government; several others were employed in banks and businesses and new industries. They bettered their prospects as months passed; most of them took up residence in Karachi which was then the capital of Pakistan;others settled in Hyderabad (Sind). All those coming from East Punjab went to Lahore and a few settled in Peshawar. They number around 30 million; of these 22 million, mainly Urdu-speaking, hailed mainly from UP, Bihar, Rajasthan, the erstwhile Nizam's dominion of Hyderabad and Delhi; they now live in the province of Sind; initially they lived a miserable existence in ghettoes since they were not easily accepted by the local Sindhis. That did not bother the Mohajirs then for they were aligned with the administration. The Urdu-speaking officers who had opted for Pakistan were sympathetic to them. They naturally looked after the Mohajirs who were mostly their kith and kin. Moreover, the first Prime Minister Liaquat Ali Khan was from UP, his mother tongue was Urdu; only in the army was there a preponderance of Punjabis and Pathans. The Mohajirs nevertheless controlled the bureaucracy until Ayub Khan imposed his rule. He was a son of the soil, a proud Pathan who systematically purged the Mohajirs from the bureaucratic set-up and filled their places with Punjabi and Frontier officers. From then on, the troubles of Mohajirs began; they were isolated and kept out of profitable jobs and influential positions.

The Mohajirs who had settled in Sind were gradually ousted from lucrative jobs; they were replaced by the local Sindhi officers and the Punjabi civil servants. They therefore had to organise themselves under the banner of their newly formed Muttahida Quami Movement (MQM) to safeguard their rights and interests. Soon they became a political force, winning a sizeable number of seats both in the Sind Provincial Assembly and the Pakistan National Assembly. Their rising clout was not liked by the Punjabi ruling elite; they embarked on the worst atrocities against them even subjecting them to physical torture; many of their activists were killed. Their undisputed leader, Altaf Hussain Qureshi escaped several assassination attempts and had to flee to London where he has been in exile for many years now. This has forced him to publicly declare that partition had been "the biggest blunder in the history of mankind".[2] According to one of the leading members of the MQM, Syed Ahmed Tariq Mir, "Some 20,000 Rangers, a huge force of police, Frontier constabulary and over 3,000 plainclothes intelligence men have been deployed in Karachi to suppress the Mohajirs."[3] He cited many cases of brutalities and rape by the anti-Mohajir elements, financed by vested interests. The MQM delegation visiting London recently showed videotapes of how the Pakistan government sent armed personnel to Karachi who mercilessly beat Mohajirs and mutilated their bodies. They pointed out that more than 15,000 MQM activists and supporters had been killed and many had been sent to unknown places. More than 2,000 Mohajirs, including prominent members of the provincial and national assemblies, had been incarcerated and subjected to rigorous hardship.

The woes of Mohajirs have multiplied with every successive government; they are being looked upon as a nuisance and attempts have been made to paralyse them everywhere. Borders have been sealed so that there is no influx of their relations and friends from India. According to Mir: "They ordered the closure of borders to prevent more of us coming from India so that we do not become numerically bigger." He said. "Israel's borders have not been closed since the state was formed in 1948. Jews from all over the world can go there and live as rightful citizens. Pakistan is unwilling to accept even 2,50,000 of its nationals stranded in Bangladesh and they continue to live in appalling conditions in Red Cross camps near Dhaka, even though many still fly Pakistani flags on top of their tents."[4] As real power is vested in the army, dominated by the Punjabis, Mohajirs are invariably suppressed. They are treated as aliens and given no consideration. That is why Mir has frankly told the Indian Muslims that, as compared to the plight of Mohajirs in Pakistan, they are in a much better position because India's democratic set-up provides them enough scope for development. He added: "They have a lesson to learn from our plight. They should not think the other side (meaning ours) is greener. They should know what is happening to their brothers and sisters in Pakistan. They are better off in India than we in Pakistan."[5] Benazir Bhutto first entered into a pact with the MQM but later betrayed them. They then aligned themselves with Nawaz Sharif and his Muslim League but they fared no better; on the contrary atrocities against them increased. Hence the Mohajirs lost all hope of getting justice or fairplay from the rulers of Pakistan — whether civilian or soldiers. They have been compelled to rise and revolt against the establishment.

Altaf Husain, who now operates from London, has attracted considerable attention; he has become the focal point of all the opponents of the Punjabi-dominated ruling clique. They comprise the Sindhis, Baluchis and Pathans. At first the Pathans were suspicious of the Mohajirs but they have now joined them and are presenting a united front against the rulers. On the eve of the twenty-first century the dissident leaders from Sind, the Frontier and Baluchistan met in London at Acton Town Hall and decided to launch along with the Mohajirs the "Pakistan Oppressed Nations' Movement". Their leaders repudiated the notion propounded by Jinnah that Pakistan was a nation and pointed out that Sindhis, Pathans, Baluchis and Mohajirs each of them constituted a nation with their different characteristics. They could not be lumped together and made to live under the domination of the Punjabis. They demanded *azadi*; in the words of the fiery leader of the Pathans, Sardar Ataullah Mengal, "we are one kind of people, our rulers are another kind."

Mahmood Khan Achakzai who heads the largest political party in the Frontier — Pashtoon Awami Party — was more bitter. He declared: "Pakistan is heading towards destruction because of its colonial ways. It just cannot go on like this. We Pathans did not surrender to the British; we certainly will not surrender to the ISI. No one can make slaves of us."[6] Similar sentiments were expressed by Syed Imdad Shah, the son of the legendary G.M.Sayed: "Sindhis will never accept Islamisation of our province. We have always been a secular people and we want a secular state."[7]

Altaf Hussain repeated in his presidential address that division of India had ruined every one of them; what was created turned out to be "the Titanic of the Islamic ummah". He explained, "The Titanic didn't sink suddenly. It sank slowly. It shot off distress flames. But nobody came. But our plight isn't a film, it's a fact." Their flames of revolt, he said, would engulf Pakistan; if it wanted to save itself it could only be through a change in its attitude towards the non-Punjabis: "They didn't hear the truth in '71, and Pakistan broke. If they treat us like slaves, a time will come when we'll get independence and they will be without slaves."[8] And like the Titanic they too will sink.

The meeting adopted a resolution which described Pakistan as a "multinational entity" and said that "the majority of the Muslim population of Pakistan divorced itself from Jinnah's Pakistan, created by the Muslims of the subcontinent; thereby the very premise of the existence of the remaining part of Pakistan was lost in '71." The resolution characterised the three evils of Pakistan as the army, bureaucracy and the intelligence agencies "all hailing from Punjab who were responsible for the dismemberment of the country in 1971. They have invaded the Balochs, the Pashtoons, the Sindhis and finally they have assaulted the descendants of the creators of Pakistan, that is, the Mohajirs."[9] The resolution further stated that Pakistan's smaller nations "have come to the conclusion that in the existing set-up they can't attain their fundamental rights."[10] They had to protect their ideology and so declared that they would not rest until they had freed themselves from the iron clutches of the Punjabis who had monopolised public life and deprived all others from obtaining any place in the power structure of Pakistan.

Altaf Hussain also disclosed that he had so far avoided appealing to Indian Muslims to help them lest he and his Mohajirs were accused by the Pakistan ruling clique as "traitors"; but as the Muslims in India were their own kith and kin they had to apprise them of the torture and persecution their brethren were subjected to in Pakistan. That was the reason their leader sent a delegation on behalf of the MQM headed by Khalid Maqbool Siddiqui — who had resigned as Minister of Industries in the Nawaz Sharif government — in protest against the harassment of the Mohajirs by the police and the army. Siddiqui met several important leaders in India, informing them of the plight of the Mohajirs in Pakistan. In an exclusive interview to *The Times of India*, he explained why Mohajirs had risen against the establishment. He had been instructed by his leader Altaf Hussain to make it clear to all concerned in India that their experience had brought them to the conclusion that "partition was the biggest mistake in history".[11] Siddiqui elaborated: "It was not a casual remark: It is a reflection of many years of experience, study and pain experienced by Altaf Hussain and many of his compatriots. He was referring to the root cause when he made this remark. It was to emphasise the magnitude of the suffering people have undergone in terms of life and property, both in India and Pakistan. In Pakistan, the effects of the division are visible even today after 53 years. You can say the MQM has decided to step up its campaign. We brought together acknowledged leaders of the Balochs, the Pathans and the Sindhis. These national minorities realise the need to come together. It is history in the making. It is a sincere effort, let me assure you. We have a joint platform. It is too early to say how we will work from here on. But it is the first step towards a joint struggle."[12]

Siddiqui was asked why they had described minorities in Pakistan as nationalities. He explained: "They are actually sub-nationalities, distinct from one another. The point we underscore is that they have common problems and they have a common adversary: the majority Punjab province and the dominant Punjabis are all-pervasive as a political class and in civil and military bureaucracy. When we criticise the Punjabi it is not so much people of that province but the ruling class which has exploited the minorities. You will be shocked to know that from provincial chief ministers onwards, even the police SHOs are selected by their principal instrument, the ISI."[13]

In the context of the change in the outlook of Mohajirs, who were in the vanguard of the Pakistan movement in undivided India, Siddiqui was asked how the younger generation of Mohajirs now look at India. He pointed out: "There is a sea-change with the change of generations and with the advent of technology and media. Our elders saw

Pakistan as a mission and worked for its success. But the young do not have that mission. They have an identity crisis. A young Mohajir sees that five decades of separation has harmed both India and Pakistan — Pakistan more so. You have become the world's largest democracy, but we have missed the bus. You have sustained your plurality, while we have witnessed repression."[14]

Siddiqui was asked: Why did he and his delegation come to India? What did he expect from this country? He clarified: "Our expectations are from both India and Indians. They should take a proactive role to help us restructure our polity. Altafbhai will soon address Indians, the Indian Muslims in particular — even more particularly, Jammu and Kashmir Muslims, especially a section that wants to be merged with Pakistan. Draw a lesson from us, he would tell them: Do you want liberation or death? Do you want to become a colony of Pakistan? Siddiqui said if India did not help them, the whole region would be destabilised and Talibanised." He explained, "After 53 years, Pakistan is being ruled by 46 families. A population of 130 million is being held hostage. We want India's help because it is no use treating the symptoms alone without tackling the root cause."[15]

The most pitiable plight has been of the immigrants who on the formation of Pakistan went to East Pakistan or Bangladesh. They came from the neighbouring Hindu-majority provinces of Rajasthan, Madhya Pradesh and Bihar, mostly from Bihar. The nearness of the distance attracted them. These Urdu-speaking people were inspired by Islamic sentiments. For twenty-five years the establishment, dominated by persons from West Pakistan, looked upon them with favour; they were more liked than the native Bengalis who differ in many respects, especially socially and culturally from the Urdu

speaking non-Bengalis who were contemptuously referred to
as Biharis. They also lived as aliens and behaved towards the
Bengalis with contempt and did not mix freely with them. Firoz
Khan Noon, the then Governor of East Pakistan, once
described them as "half Muslims", as he found them more at
home with the Hindu Bengalis. Maulana Bhashani, the
firebrand leader of the rebellious Bengalis, retorted: "Should
we bare our dhotis to prove to him that we are Muslims?"

Against this background there was the massive anti-
West Pakistan upsurge at the end of 1971, primarily on the
question of language; it transformed eventually into a
movement for independence under Shaikh Mujibur Rehman.
The Bihari migrants opposed it and actively supported the West
Pakistanis in their oppressive measures against the agitated
Bengalis. When the army cracked down on the Mukti Bahinis,
these Biharis acted as spies and fifth columnists. They began
to be despised and hated by the local Bengalis. Hence when
the Punjabi-dominated army was defeated and Bangladesh
came into existence as an independent country, they were the
first target of the Mukti Bahini and the Bengali freedom
fighters. It was indeed shocking that Muslims of both the wings
of Pakistan who had boasted of an Islamic brotherhood, and
on that basis had sworn their solidarity in demanding a separate
Muslim homeland, indulged in the worst kind of genocide
against one another.

Anthony Mascarenhas, special correspondent of
London's *Sunday Times* was witness to the inhuman atrocities
committed by the Pakistani army against the rebellious
Bengalis. He has described how "hundreds of professors,
doctors and teachers — the cream of the intellectual set —
have vanished overnight after being taken to military centres
'for questioning'. So has the flower of Bengali youth been

scoured away by the dreadful 'cleansing process' undertaken by the army — several hundred unsuspecting Bengalis were shot off for 'violating curfew' although curfew had not been publicly announced... I heard the otherwise honourable men, all good chaps, joking about the day's kill and with a friendly rivalry keeping track on the top score... the Nazi style pogroms were intended, in the context of the present Pakistani regime, as a military answer to what was essentially a political regime of its own making...the obliteration of Bengali language and culture."[16]

After the advent of Bangladesh and the ouster of the Punjab-dominated bureaucracy and armed personnel, the Bengali freedom fighters went amuck and took their vengeance on the Biharis, who had aided and abetted the former. The two authors Matiur Rehman and Naeem Hasan in their book *Iron Bars of Freedom* have poignantly described how "within hours of surrender of Dacca to the Indian army, the Mukti Bahini unleashed a war of retribution throughout the country. The planned cold-blooded killings that followed and which resulted in the loss of thousands of lives... the victims were unarmed civilians, Biharis and the vanquished para-military personnel... thousands were 'lynched, flogged, flayed, mutilated, cleaved and butchered' simply because they had chosen to stay loyal to their erstwhile state — Pakistan. The aftermath had been terrible... Those non-Bengalis who survived the holocaust were turned into aliens, deprived of their belongings, possessions, jobs and safety." Abul Fazal, Vice-Chancellor of Chittagong University and a noted Bangladeshi scholar cried out, "They [the Biharis] are utterly helpless and dispossessed. Most of them are women and children. They have no means of livelihood, no occupations, or anything to cling to. They cannot envisage a future. This is a queer but pathetic problem. Theirs is a human problem. When some of them are found in bad health, wearing tattered garments, hungry and helpless, begging alms with tearful eyes in streets and market place, this morbid scene appears to me as a great insult to humanity..."[17]

So it has been for the last thirty years. These Biharis are an unwanted and harassed lot in Bangladesh; they are eager to go to Pakistan. They have begged of its authorities to rescue them and give them shelter in any small corner of Pakistan. Some governments had expressed sympathy with their plight but no one did anything to alleviate their suffering despite the offers of financial assistance from Saudi Arabia and several other Muslim countries. No Pakistani ruler, civilian or military, whether Bhutto, Zia, Benazir, Sharif or Musharraf came forward to rescue them; they continue to rot in places where they are detested. No religious or secular organisation in Pakistan has offered to rehabilitate them. None of them, whether devout Muslims of Sind, Punjab, the Frontier or Baluchistan have condescended to lend them a helping hand and provide them some kind of a home somewhere in Pakistan.

M.P. Bhandara, a former member of the National Assembly of Pakistan in a scathing attack on the attitude of Pakistan towards these forlorn and oppressed people, has pointed out in an article in *Dawn*, the newspaper founded by Jinnah, "The non-repatriation of Bihari Pakistanis by Pakistan since the creation of Bangladesh in 1971 is a negation of the so-called Two-Nation theory which was and is the ideological basis for Pakistan; it is also a silent but solemn rebuttal of our high-pitched claims of Islamisation. And at the level of common human decency a shame."[18] Bhandara ridicules the justification of the successive Pakistani governments for refusing to rehabilitate the hapless Biharis and observes, "However, notwithstanding the legal, ideological and humane credentials of these people to be recognised as our citizens, Pakistan refuses on specious, legalistic, hair-splitting grounds to accept them on the plea that they had migrated to East Pakistan, as if it was never a part of Pakistan. They, therefore, exist in a virtual no man's land in Bangladesh without flag, honour, passport or resources. Indeed, they are the true orphans of Pakistan's break-up."[19]

Bhandara is amazed at the hypocrisy of the Pakistani authorities, who under pressure from America, allowed millions of Afghans to seek refuge in Pakistan and continue to do so. Furthermore, what is surprising is that while they gave shelter to thousands of Bosnians and Kosovaras, they refuse to offer the same facilities to their own Biharis who had sacrificed their all for the attainment of Pakistan. As he puts it, "It is not only a case of double standards but a case of triple-decker values of convenience. Pakistan was conceived to be a homeland of Muslims of British India just as Israel was and is a homeland for Jews from the world over. But it might be said to the credit of Israel that it still keeps its doors open for any Jew wishing to enter the Jewish state from anywhere. Pakistan has shut the door for the Muslims of the subcontinent, including those claiming to be its own citizens."[20]

Bhandara, with the editorial endorsement of *Dawn,* concludes: "The Two-Nation theory falls if the premise of the homeland is no longer available. And its credentials as an Islamic state are dubious if Muslims of the subcontinent, persecuted on grounds of ethnicity or religion cannot enter."[21] Finally he rightly questions the claim of Pakistan for the accession of the territory of Jammu and Kashmir by pointing out its callous treatment of the Biharis. On a bitterly critical note he concludes, "On this analogy of a cynical concern for humans, our interest would appear to be more in the real estate of Kashmir and its geographical disposition than in the Kashmiris."[22]

Pakistan has, all along, concentrated on the dissidents in the Valley of Kashmir, describing them as freedom fighters; but has wisely kept away from inciting Indian Muslims who have stoutly opposed its ill-conceived design to annex Kashmir. They have defended the stand of India and refused to lend any support to the band of their co-religionists in Kashmir who have been struggling to free the state from its affiliation with India. These dissidents are aware that Indian Muslims will never provide them any help, moral or material, and on the contrary, foil every attempt to break Kashmir's ties with India. They will do everything in their power to preserve and protect the secular fabric of their country. In a poem in Urdu which I composed in the wake of Pakistan's aggression in 1965 I have tried to voice the unflinching determination of Indian Muslims on this issue; its English translation runs as follows:

I swear by the blood of Gandhi and by
our martyrs of freedom,
I swear by the honour of Nehru and by
the swear of our peasants and workers;
The sun's rays may turn cold and the oceans may go dry,
The stars in the sky may lose their shine
The monsoon clouds may shower no rains
And the chirping birds may sing no more.
All of that is possible, but not this —
No one can take away Jammu and Kashmir from us,
No one dare strike yet another blow to our unity.

TWENTY

The Historic Blunder

What did the Muslims of the subcontinent gain by the creation of Pakistan? It has been universally regarded as the most precious gift Jinnah gave them. He alone was undoubtedly its sole founder. Single-handedly he fought for it and the entire credit for its formation must go to him. But so should the blame, for the dreadful consequences that followed. An indepth analysis of Jinnah's upbringing, training and outlook — nay his personality as a whole — as has been brought out in this retrospect, establishes beyond doubt that he was never motivated in any of his actions all through his public life by love for Islam. Right from his childhood he had no involvement with his religion because the Aga Khani sect to which he and his family belonged had strong non-Islamic influence in its practices. Moreover Jinnah had never shown any religious inclination. God had never interested him. He took up the cause of the Muslims only because it helped him politically; unfortunately Indian politics could never rise above its communal moorings. At first he

aligned himself with the Hindus and worked incessantly for
Hindu-Muslim unity. That established him as the best link
between the two communities and gave him an added
advantage in pursuing his brand of politics. Later, with the
advent of Gandhi, the political environment changed and
Jinnah was sidelined as a result of his aversion to mass agitation;
he then concentrated all his energy in rebuilding his leadership
by associating with the anti-Gandhi forces. Being a successful
lawyer, he continued to be admired for his forensic abilities
and brilliant advocacy. And although the Congress had grown
averse to him it could also not completely ignore him.

Nevertheless in the latter part of his political career he
had indeed lost the clout that he earlier enjoyed; and that was
basically on several counts: The generality of the Muslims
felt alienated from him after he refused to support the Khilafat
movement. Besides he was out of place with leaders who
quoted the Quran and spoke in Urdu. He was ignorant of both.
His whole being revolted against the domination of politics
by the mullahs and the maulanas among the Muslims and the
Mahatma and the pundits among the Hindus. He told Gandhi
bluntly that his ways would bring nothing but ruin to the
country. He tried to resurrect his leadership by making the
League the instrument of his politics; but then the organisation
did not have the image nor the influence to enable him to do
so. Because of Gandhi's support to the Khilafat movement,
most of the politically-minded Muslims continued to be with
the Congress.

Though isolated, Jinnah did not give up his efforts to
unite the Hindus and the Muslims to obtain constitutional
reforms, safeguarding the interests of the Muslims. The worst
blow that he suffered was the rejection of his amendments to
the Nehru Report of 1928. Until then he had struggled

unfailingly to arrive at a consensus on Hindu-Muslim differences but now, under the changed circumstances, every move he made became suspect. At first he was distrusted by the Hindus but later even the Muslims doubted his motives. Besides other Muslim leaders like the Aga Khan and Sir Fazl-i-Husain had meanwhile also appeared on the scene at that time and they managed to oust him. Consequently he was so disheartened that he decided to give up politics and retire in London. There too, he made futile efforts to find new political pastures by trying to enter the House of Commons.

Jinnah however could not rest content for long; his burning desire was to be in the limelight and this drove him to regain his position. He went back to India with a new determination. From an avowed nationalist, he became an arch communalist. He took an aggressively anti-Hindu stand and concentrated all his energies on mobilising the Muslims. He made it his mission to unite the Muslims and activate the moribund League. He became a born-again Muslim hoping to rise on the convenient shoulders of communalism.

The task was not easy; he lacked the necessary cultural bearing to woo the Muslims. He had no emotional attachment to their sacred places nor to their customs, language and conventions. The nexus to connect with them was missing. He had no doubt fought for them in the past but he had done so by cooperating with the Hindus and working for a united front. Later when he took over the communal plank, he had to undo all that he had done in the past. In the process he discarded the Hindus but he could not totally align with the practising Muslims. He was too deeply entrenched in his western style of living and thinking to give it up. He could not easily mix with the illiterate Muslim masses; he felt comfortable only among the western-educated elite. The poor and the downtrodden

Muslims failed to interest him; even when he put on the exclusively communal garb and reorganised the League he relied more on the lordly nawabs and the rich and indolent jagirdars. Iqbal had cautioned him a year before his death in a letter dated May 28, 1937: "The League will have to finally decide whether it will remain a body representing the upper classes of Indian Muslims or Muslim masses.... The question therefore is: how is it possible to solve the problem of Muslim poverty? And the whole future of the League depends on the League's activity to solve this question. If the League can give no such promises I am sure the Muslim masses will remain indifferent to it as before."[1]

Jinnah did not however heed the poet's advice; he was mainly interested in building an exclusive platform for himself. And within no time he managed to gather the Muslims under his leadership without changing either his thinking or his approach. His lack of knowledge of Islam and his inability to speak Urdu proved no hindrance. His contempt for the masses remained unchanged. An incident, which I have narrated in my book, *Price of Partition* confirms it. It happened at the mammoth public meeting, which the League had organised to celebrate the Deliverance Day on the exit of the Congress ministries in 1939. Just before the meeting Jinnah's behaviour startled me beyond comprehension. He arrived at the specified time. He was always punctual. He surveyed the scene and when he could not see the press seated prominently in the front rows, he lost his temper. He turned to the organisers and shouted angrily: "Where is the press?" and then in full hearing of the public since the mike was on the dais, he thundered: "Do you think I have come to address these donkeys?" He wanted his speech to be conveyed more to the world than to the assembled crowd. Despite the handicap of being a Muslim and the arrogance in his approach he managed to become the darling of the Muslims. He exploited their religious leanings and inculcated in them the fear of Hindu domination. He coined the Two-Nation theory, cleverly stressing on the vital differences between Hindus and Muslims. He convinced Muslims that the Hindus would never share power with them. Their sole objective, he told them, was to oust the British, establish Hindu raj and subjugate them, so as to avenge the alleged atrocities committed by the medieval Muslim rulers.

In building a new leadership for himself, on the basis of Muslim separatism that he had earlier abhorred, Jinnah deliberately ignored the various commonalities between Hindus and Muslims. In the earlier phase of his public life he often spoke of how the two lived together peacefully for centuries despite some differences, even hostilities. In those days, he never let go an opportunity to emphasise that the two communities showed respect and consideration for one another and managed the contradictions in their relationship with goodwill and harmony. Their heroes and festivals, he said, might have been different but they never caused any major conflict on either side. There was a silent and peaceful acceptance of the diversities and differences in their approach on vital matters. Jinnah was then of the opinion that the so-called Hindu-Muslim riots were the products of the British raj; during the Muslim rule, there might have been wars between Muslim and Hindu rulers, but there was never any discord between the ordinary people of the two communities. The elite might have at times experienced some tension and animosity among themselves but the people at large had always lived in peaceful co-existence.

Jinnah had sworn by these facts all along until the last seven or eight years of his life, but he brazenly denied them as he embarked on his new role as defender of the faithful. He then began propagating that there was little in common between Hindus and Muslims and that they could never live and work together. He misrepresented Gandhi's call for *Ram Rajya* among Muslims and asked them to demand a separate state for themselves. This earned him a positive response which helped him assume the role of their sole spokesman. He did not mind using any means to achieve this end. John Gunther in his celebrated work *Inside Asia* has commented: "His opposition to the Hindus is bitter and inflamed; he tours the country making attacks on Congress, which splits and weakens nationalist sentiment. Jinnah says that he was driven into communalism and the resurrection of the Moslem League by the intransigence of the Hindus, but his own intense political ambition had much to do with it."[2]

And thus he took charge of the League and mobilised the Muslims under its aegis and with his mesmerising technique, he galvanised them into a force to reckon with. He made himself so politically invulnerable that the British accepted him as the authentic representative of the Muslims and eventually the Congress too conceded that status to him, even if unwillingly. He felt truly elevated when he was equated with Gandhi. This was exactly what he had aimed for ever since he returned from London in the early thirties. He steadfastly pursued his objective to partition the country. He used every political means and organisational measure to counter his opponents and often had the better of them. He did not deviate from his armchair politics but still managed to win over the Muslim masses.

Sometimes when his detractors questioned him on what sacrifice he would be ready to make for the Muslims, he scoffed at them saying he did not believe in aping Gandhi whose methods of non-cooperation and mass agitation he detested.

He missed no opportunity to pour venom on the Congress and the Hindus and always kept the British on his side; within the League he was able to have complete sway. This he did surprisingly by maintaining a distance from all. He enjoyed being eulogised; his monumental ego brooked no opposition. He thrived on his command being unquestionably obeyed. His vanity was overbearing; he had contempt for all those who disagreed with him. In the evening of his life, when he was obsessed with his pet scheme of Pakistan, he had convinced himself that it was the solution. He refused to listen to any argument against it. Nor was he deterred by the mounting opposition unleashed by his opponents. The more they questioned him about the viability of Pakistan the more dogmatic he became in pursuing it.

Jinnah's weapon was not logic but debating skills in which few could equal him. Also few could match his organising capacity. He adhered firmly to the constitutional path; he did not encourage illegal agitations. Only once when he was utterly frustrated, after the failure of his negotiations with Viceroy Wavell, did he agree, under pressure from his colleagues, to declare "Direct Action"; it unfortunately resulted in more death and destruction of the Muslims. This reaffirmed his resolve not to ever deviate from the constitutional path. He genuinely regretted having come down from the politics of the ivory tower to that of the marketplace. There are, indeed, few instances in history where a leader had been able to achieve so much by doing so little, except through play of words. He once remarked that he got Pakistan by using just the services of his secretary and typewriter.

Jinnah has been credited with continuing the process of Muslim separatism which, it is said, was first started by Sir Syed Ahmad Khan, the pre-eminent Muslim leader of the late nineteenth century. It is true that the venerable Syed asked the Muslims not to join the Hindus in promoting the Congress and spoke of their differences. But that was because he did not want the British to target Muslims once again as they had done earlier after the revolt of 1857. Otherwise he was all for Hindu-Muslim collaboration and often described them as the two beautiful eyes on the face of India; if one was hurt, he said, the other was bound to be affected.

Allama Iqbal, the poet-philosopher of Islam, has been hailed, after the creation of Pakistan, as its mentor on the grounds that in his presidential address to the League in 1930 he had advocated the formation of a consolidated Muslim north-west state. But this according to Iqbal was to be within India, and not out of it. A year later, in his speech at the Round Table Conference in 1931 Iqbal pleaded for an All-India Federation in which he pointed out: "Muslims would get majority rights in five out of eleven Indian provinces with full residuary powers and one-third share of seats in the total in the house of the Federal Assembly."[3] In his letter to *The Times*, London, dated October 12, 1931 Iqbal refuted the charge made by the British journalist Edward Thompson that he was endangering the defence of the country by asking for the division of India. He explained: "I am all for a redistribution of India into provinces with effective majorities of one community or another on lines as advocated both by the Nehru and Simon Reports."[4] Hence the claim that there was a continuation of the struggle by the Muslims for some kind of a separate and independent state has no basis. It was Jinnah alone who worked for it and in consequence brought about the division of the country which in the process dismembered a once vibrant and united Muslim community and split it into three parts, destroying their common historical bond.

In retrospect what emerges unmistakably is Jinnah's no-holds barred campaign from 1937 onwards to foster Hindu-Muslim hostilities. His politics then consisted of creating as big a barrier between the two communities as was possible by propagating his Two-Nation theory. To justify it, he talked of Hindu domination and raised the slogan of "Islam in danger". He deliberately added obstacle after obstacle to frustrate reconciliation with the Hindus; he pursued with fearless determination the campaign for a separate state irrespective of the cost that the Muslims themselves would have to pay. Though he fully exploited Islam, he was never motivated by a religious urge. It was a purely political move to gain his obsessive ambition. And yet, he played his game so dexterously that he not only amassed a huge following of the illiterate masses but also gathered round him such lieutenants who obeyed him blindly. He silenced his opponents and emerged as the unchallenged leader — the Quaid-i-Azam or the Great Leader.

Jinnah had no doubt used Islam to obtain his Pakistan but as soon as it came into existence he clarified that he would run the newly-born state on modern, western lines. He was also not enamoured of the parliamentary system which he so often denounced. He was all for the presidential system though he did not spell it out. He believed in concentrating all powers in his hands. He made that clear when he appointed himself as Governor-General. He saw to it that the politicians who gathered round him, the bureaucrats who came to him, the colonels and generals who saluted him, followed his diktat. He ruled as the British viceroys did. That was the reason he retained the administrative set-up of the colonial masters who loved pomp and pageantry and showed little interest in the welfare of the masses. Jinnah imitated their style of functioning and systematically discouraged every move to Islamise Pakistan. Those who succeeded him followed faithfully in his footsteps.

If this was to be the outcome, what then had the fight for Pakistan been all about? By the time Jinnah came out with his separatist demand, Hindus had, by and large, agreed to concede more than his "Fourteen Points". His grievances which were earlier scoffed at were readily accepted. His conditions for settlement were all granted. But Jinnah thrived on conflicts. Wavell became so exasperated while negotiating with him that he wrote about him in his journal: "narrow and arrogant... constitutionally incapable of friendly cooperation with the other party."[5] True, wisdom dawned on the Hindu leadership rather late; but the alternative that Jinnah came out with was worse than the disease. It was the outcome of his fanaticism. He told Mountbatten not to decry fanatics. "If I hadn't been a fanatic, there never would have been Pakistan."[6]

It must, however, be admitted that until Jinnah began his aggressive anti-Hindu campaign, the protagonists of Hindu political supremacy had been carrying on the most hateful propaganda against the Muslims, describing them as traitors to India and the real enemies of Hinduism. They maligned Gandhi systematically for breaking communal barriers and trying to cement the bonds between the two communities. This was done not only by self-proclaimed Muslim baiters like Veer Savarkar and Bhai Parmanand but also by a number of prominent leaders of the Congress from Lala Lajpat Rai to Ravi Shankar Shukla. The British also encouraged such denunciation of the Muslims by the Hindus. It suited their policy of keeping alive the existing inter-communal hostility. Tagore became concerned about this unfortunate development and reminded the Hindus: "Some time ago this cleavage between Hindus and Muslims was hardly as pronounced as now. We were so mingled together that we did not perceive our difference. The absence of a feeling of separateness was, however, a negative, not a positive fact. In other words, we were not conscious of our differences, not because there were none. The fact was that we were much in a torpor which bred a lack of awareness. A day came when the Hindu started being conscious of the glory of Hinduhood. He would no doubt have been highly pleased if the Muslim had then acknowledged his glory and kept quiet, but the Muslimhood of the Muslim started asserting itself for the same reason as the Hinduhood of the Hindu. Now he wants to be strong, not by merging with the Hindu, but by being a Muslim."[7]

Jinnah could succeed with his Two-Nation theory by referring to this scurrilous anti-Muslim thesis that had been built up over the decades; it helped him considerably to convince Muslims that they were really hated by the Hindus and therefore any collaboration with them would only result in their subjugation. He simplified his argument by dividing the Hindus and the Muslims into two groups as enemies and friends. This naturally caused the most intense antagonism between them especially in the political arena. As Carl Schmitt has observed: "The political is the most intense and extreme antagonism, and every concrete antagonism becomes that much the more political the closer it approaches the most extreme point that of the friend-enemy grouping."[8] This syndrome of "us" and "they" got so embedded in the psyche of both Hindus and Muslims that the cleavage became the biggest obstacle to communal unity and eventually resulted in the creation of Pakistan.

Pakistan however brought no relief to the Muslims; it neither freed the Muslims from Hindu domination nor did it provide them with an exclusively Islamic dispensation. Even in the state that Jinnah created, the Muslims are faring no better than their co-religionists in India. In fact, in many respects the former are the losers; they have lost several basic human rights. They hardly enjoy any democratic freedom as such and even the rule of law is not properly enforced. The Muslim brotherhood by which Jinnah swore, collapsed when the two wings of Pakistan fell apart. And still fanaticism has so gripped Pakistan that it cannot be got rid of; in the name of Shariah virtual hell has been unleashed. Men are told to keep the beard and women to be in purdah. Mixing of men and women is frowned upon because it is loudly proclaimed that "the freedom of women which allows them to work in every field of life with men is the main reason for social degradation."[9] Never before were the traditions of Islam so abused.

The Muslims who migrated to Pakistan as the legendary Urdu poet Josh Malihabadi said, faced the same fate as the martyred grandson of the Prophet — Imam Husain. The rest of the people are also harassed and troubled. Instead of solving their problems the rulers have created such unstable and insecure conditions that most of them live in constant fear. The crisis in neighbouring Afghanistan has added to their troubles; the billions of dollars that America poured into Pakistan to help crush communism in Afghanistan have been misused by unscrupulous elements; they have been importing narcotics and arms and supporting the training of the so-called mujahideen to indulge in terrorism. They have financed the establishment of madrasas which have become live centres of militancy. Their trainees indulge in senseless murders. They have created the Talibans, who captured Afghanistan and have set up such a ruthless regime there that according to a UN official "the country is facing drought year after year, scorching its earth". "Millions of refugees," reports *Time* magazine, "are pouring into camps, that offer little food, water or medical aid."[10] And this has been brought about by the financial support provided by America to them.

Their latest act of vandalism has been the destruction of Buddha's statues at Bamiyan. It has been reminiscent of the carnage of their ancestors, Halaku and Ghenghiz Khan. This is in clear violation of Quranic injunctions and has been condemned by Muslims the world over. The one-eyed Mullah Mohammad Omar was trained in a Karachi madrasa; his group was armed by the ISI; hence Pakistan cannot disown him; someone has sarcastically remarked about him that: "With the benevolent Buddhas demolished, it might not be a bad idea to display in Bamiyan, a relic of the Stone Age and name it Mullah Omar." His Talibans have started to spread their oppressive wings in Pakistan also; their so-called jihad is striking the innocent and the helpless. Ayaz Amir has observed in *Dawn*: "Cannot they assess the dangers of a *jihad* gone rampant, a *jihad* whose symbols are now perhaps more evident in Pakistan than in Kashmir?"[11]

This is the result of Jinnah's politics; he had vowed that he would provide the Muslims a separate homeland to free them from Hindu domination. But what has really happened is that they have been permanently enslaved — two-thirds of them to the Hindus and the remaining one-third which constitute Pakistan to the power-brokers and drug dealers. As the noted Pakistani author, Ahmed Rashid has pointed out: "Pakistan has become the hotbed of the biggest smuggling racket in the world... enmeshed with Pakistani smugglers, transporters, drug barons, bureaucrats, politicians and army officers...."

The scandals about them are so startling that one wonders how a state could fall so low. Its citizens are denied even basic rights of existence: jobs, housing, health services. Z.A. Bhutto recognised the reality of the situation and was able to win elections on the assurance of *roti, kapda aur makan* — to the people. But he failed to fulfil it; so have all the other leaders. Meanwhile the economic condition in Pakistan has gone from bad to worse. Most of the earning members of families have been fleeing to the Gulf and Saudi Arabia for years, in search of employment; the more educated ones are migrating to UK and USA. According to the latest report published by *The Observer*, London: "Pakistan is facing a massive brain drain as record numbers of people desperate to leave their politically unstable, economically chaotic country swamp foreign embassies with visa applications.....The biggest number of applications for British visas are from Pakistan. And Canada, the destination of first choice for Pakistanis, has received 40 per cent more immigrant visa applications in the first quarter of this year than in the same period last year. Doctors, lawyers and IT professionals are leading the exodus, but labourers and farmhands are joining the queues of malnourished people who gather daily outside the US embassy in Islamabad."[12]

To quote Najam Sethi, the distinguished editor of the well-known Pakistani weekly *Friday Times*, "Should Musharraf become the President, he would traverse a much-trodden path in Pakistan's sad history during which the presidency has housed all sorts of conspirators (Iskander Mirza, Ghulam Ishaq Khan), usurpers (Generals Ayub, Yahya, Zia), stooges (Chaudhry Fazal Elahi, Rafiq Tarar) and misfits (Farooq Leghari)."[13] And Sethi asked those who still look for the glory of Islam in Pakistan: "What is so Islamic about our country when Sunnis and Shias, and now Deobandis and Brelvis, are killing each other so wantonly, when we are so devoid of a sense of brotherhood and tolerance, when there is no justice for the poor and destitute, when our women are relegated to second-class citizenship?"[14]

The rulers now boast of the power that the nuclear bombs have given them; but according to Zia Mian, a Pakistan scholar, who works as a research scientist at Princeton University, USA, "For 30 years, Pakistani leaders have believed their salvation lay in one single thing: the Bomb. Now, once the idea has been rendered into reality, it is plain the Bomb has failed Pakistan. It has been unable to cement the fissures in a crumbling state and society fast approaching ruin. Rather, it has hastened the collapse by removing all illusions."[15]

And yet there are some Muslims in Kashmir who are agitating to be part of such a state which most Pakistani intellectuals themselves have pronounced "a failed state". Its ruling clique has already committed three aggressions against India to annex the Valley but having failed, they have now in the last decade, resorted to cross-border terrorism. Their aim is to grab the region; it is not to bring prosperity to the Muslim of Kashmir who should not be deluded by the call of Muslim brotherhood. They must realise that their joining Pakistan will generate such an emotional outrage among Hindus that no secular framework, however powerful, will be able to control the holocaust which will be unleashed against the Muslims in India, who today number more than the Muslims in Pakistan.

Moreover the callous attitude of the rulers of Pakistan to the two million Biharis who are facing dire conditions in Bangladesh should open the eyes of Kashmiris about what would be their fate. As it is Pakistan's hostile attitude to India and support to the mujahideen who operate in Kashmir has put Indian Muslims under a veil of suspicion bordering on distrust. The Islamic bond is misrepresented to cast aspersions on the latter's loyalty to their country. The ISI and its band of mujahideen have failed in their murderous designs but they have helped indirectly the forces within India who would like to eliminate Indian Muslims and destabilise the secular edifice of the Republic.

In united India, Muslims had enjoyed far more power — in five out of the eleven provinces they had their own governments. They played a major part in the affairs at the Centre. They have lost it all since partition. In united India, as the passage of time has revealed, they would have had a much better existence; casteism among the Hindus would have ensured the Muslims a secure future. The Nobel laureate Dr. Amartya Sen, in his Dorab Tata Memorial lecture (February 2001) explained that while numerically Hindus might be a vast majority, they could not enjoy a privileged position as their so-called unity encountered heterodoxy at every step in matters of belief. Another significant observation has been made by the widely read columnist Kuldip Nayar: "Mrs. Margaret Thatcher was Great Britain's Prime Minister when I was India's High Commissioner in London. The Soviet Union was breaking up at that time, and Mr. Gorbachev had asked Mrs. Thatcher how he could save his country from disintegration. She told me that she had advised him: 'Go to your friend, India. Learn from them how they have lived together for centuries, despite numerous religions, regions, castes and languages'."[16] Jinnah was fully aware of this truth; in fact he lived through it and admitted it publicly on several occasions until the last few years of his life when he took the separatist path in order to resurrect his fallen leadership.

There is also the presence among the Hindus of the liberal segment which would never have allowed the composite character of united India to be destroyed. Nor would a fair number of them have permitted the dilution of India's progressive and secular character. They may not be large in number but they are certainly salient. Jinnah deliberately blacked out these facts and exaggerated the differences between Hindus and Muslims. He also gave a twisted meaning to democracy by stressing that it functioned not on political but religious groupings. He discounted parallelism which is the kernel of India's continuous centuries-old heritage. His Two-Nation theory was a travesty of the country's glorious past and a repudiation of its modern political upbringing. Through the inculcation of hatred and the flow of bloodshed, the state that he founded has got trapped in its own contamination. It continues to function under its shadow. In the result it is more the Pakistanis than the Indians who are the sufferers; its traders, artists, authors, poets, musicians and a whole lot of enterprising people in different fields are being denied the vast advantages that its big neighbour with unlimited opportunities could have given them. Most of them, when they visit India, become nostalgic and genuinely regret the historic loss.

The so-called mujahideen, whom Musharraf described as freedom fighters during his visit to India are not only killing innocent citizens in Jammu and Kashmir but they have also become a menace to ordinary Pakistanis. As the well-known Pakistan writer A.B. Jafri has explained in his article in *Dawn*: "To be fair, one must concede that the *jihadis* are a fairly frank lot, if not downright audacious. They call themselves by names like Sipah (army), Lashkar (expeditionary force), Jaish (brigade), Harakat (movement wielding arms), and of course *jihadis* (holy warriors). Most of them have their recruiting outfits, their exclusive schools to teach their sectarian doctrine (gospel), and also to train their alumni in the use of lethal arms. There is nothing very secretive about them." He further adds: "The fundamentalists that we have around us do not abide by the normal laws. They operate regardless of the law, often in deliberate disregard and defiance of it. They justify their existence and their militant conduct on the basis of what they claim to be super-laws or the laws of supra-state power." Jafri concludes: "The point to stress is that any talk of peace and stability in the country will sound like a cruel joke so long as all these heavily armed and motivated *jihadis, lashkars, sipahs* and militias exist in our midst."[17]

Which section of the Muslims of undivided India then really gained by partition and the consequent dismemberment of their united community? How could reason and even one's own selfish interest have been so submerged by fanaticism? The renowned Urdu poet Faiz Ahmed Faiz, a progressive with communist leanings was carried away by the intellectual fraud that the Indian communists played in legitimising Jinnah's demand. They argued that even religious communities had the right of self-determination and distorted facts to affirm that Indian Muslims were a nation who were entitled to have a separate homeland. This was a repudiation of the policies and programmes of Gandhi; they coined a counter to the Gandhian concept of one nation by endorsing Jinnah's Two-Nation theory. They hoped that it would bring them popular Muslim support. It was an alarming performance which they justified by distorting Marxism. The damage it did was enormous because it swayed a large number of Muslim intellectuals and the middle classes to favour the demand of Pakistan. It rationalised religious bigotry and legitimised communal fanaticism. Faiz and many of his compatriots, who had a considerable following among the younger Muslim generation, were misled. However the aftermath of partition and the miseries that it brought in its wake to the helpless poor and downtrodden millions pricked their conscience; many of them later admitted that they were grossly mistaken. In a poem which Faiz wrote in anguish and which has become a classic in Urdu literature he expressed his outrage on the tragic outcome:

> This leprous daylight, dawn night's fangs have mangled,
> — This is not that long-looked-for break of day,
> Not that clear dawn in quest of which our comrades
> Set out, believing that in heaven's wide reach
> Somewhere must be the stars' last halting-place,
> Somewhere the shore of night's slow-washing tide,
> Somewhere the anchorage of the ship of pain.
> When they set out, those friends, taking youth's secret
> Pathways, how many hands plucked at their sleeves!
> From panting casements of the land of beauty
> Soft arms invoked them, flesh cried out to them;
> But dearer was the lure of dawn's bright cheek,
> Closer them hung her robe of shimmering rays;
> Light-winged their longing, feather-light their toil.
> But now, word goes, day's first faint birth from darkness
> Is finished, and wandering feet stand at their goal;
> Our leaders' ways are altering, festive looks
> Are now in fashion, discontent reproved.
> Yet still no physic offered to unslaked eye
> Or fevered heart or soul works any cure.
> Where did that sweet breeze blow from, then — where has it
> Gone, and the roadside lamp not flickered once?
> Night's heaviness is unlessened yet, the hour
> Of mind and spirit's ransom has not struck.
> Let us go on, our goal is not yet reached. [18]

But how could they ever reach it? The goal itself is lost in the debris of the past. As Nirad C. Chaudhuri has rightly observed, "I do not know of any nation which is held so relentlessly in the clutches of the past and is yet so incapable of contemplating and understanding it and consequently profiting by its lessons." This applies much more to the Muslims than any other segment of the society which constituted united India.

On hindsight the entire development which brought about the tragic end sounds so ironical. Nehru disliked Jinnah and pushed him to the wall. Gandhi tried his best to mollify the League President but the two leaders thought and worked at cross-purposes. Azad was ignored. Patel was misled. From 1940 to 1947 every effort to bring the Congress and the League together failed because neither party trusted the other. Moreover Jinnah's obstinacy and intransigence remained a stumbling block. Finally Mountbatten showed them the easy way out and made them opt for the division of the country. The Quaid-i-Azam claimed that he had at last freed the Muslims from Hindu domination; he boasted that he had given them a state of their own. That has, however, in a short period of fifty years, proved to be a millstone round their neck. Likewise the Hindus have gained even less by ridding themselves of two-thirds of the Muslims; their security is constantly threatened and their stability crippled. In the result what is left behind for both the contending communities is the legacy of hate that is eating into the vitals of their beings. The more I think of the dreadful partition and the consequent sufferings that it has brought in its wake to our two peoples, the more inclined I am to ask the question, which one of the greatest philosophers of our times, Bertrand Russell asked: "Are we to continue entrusting our affairs to men without sympathy, without knowledge, without imagination, and having nothing to recommend them except methodical hatred and skill in vituperation?"[19] Unless we get out of their clutches, the past will haunt us, the present will continue to be unsettled and the future endangered for all times.

There is no denying the fact that a large number of both Hindus and Muslims of South Asia have gone through hell in the last more than fifty years; the historic blunder that the leadership committed in agreeing to partition has left behind the baggage of hatred and ill-will which has irretrievably entrapped them. They need to free themselves from its entanglement and create a different environment of mutual goodwill, harmony and accommodation. Long ago Iqbal urged upon both Hindus and Muslims to jointly build a *naya shavala* or a new altar of unity with its columns touching the skies. He expressed this in a soul-stirring poem. It has been rendered beautifully into the English by Prof. V.G. Kiernan who has been a professor of history at the University of Edinburgh. The poem ends with a message which provides us with abiding hope:

Come, let us lift suspicion's thick curtains once again,
Unite once more the sundered, wipe clean division's stain.[20]

Notes

Chapter I: Early Years

1. Wolpert, Stanley, *Jinnah of Pakistan*, New York, 1984, p. 9.
2. Qureshi, Saleem (ed.), *Jinnah: The Founder of Pakistan*, Karachi, 1999, p. 4.

Chapter II: Political Initiation

1. Wolpert, Stanley, *Jinnah of Pakistan*, New York, 1984, p. 27.
2. Zakaria, Rafiq, *Rise of Muslims in Indian Politics*, New Delhi, 1970, p. 106.
3. Wolpert, Stanley, *Jinnah of Pakistan*, New York, 1984, p. 26.
4. Ibid., p. 27.
5. Ibid., pp. 32-33.
6. Dwarkadas, Kanji, *India's Fight for Freedom 1913-1937 - An Eyewitness Story*, Bombay, 1966, p. 63.

Chapter III : Efforts at Unity

1. Bolitho, Hector, *Jinnah: Creator of Pakistan*, London, 1954, p. 153.
2. Wolpert, Stanley, *Jinnah of Pakistan*, New York, 1984, pp. 46-47.

3. Ibid., pp. 47-48.

4. Bandopadhaya, Sailesh Kumar, *Quaid-I-Azam, Mohammad Ali Jinnah and the Creation of Pakistan,* New Delhi, 1991, p. 29.

5. Ahmed, Akbar S., *Jinnah, Pakistan and Islamic Identity: The Search for Saladin,* New York, 1997, p. 152.

6. Wolpert Stanley, *Jinnah of Pakistan,* New York, 1984, p. 50.

7. Ibid., p. 51.

8. Ibid., p. 52.

9. Bandopadhaya, Sailesh Kumar, *Quaid-i-Azam, Mohammad Ali Jinnah and the Creation of Pakistan,* New Delhi, 1991, p. 81.

Chapter IV: The Lean Period

1. Bandopadhaya, Sailesh Kumar, *Quaid-I-Azam, Mohammad Ali Jinnah and the Creation of Pakistan,* New Delhi, 1991, pp. 41-42.

2. Ibid., p. 44.

3. Wolpert, Stanley, *Jinnah of Pakistan,* New York, 1984, p. 85.

4. Bolitho, Hector, *Jinnah: Creator of Pakistan,* London, 1954, p. 85.

5. Chagla, M.C., *Roses in December – An Autobiography,* Bombay, 1973, pp. 118-19.

6. Bandopadhaya, Sailesh Kumar, *Quaid-I-Azam, Mohammad Ali Jinnah and the Creation of Pakistan,* New Delhi, 1991, pp. 52-53.

7. Ibid., p. 54.

8. Pirzada, Syed Sharifuddin, *The Collected Works of Quaid-e-Azam Mohammad Ali Jinnah, Vol. II, 1921-1926,* Karachi, 1986 p. 429.

Chapter V: Decline of Clout

1. Pirzada, Syed Sharifuddin, *The Collected Works of Quaid-e-Azam Mohammad Ali Jinnah, Vol. II, 1921-1926,* Karachi, 1986, pp. 363, 368.

2. Ibid., pp. 368-69, 372.

3. Ibid., p. 267.

4. Pirzada, Syed Sharifuddin, *The Collected Works of Quaid-e-Azam Mohammad Ali Jinnah, Vol. III, 1926-1931,* Karachi, 1986, p. 205.

5. Ibid., p. 258.

6. Ibid., p. 219.

7. Ibid., p. 224.

Chapter VI: Temporary Retirement

1. Pirzada, Syed Sharifuddin, *The Collected Works of Quaid-e-Azam Mohammad Ali Jinnah, Vol. III, 1926-1931,* Karachi, 1986, pp. 316-19.
2. Wolpert, Stanley, *Jinnah of Pakistan,* New York, 1984, p. 100.
3. Ibid., pp. 100-01.
4. Ibid., p. 101.
5. Bandopadhaya, Sailesh Kumar, *Quaid-I-Azam –Mohammad Ali Jinnah and the Creation of Pakistan,* New Delhi, 1991, p. 70.
6. Ibid., p. 75.
7. Pirzada, Syed Sharifuddin, *The Collected Works of Quaid-e-Azam Mohammad Ali Jinnah, Vol. III, 1926-1931,* Karachi, 1986, p. 324.
8. Ibid., p. 326.
9. Bandopadhaya, Sailesh Kumar, *Quaid-I-Azam–Mohammad Ali Jinnah and the Creation of Pakistan,* New Delhi, 1991, pp. 73-74.
10. Wolpert, Stanley, *Jinnah of Pakistan,* New York, 1984, pp.105-06.
11. Bandopadhaya, Sailesh Kumar, *Quaid-i-Azam – Mohammad Ali Jinnah and the Creation of Pakistan,* New Delhi, 1991, p. 81.

Chapter VII: Undoing the Past

1. Pirzada, Syed Sharifuddin, *The Collected Works of Quaid-e-Azam Mohammad Ali Jinnah, Vol. III, 1926-1931,* Karachi, 1986, p. 415.
2. Ibid., p. 418.
3. Ibid., pp. 421-22.
4. Ibid., p. 500.
5. Bandopadhaya, Sailesh Kumar, *Quaid-i-Azam — Mohammad Ali Jinnah and the Creation of Pakistan,* New Delhi, 1991, p. 83.
6. Ibid., p. 88.

7. Bolitho, Hector, *Jinnah — Creator of Pakistan*, London, 1954, p. 101.
8. *The Memoirs of Aga Khan — World Enough and Time*, London, 1954, p. 229.
9. Moore, R.J., *The Crisis of Indian Unity, 1917-1940*, Delhi, 1974, pp. 241-42
10. Wolpert, Stanley, *Jinnah of Pakistan*, New York, 1984, p.126.

Chapter VIII: Preparing for Separation

1. Chagla, M.C., *Roses in December – An Autobiography*, Bombay, 1973, pp. 103-04.
2. Moore, R.J., *Churchill, Cripps, and India – 1939-1945*, London, 1979, p. 1.
3. Pirzada, Syed Sharifuddin, *Foundations of Pakistan – All- India Muslim League Documents: 1906-1947, Vol. II*, New Delhi, 1982, pp. 266-67.
4. Ibid., p. 267.
5. Ibid., pp. 267-68.
6. Ibid., p. 273.
7. Kamal, Khursheed (ed.), *A Documentary Record of the Congress Government:* 1937-39.(*Related to Muslims under Congress Rule*), *Vol. I*, New Delhi, n.d., pp. 139-40.
8. Chandra, Kailash, *Jinnah and the Communal Problem in India*, Delhi, 1986, pp. 34-35.
9. Bolitho, Hector, *Jinnah: Creator of Pakistan*, London, 1954, pp. 115-16.
10. Ibid., pp. 116-17.
11. Ibid., p. 117.
12. Pirzada, Syed Sharifuddin, *Foundations of Pakistan – All-India Muslim League Documents: 1906-1947, Vol. II*, New Delhi, 1982, p. 304.
13. *Frontline*, April 13, 2001.

Chapter IX: Demand for Pakistan

1. Saiyid, Matlubul Hasan, *The Political Study of Mohammad Ali Jinnah, Vol. II,* Delhi, 1986, pp. 688-89.
2. Philips, C.H. & Wainwright, Mary Doreen (eds.), *The Partition of India, Policies and Perspectives, 1935-1947*, London, 1970, p. 209.

3. Ibid.

4. Wolpert, Stanley *Jinnah of Pakistan*, New York, 1984, p. 191.

5. Ibid., p. 207.

6. Moore, R.J., *Churchill, Cripps, and India, 1939-1945*, New York, 1979, p. 28.

7. Wolpert, Stanley, *Jinnah of Pakistan*, New York, 1984, p. 196.

Chapter X: Encounter with Gandhi

1. Wolpert, Stanley, *Jinnah of Pakistan*, New York, 1984, pp. 228-29.

2. Ibid., p. 229.

3. Majumdar, S.K., *Jinnah and Gandhi – Their Role in India's Quest for Freedom*, Calcutta, 1966, p. 212.

4. Wolpert, Stanley, *Jinnah of Pakistan*, New York, 1984, p. 231.

5. Ibid., p. 234.

6. Ibid., p. 236.

7. Tendulkar, D.G., *Mahatma: Life of Mohandas Karamchand Gandhi, Vol. VI, 1940-1945*, Bombay, 1953, p. 345.

8. Ibid., pp. 348-49.

9. Ibid., p. 349.

10. Ibid., p. 354.

11. Wolpert, Stanley, *Jinnah of Pakistan*, New York, 1984, p. 239.

12. Merriam, Allen Hayes, *Gandhi Vs Jinnah: The Debate Over the Partition of India*, Calcutta, 1980, p. 117.

13. Bolitho, Hector, *Jinnah -- Creator of Pakistan*, London, 1954, p. 153.

14. Zakaria, Rafiq, *The Price of Partition*, Mumbai, 1998, pp. 174-75.

Chapter XI: Viceregal Endeavours

1. Moore, R.J., *Churchill, Cripps, and India, 1939-1945*, New York, 1979, p. 140.

2. Wolpert, Stanley, *Jinnah of Pakistan*, New York, 1984, p. 244.

3. Ibid., p. 245.

4. Ibid.

5. Pyarelal, *Mahatma Gandhi: The Last Phase, Vol. I*, Ahmedabad, 1956, p. 137.

6. Wolpert, Stanley, *Jinnah of Pakistan*, New York, 1984, p. 247.

7. Ibid., p. 255.

8. This was the gist of the dialogue which the Mission had with Jinnah and which was narrated to me by Lord Alexander, a member of the Mission who I met soon after the Lordship's return to London.

9. Bandopadhaya, Sailesh Kumar, *Quaid-I-Azam, Muhammad Ali Jinnah and The Creation of Pakistan*, New Delhi, 1991, p. 250.

Chapter XII: Failure of Negotiations

1. Bandopadhaya, Sailesh Kumar, *Quaid-I-Azam, Muhammad Ali Jinnah and the Creation of Pakistan*, New Delhi, 1991, p. 256.

2. Ibid., p. 257.

3. Ibid,. p. 258.

4. Ibid., p. 260.

5. Ibid., p. 261.

6. Speech at prayer meeting, May 17, 1946, *Collective Works of Mahatma Gandhi*, Vol. 84, p. 155.

7. Wolpert, Stanley, *Jinnah of Pakistan*, New York, 1984, p. 271

8. Ibid., pp. 271-72.

9. Majumdar, S.K., *Jinnah and Gandhi – Their Role in India's Quest for Freedom*, Calcutta, 1966, pp. 225-26.

10. Ibid., p. 227.

11. Ibid., p. 228.

12. Ibid., pp. 228-29.

13. Ibid., p. 230.

14. Wolpert, Stanley, *Jinnah of Pakistan*, New York, 1984, p. 282

15. Singh, Anita Inder, *The Origins of the Partition of India, 1936-1947*, Delhi, 1987, p. 181.

16. Wolpert, Stanley, *Jinnah of Pakistan*, New York, 1984, p. 282.

17. Wright, William Aldis, *The Complete Works of William Shakespeare*, New York, 1936, p. 470.

Chapter XIII: Surrender to Partition

1. Wolpert, Stanley, *Jinnah of Pakistan*, New York, 1984, p. 292.
2. Majumdar, S.K., *Jinnah and Gandhi — Their Role in India's Quest for Freedom*, Calcutta, 1966, pp. 243-44.
3. Ibid., p. 244.
4. Moore, R.J., *Escape From Empire — The Attlee Government and the Indian Problem*, New York, 1983, p. 206.
5. Majumdar, S.K., *Jinnah and Gandhi — Their Role in India's Quest for Freedom*, Calcutta, 1966, p. 246.
6. Wolpert, Stanley, *Jinnah of Pakistan*, New York, 1984, pp. 303-04.
7. Bandopadhaya, Sailesh Kumar, *Quaid-I-Azam, Muhammad Ali Jinnah and the Creation of Pakistan*, New Delhi, 1991, p. 307.
8. Majumdar, S.K., *Jinnah and Gandhi —Their Role in India's Quest for Freedom*, Calcutta, 1966, p. 250.

Chapter XIV: Creation of Pakistan

1. Collins, Larry and Lapierre, Dominique, *Freedom at Midnight*, New Delhi,1976, pp. 103-05.
2. Zakaria, Rafiq, *the Price of Partition*, Mumbai, 1998, pp. 152-53.
3. *The Indian Post*, May 7, 1989.
4. Majumdar, S.K., *Jinnah and Gandhi —Their Role in India's Quest for Freedom*, Calcutta, 1966, pp. 254-55.
5. Lohia, Rammanohar, *Guilty Men of India's Partition*, Allahabad, 1960, pp. 9-11.
6. Thomas, Benjamin. P, *Abraham Lincoln*, New York, 1968, p. 377.
7. Ibid., p. 258.
8. Nichols, Beverley, *Verdict on India*, Bombay, 1944, p. 188.

Chapter XV: The Grim Aftermath

1. Majumdar, S.K., *Jinnah and Gandhi – Their Role in India's Quest for Freedom*, Calcutta, 1966, pp. 287-88.
2. Royle, Trevor, *The Last Days of the Raj*, Britain, 1989, p. 229.
3. Qureshi, Saleem (ed.), *Jinnah: The Founder of Pakistan*, Karachi, 1999, p. 32.

4. Azad, Abul Kalam, *India's Maulana, Centenary Edition, Vol.2,* New Delhi, 1990, pp. 170-73.
5. Ibid.
6. Ibid.
7. Ibid.
8. Campbell-Johnson, Alan, *Mission with Mountbatten,* Bombay, 1951, p.113.
9. *Indian Express,* November 26, 2000.

Chapter XVI: Authoritarian Misrule

1. Zakaria, Rafiq, *The Price of Partition,* Mumbai, 1998, p. 166
2. Khan, Wali, *Facts are Facts—The Untold Story of India's Partition,* New Delhi, 1987, p. 158.
3. Weiss, Anita M. (ed.), *Islamic Reassertion in Pakistan,* New York, 1986, p. 42.
4. Iqbal, Afzal, *Islamization of Pakistan,* Delhi, 1984, p. 25.
5. Ali, Tariq, *Can Pakistan Survive? The Death of a State,* Middlesex, 1983, pp. 42-43.
6. Wolpert, Stanley, *Jinnah of Pakistan,* New York, 1984, p. 355.
7. Iqbal, Afzal, *Islamization of Pakistan,* Delhi, 1984, p. 26.
8. Hidayatullah, M. and Hidayatullah, Arshad, (eds.), *Mulla's Principles of Mahomedan Law,* Bombay, 1977, p. 141.
9. Wolpert, Stanley, *Jinnah of Pakistan,* New York, 1984, p. 361.
10. Ibid., pp. 359-60.

Chapter XVII: The Struggle to Survive

1. Weiss, Anita M.(ed.), *Islamic Reassertion in Pakistan,* New York, 1986, pp. 43-44.
2. Binder, Leonard, *Religion and Politics in Pakistan,* Berkeley, 1963, p. 144.
3. Sayed, G.M., *Struggle for New Sind,* Karachi, 1949 as quoted by Tariq Ali in his book, *Can Pakistan Survive,* Middlesex, 1983, p. 44.
4. Binder, Leonard, *Religion and Politics in Pakistan,* Berkeley, 1963, p. 140.
5. Iqbal, Afzal, *Islamization of Pakistan,* Delhi, 1984, p. 59.
6. Ibid., pp. 59-60.

7. Binder, Leonard, *Religion and Politics in Pakistan*, Berkeley, 1963, p. 163.
8. Iqbal, Afzal, *Islamization of Pakistan*, Delhi, 1984, p. 67.
9. Ibid., p. 68.
10. Munir, Muhammad, *From Jinnah to Zia*, Lahore, 1979, p. 52.
11. Ibid., pp. 46-47.
12. Ibid., p. 65.
13. *The Asian Age*, April 15, 2001.
14. Choudhury, Golam.W, *Pakistan—Transition from Military to Civilian Rule*, Essex, 1988, p. 156.
15. Khan, Mohammad Ayub, *Friends Not Masters – A Political Autobiography*, London, 1967, pp. 54-55.
16. Ibid., p. 70.
17. Jahan, Rounaq, *Pakistan: Failure in National Integration*, New York, 1972, p. 55.
18. Khan, Mohammad Ayub, *Friends Not Masters – A Political Autobiography*, London, 1967, p. 49.
19. Iqbal, Afzal, *Islamization of Pakistan*, Delhi, 1984, p. 74.
20. Ibid., pp. 80-81.

Chapter XVIII: The Fanatical Fringe

1. Khan, Mohammad Asghar, *Generals in Politics, Pakistan 1958-1982*, New Delhi, 1983, pp. 160-61.
2. *Mainstream*, December 2, 2000.
3. Ibid.
4. *India Today*, August 21, 2000.
5. *On the Abyss–Pakistan After the Coup*, HarperCollins, New Delhi, 2000, pp. 5-6.
6. *The Asian Age*, February 2, 2000.
7. *Indian Express*, April 23, 2001.
8. *On the Abyss–Pakistan After the Coup*, HarperCollins, New Delhi, 2000, p. 85.
9. Ibid., p. 92.
10. Firestone, Reuven, *Jihad: The Origin of Holy War in Islam*, New York, 1999, p. 17.

11. *On the Abyss – Pakistan After the Coup*, HarperCollins, New Delhi, 2000, p. 102.
12. *The Times of India*, January 16, 2001.
13. Ibid., April 29, 2001

Chapter XIX: Victims of Partition

1. Azad, Abul Kalam, *India's Maulana, Centenary Edition, Vol. 2*, New Delhi, 1990, p. 173.
2. *The Economic Times*, October 3, 2000.
3. Ibid.
4. Ibid.
5. Ibid.
6. *Outlook*, October 2, 2000.
7. Ibid.
8. Ibid.
9. Ibid.
10. Ibid.
11. *The Times of India*, October 5, 2000.
12. Ibid.
13. Ibid.
14. Ibid.
15. Ibid.
16. Mascarenhas, Anthony, *The Rape of Bangla Desh*, Delhi, n.d., pp. 115, 118 and 120.
17. Rahman, Matiur and Hasan, Naeem, *Iron Bars of Freedom*, London, 1980, pp. 10, 14.
18. *The Asian Age*, April 30, 1999.
19. Ibid.
20. Ibid.
21. Ibid.
22. Ibid.

Chapter XX: The Historic Blunder

1. *Letters of Iqbal to Jinnah,* published by Sh. Muhammad Ashraf, Lahore, 1942, pp. 16-18.

2. Gunther, John, *Inside Asia,* New York, 1942, p. 486.

3. Zakaria, Rafiq, *Iqbal: The Poet and the Politician,* New Delhi, 1993, p. 81.

4. Ibid., p. 88.

5. Wolpert, Stanley, *Jinnah of Pakistan,* New York, 1984, p. 245.

6. Bolitho, Hector, *Jinnah, Creator of Pakistan,* London, 1954, p. 167.

7. Zakaria, Rafiq, *The Price of Partition,* Mumbai, 1998, pp. 64-65.

8. Quoted in *The Cunning of Unreason: Making Sense of Politics,* London, 2000, p. 10.9

9. *Indian Express,* Mumbai, April 12, 2001.

10. *Time Magazine,* February 26, 2001.

11. *The Asian Age,* Mumbai, February 26, 2001.

12. *The Observer,* Mumbai, July 1, 2001.

13. *Deccan Chronicle,* Hyderabad, March 4, 2001.

14. Najam Sethi's editorial in *Friday Times,* June 15-21, 2001.

15. *Outlook,* Mumbai, July 23, 2001

16. Quoted in *Jetwings for the Well-informed Traveller,* March 2001.

17. Article in *Dawn.* Reproduced in *The Asian Age,* Mumbai, August 2, 2001.

18. Kiernan, V.G. (translated), *Poems by Faiz Ahmad Faiz,* New Delhi, 1958, pp. 41-42.

19. Burnett, Whit (ed.), *This is My Philosophy,* New York, 1957, p. 6.

20. Kiernan, V.G. (translated), *Poems from Iqbal,* Karachi, 2000, p. 18.

Bibliography

Aga Khan, *The Memoirs of Aga Khan-World Enough and Time*, London, 1954

Agwani, M.S., *Islamic Fundamentalism in India*, Chandigarh, 1986

Ahmad, Jamil-ud-Din (ed.), *Some Recent Speeches and Writings of Mr. Jinnah*, Lahore, 1942

Ahmed, Akbar S., *Jinnah, Pakistan and Islamic Identity — The search for Saladin*, London, 1997

——————————, *Resistance & Control in Pakistan*, London, 1991

——————————, *Pakistan Society*, New York, 1986

Ahmed, Ishtiaq, *The Concept of an Islamic State: An Analysis of the Ideological Controversy in Pakistan*, London, 1987

Ahmed, Sayed Riaz, *Maulana Maududi and the Islamic State*, Lahore, 1976

Aiyar, Mani Shankar, *Pakistan Papers*, New Delhi, 1994

Akbar, M.J., *India: The Siege Within — Challenge to a Nations's Unity*, England, 1985

————————, *Kashmir Behind the Vale*, New Delhi, 1991

Ali, Tariq, *Can Pakistan Survive? The Death of a State*, Middlesex, 1983

Ambedkar, Dr. B.R., *Pakistan or Partition of India*, Bombay, 1945

————————, *Ranade, Gandhi & Jinnah*, Bombay, 1943

Ansari, Iqbal A. (ed.), *Muslim Situation in India*, New Delhi, 1989

Ashraf, Sh. Muhammad, *Letters of Iqbal to Jinnah*, Lahore, 1942

Azad, Abul Kalam, *India's Maulana, Centenary Edition, Vol.2*, New Delhi, 1990

————————, *India Wins Freedom*, New York, 1959

Aziz, K.K., *The Making of Pakistan: A Study in Nationalism*, New Delhi, 1988

————————, *History of Partition of India: Origin & Development of the Idea of Pakistan, Vol. I to IV*, New Delhi, 1988

Baig, M.R.A., *The Muslim Dilemma in India*, Delhi, 1974

Bajaj, Jitendra (ed.), *Ayodhya and the Future India*, Madras, 1993

Bandopadhaya, Sailesh Kumar, *Quaid-I-Azam Mohammad Ali Jinnah and the Creation of Pakistan*, New Delhi, 1991

Binder, Leonard, *Religion and Politics in Pakistan*, Berkeley, 1963

Bolitho, Hector, *Jinnah: Creator of Pakistan*, London,1954

Bourke, Margaret White, *Halfway to Freedom*, New York, 1949

Bulliet, Richard, W., *Islam — The View from the Edge*, New York, 1994

Burki, Shahid Javed, *Pakistan Under Bhutto, 1971-1977*, 1980

Butani, D.H., *The Future of Pakistan*, New Delhi, 1984

Campbell-Johnson, Alan, *Mission with Mountbatten*, Bombay, 1951

Chagla, M.C., *Roses in December*, Bombay, 1973

Chandra, Bipin, *Communalism in Modern India*, New Delhi, 1984

Chandra, Kailash, *Jinnah and the Communal Problem in India*, Delhi, 1986

Chopra, P.N., *Role of Indian Muslims in the Struggle for Freedom*, New Delhi, 1979

Choudhary, Zahid, *Pakistan Kaise Bana* (Urdu Text), *Vols. I and II*, Lahore, 1989

Choudhury, Golam W., *Pakistan — Transition from Military to Civilian Rule*, Essex, 1988

Collins, Larry and Lapierre, Dominique, *Freedom at Midnight*, New Delhi, 1976

——————, *Mountbatten and the Partition of India: March 22-August 15, 1947, Vol.1*, New Delhi, 1982

——————, *Mountbatten and Independent of India: 16 August 1947-18 June 1948*, Ghaziabad, 1984

Dunn, John, *The Cunning of Unreason — Making Sense of Politics*, London, 2000

Dwarkadas, Kanji, *India's Fight for Freedom 1913-1937 — An Eyewitness Story*, Bombay, 1966

——————, *Ruttie Jinnah — The Story of a Great Friendship*, Bombay, n.d.

Edwardes, M., *The Last Years of British India*, London, 1963

Firestone, Reuven, *Jihad: The Origin of Holy War in Islam*, New York, 1999

Gajendragadkar, P.B., *Kashmir: Retrospect and Prospect*, Bombay, 1967

Gandhi, M.K., *Communal Unity*, Ahmedabad, 1949

——————, *The Hindu-Muslim Unity*, Bombay, 1965

Glendevon, John, *The Viceroy at Bay*, London, 1971

Gopal, Ram, *Indian Muslims: A Political History (1858-1947)*, Bombay, 1959

Gottlieb, Gidon, *Nation Against State*, New York, 1993

Graham, Bruce, *Hindu Nationalism and Indian Politics*, New Delhi, 1993

Graham, G.F.I, *Life & Work of Sir Syed Ahmed Khan*, London, 1909

Gunther, John, *Inside Asia*, New York, 1938

Hameed, Syeda Saiyidain, *Islamic Seal on India's Independence, Abul Kalam Azad - a Fresh Look*, Karachi, 1998

Haq, Mushirul, *Muslim Politics in Modern India 1857-1947*, Meerut, 1970

——————, *Islam in Secular India*, Simla, 1972

Hardy, Peter, *Partners in Freedom and True Muslims: The Political Thought of Some Muslim Scholars in British India 1912-1947,* Lund, 1971

Harman, S., *Plight of Muslims in India*, London 1976

Harris, M.A., *Quaid-i-Azam*, Karachi, n.d.

Hasan, Khalid Shamsul, *Quaid-i-Azam's Unrealised Dream*, Karachi, 1991

Hasan, Mushirul, *India's Partition Process, Strategy & Mobilization*, Delhi, 1993

Hasan, Qamar, *Muslims In India, Attitudes, Adjustments and Reactions,* New Delhi, 1988

Hidayatullah, M. & Hidayatullah, Arshad, *Mulla's Principles of Mahomedan Law*, Bombay, 1977

Husain, Azim, *Fazl-i-Husain — A Political Biography*, Bombay, 1946

Hussain, Mushahid, *Pakistan's Politics: The Zia Years*, Delhi, 1991

Ikram, S.M., *Modern Muslim India & the Birth of Pakistan*, Lahore, 1970

Imam, Zafar, (ed.), *Muslims in India*, New Delhi, 1975

Iqbal, Afzal, *Islamization of Pakistan*, Delhi, 1984

Iqbal, Javid, *Ideology of Pakistan,* Lahore, 1971

Jahan, Rounaq, *Pakistan: Failure in National Integration*, New York, 1972

Jain, Girilal, *Pakistan Military Elite*, Delhi, n.d.

——————, *The Hindu Phenomenon*, New Delhi, 1994

Jalal, Ayesha, *The Sole Spokesman: Jinnah, the Muslim League and the Demand for Pakistan,* Cambridge, 1985

Jinnah, Mohammed Ali, *Quaid-i-Azam Mohammed Ali Jinnah: Speeches as Governor-General of Pakistan, 1947-48,* Karachi, 1948

Kamal, Khursheed (ed.), *A Documentary Record of the Congress Government: 1937-39. (Related to Muslims Under Congress Rule) Vol.I*, New Delhi, n.d.

Kaura, Uma, *Muslims and Indian Nationalism: Emergence of the Demand for India's Partition, 1928-40*, New Delhi, 1977

Khalid, Sayeed B., *Pakistan: The Formative Phase, 1857-1948*, Oxford, 1968

Khaliquzzaman, Choudhry, *Pathway to Pakistan*, Lahore, 1961

Khan, M. Asghar, *Pakistan at the Crossroads*, Lahore, 1969

——————, *Generals in Politics: Pakistan 1958-1982*, New Delhi, 1983

Khan, Mohammad Ayub, *Friends Not Masters — A Political Autobiography*, London, 1967

Khan, Shafique Ali, *Two Nation Theory as a Concept, Strategy & Ideology*, Karachi, 1973

Khan, Wali, *Facts are Facts — The Untold Story of India's Partition*, New Delhi, 1987

Kiernan, V.G. (translated) *Poems by Faiz Ahmad Faiz*, New Delhi, 1958

——————, (translated), *Poems from Iqbal*, Karachi, 2000

Lohia, Rammanohar, *Guilty Men of India's Partition*, Allahabad, 1960

Lumby, E.W.R., *The Transfer of Power in India, 1945-47*, London, 1954

Majumdar, S.K., *Jinnah and Gandhi—Their Role in India's Quest for Freedom*, Calcutta, 1966

Malkani, K.R., *The Politics of Ayodhya And Hindu-Muslim Relations*, New Delhi, 1993

Mascarenhas, Anthony, *Bangladesh: A Legacy of Blood*, London, 1986

——————, *The Rape of Bangla Desh*, Delhi, n.d.

Mathur, Y.B., *Muslims and Changing India*, New Delhi, 1972

Mehta, Ashok and A. Patwardhan, *The Communal Triangle in India*, Allahabad, 1942

Menon, V.P., *The Transfer of Power in India*, Bombay, 1957

Merriam, Allen Hayes, *Gandhi vs Jinnah, The Debate over the Partition of India*, Calcutta, 1980

Minaut, Gali, *The Khilafat Movement*, New Delhi, 1972

Moin, Shakir, *Khilafat to Partition: A Survey of Major Political Trends Among Indian Muslims during 1919-1947*, New Delhi, 1970

Moon, Penderel (ed.), *Wavell: The Viceroy's Journal*, Delhi, 1973

Moore, R.J., *The Crisis of Indian Unity 1917-1940*, Delhi, 1974

——————, *Churchill, Cripps, and India — 1939-1945*, New York, 1979

——————, *Escape from Empire: The Attlee Government and the Indian Problem*, New York, 1983

——————, *Endgames of Empire: Studies of Britain's Indian Problem*, Delhi, 1988

Mujeeb, M., *The Indian Muslims*, London, 1967

Mujtabai, F., *Hindu-Muslim Cultural Relations*, New Delhi, 1983

Munir, Muhammad, *From Jinnah to Zia*, Lahore, 1979

Munshi, K.M., *Akhand Hindustan*, Bombay, 1942

Naim, C.M.(ed.), *Iqbal, Jinnah and Pakistan*, Delhi, 1982

Nadwi, Abul Hasan Ali, *Muslims in India*, Lucknow, 1980

Nagarkar, V.V., *Genesis of Pakistan*, Bombay, 1975

Nehru, Jawaharlal, *Autobiography*, London, 1936

——————, *Discovery of India*, Calcutta, 1946

Nichols, Beverley, *Verdict on India*, Bombay, 1944

Noman, Mohammad, *Muslim India: Rise and Growth of the All-India Muslim League*, Allahabad, 1942

On the Abyss-Pakistan After the Coup, Published by Harper Collins, New Delhi, 2000

Page, David, *Prelude to Partition: The Indian Muslims and the Imperial System of Control 1920-1932,* Delhi, 1982

Philips, C.H. & Wainwright, Mary Doreen (eds.), *The Partition of India, Policies and Perspectives, 1935-1947,* London, 1970

Pirzada, Syed Sharifuddin (ed.), *Foundations of Pakistan – All-India Muslim League Documents: 1906-1924, Vol.I,* New Delhi, 1982

————————,(ed.), *Foundations of Pakistan – All-India Muslim League Documents: 1906-1947,* Vol.II, New Delhi, 1982

————————, *The Collected Works of Quaid-e-Azam Mohammad Ali Jinnah, Vol.I 1906-1921,* Karachi, 1984

————————, *The Collected Works of Quaid-e-Azam Mohammad Ali Jinnah, Vol.II 1921-1926,* Karachi, 1986

————————, *The Collected Works of Quaid-e-Azam Mohammad Ali Jinnah,Vol.III 1926-1931,* Karachi, 1986

Prasad, Rajendra, *India Divided,* Bombay, 1946

Qureshi, Ishtiaq Hussain, *The Muslim Community of the Indo-Pakistan Subcontinent,* Hague, 1962

Qureshi, Saleem (ed.), *Jinnah: The founder of Pakistan,* Karachi, 1998

Rahman, Hossainur, *Hindu-Muslim Relations in Bengal 1905-47,* Bombay, 1974

Rahman, Matiur & Hasan, Naeem, *Iron Bars of Freedom,* London, 1980

————————, (ed.), *Second Thoughts on Bangladesh,* London, 1979

Rai, Vijai Shankar, *The Last Phase of the Transfer of Power in India,* New Delhi, 1990

Rowse, A.L., *Glimpses of the Great,* Lanham, 1985

Royle, Trevor, *The Last Days of the Raj,* Britain, 1989

Saiyid, Matlubul Hasan, *The Political Study of Mohammad Ali Jinnah,Vol.I,* Delhi, 1986

————————,*The Political Study of Mohammad Ali Jinnah,Vol.II,* Delhi, 1986

Sayed, G.M., *Struggle for New Sind,* Karachi, 1949

Sayeed, Dr. Khalid Bin, *Pakistan: The Formative Phase,* Karachi, 1960

Schimmel, Annemarie, *Islam in India and Pakistan,* Leiden, 1982

Seervai, H.M., *Partition of India — Legend & Reality,* Bombay, 1989

Seshadri, H.V., *The Tragic Story of Partition,* Bangalore, 1982

Setalvad, M.C., *Secularism,* Delhi, 1967

Sharma, Rajeev (ed.), *The Pakistan Trap,* New Delhi, 2001

Singh, Anita Inder, *The Origins of the Partition of India, 1936-1947,* Delhi, 1987

Singh, Bhim Sen, *The Cripps Mission,* New Delhi, 1979

Stern, Philip Van Doren (ed.), *The Life and Writings of Abraham Lincoln,* New York, 2000

Symonds, Richard, *The Making of Pakistan,* Karachi, 1976

Talbot, Ian, *Provincial Politics and the Pakistan Movement: The Growth of the Muslim League in North-West and North-East India 1937-47,* Karachi, 1988

——————, *Inventing the Nation: India & Pakistan,* London, 2000

Thomas, Benjamin. P, *Abraham Lincoln,* New York, 1968

Thompson, Edward, *Enlist India for Freedom,* London, 1940

Umer, Muhammad, *Hindustani Tehzeeb ka Mussalmanon pur Asar* (Urdu Text), New Delhi, 1975

Wadhwa, Kamlesh Kumar, *A Hindu Nationalist, Gandhi-Muslim Conspiracy,* Poona, 1941

Waheeduz-Zaman, *Towards Pakistan,* Lahore, 1978

Weekes, Richard V., *Pakistan Birth & Growth of a Muslim Nation,* Princeton, 1964

Weiss, Anita M.(ed.), *Islamic Reassertion in Pakistan —The Application of Islamic Laws in a Modern State,* New York, 1986

Williams, L.F. Rushbrook, *The East Pakistan Tragedy*, New York, 1972

Wolpert, Stanley, *Jinnah of Pakistan*, New York, 1984

Wright, William Aldis, *The Complete Works of William Shakespeare*, New York, 1936

Zakaria, Rafiq, *Rise of Muslims in Indian Politics*, New Delhi, 1970

——————————, *Iqbal: The Poet and the Politician*, New Delhi, 1993

——————————, *The Widening Divide – An Insight into Hindu-Muslim Relations*, New Delhi, 1995

——————————, *The Price of Partition*, Mumbai, 1998

——————————, *Gandhi and the Break-up of India*, Mumbai, 1999

Index

G

H

Z